D0045896

Afterloss®

Afterloss®

A Recovery Companion for Those
Who Are Grieving

Barbara Hills LesStrang

Thomas Nelson Publishers
Nashville

Copyright © 1992 by Barbara Hills LesStrang.

Afterloss is a registered trademark of Harbor House (West) Publishers, Inc., and is used here under limited license granted by the owner.

Certain portions were published by Harbor House (West) Publishers, Inc., copyright © 1990 and 1991 and are reprinted by permission.

All rights reserved. Written permission must be secured from the publisher to use or reproduce any part of this book, except for brief quotations in critical reviews or articles.

Published in Nashville, Tennessee, by Thomas Nelson, Inc., and distributed in Canada by Lawson Falle, Ltd., Cambridge, Ontario.

Scripture quotations, unless otherwise noted, are from the NEW KING JAMES VERSION of the Bible. Copyright © 1979, 1980, 1982, Thomas Nelson, Inc., Publishers.

Scripture quotations noted NIV are from The Holy Bible: NEW INTERNATIONAL VERSION. Copyright © 1978 by the New York International Bible Society. Used by permission of Zondervan Bible Publishers.

Scripture quotations noted KJV are from the King James Version of the Bible.

Scripture quotations noted TLB are from The Living Bible (Wheaton, Illinois: Tyndale House Publishers, 1971) and are used by permission.

Library of Congress Cataloging-in-Publication Data

LesStrang, Barbara Hills.
    Afterloss : a recovery companion for those who are grieving / Barbara Hills LesStrang.
        p.   cm.
    ISBN 0-8407-7684-5
    1. Grief—Religious aspects—Christianity.   2. LesStrang, Barbara Hills.   I. Title.   II. Title: Afterloss.
    BV4905.2.L6   1992
    248.8'6—dc20   92–7975
                                                                                  CIP

Printed in the United States of America
1 2 3 4 5 6 7 — 97 96 95 94 93 92

For my darling husband,
the love of my life,
my best friend, mentor, laughing and loving companion
all these beautifully outrageous, joy-filled years.

For Mother and Daddy, John and Louise Hills,
who provided their family with the greatest gift of all.
We never knew anything but love!

For my brother, Major John Russell Hills, USAF,
whose name is now etched on a black marble wall,
whose love I will always carry in my heart.

And for our Lord God,
the giver of all true gifts,
who took this broken, grieving daughter,
and made her whole again.

For my darling husband,
the love of my life,
my best friend, mentor, laughing and loving companion
all these beautifully outrageous, joy-filled years.

For Mother and Daddy, John and Louise Hills,
who provided their family with the greatest gift of all.
We never knew anything but love!

For my brother, Major John Russell Hills, USAF,
whose name is now etched on a black marble wall,
whose love I will always carry in my heart.

And for our Lord God,
the giver of all true gifts,
who took this broken, grieving daughter,
and made her whole again.

My special appreciation to Dr. Margie Kennedy-Reeves and the Eisenhower Medical Center, Rancho Mirage, California, for providing an oasis for inspiration, healing, and recovery.

Remembering . . .

My dear friend, **Anne Ortlund,** whose inspirational writings planted the early seeds for my desire to really know God, to learn more of His ways and whose beautiful example of true, balanced womanhood continues to inspire, illumine, instruct, and guide.

Ron and Carolyn Haynes, for their vision, with gratitude not only for their suggestion that prompted this book about the *Afterloss* story, but also for their ongoing enthusiasm and encouragement throughout the project. Ron came to me when I couldn't get to him, all during the long and arduous healing of my broken leg and subsequent surgery. I'm especially grateful for their prayers and their belief that the Lord would give me the inspiration and the ability to complete this work.

Jane Jones, the consummate editor, for her brilliance and sensitivity in orchestrating our song.

The brave men and women who shared their stories of love, loss, and recovery, and who opened their hearts so willingly to let their scars of healing point the way for others who now seek their own road to recovery.

Trish Hall, *The New York Times,* who probably still has no idea of the remarkable catalyst she and her front page story were in the growth and development of the *Afterloss* ministry. **Jack Smith,** syndicated columnist, whose feature about The *Afterloss* Recovery Program is still instrumental in bringing healing and comfort to many people across America. **Jamie Bray,** *The Desert Sun,* whose accurate portrayal and beautifully written Memorial Day feature about the *Afterloss* mission played a significant role in the ultimate publication of this book. **Joan Snyder Boiko,** *The Desert Post,* whose own sensitivity was reflected in her feature that captured the heart and soul of the *Afterloss* mission.

Beverlee Kelley, my special friend and consultant, who made me believe that I, too, could learn to understand and operate a Macintosh computer and its many programs and then stayed nearby and taught and encouraged me each challenging step of the way. **Huck Finn,** our friend and consultant, who came any hour of the day to bail us out of various mishaps and battle electronic gremlins that tried to confound or otherwise spoil the *Afterloss* mission. **Steve Franklin,** a most talented troubleshooter, who has helped in countless other ways as we continue to be about our Father's business. **Scott and Salwa Schmidt** and the members of their Print Shop family for grasping the excitement and our ongoing commitment to printed excellence for the *Afterloss* project.

Phyllis Jaquett, one of God's special angels, with my deep gratitude for providing invaluable editorial assistance and encouragement during the final stages of this manuscript and for her insight into her journey from "the bewildering limbo of grief back to the world of the living." **Mary V. O'Gorman,** whose salutary suggestions contributed much to the *Afterloss* project. Our beautiful **Jan Cysewski,** with her willing and loving heart, who cared for us all during the writing of this manuscript.

Our magnificent seven, **Michelle, Diane, Steven, Paul, Linda, David, and Christian** and their families for their encouragement, prayerful support, assistance, and love.

And finally with a special tribute, **Betty Hawkins,** my beautiful sister-in-Christ, who has surpassed every definition and every expectation of what a true friend is or could ever be. Her joy and belief in the mission and ministry of *Afterloss* have been a vital link in the birth and growth of this recovery program. Her prayerful support, often on bended knee right beside me, continually leaves me in awe of what a blessed gift a true friend is.

Foreword

It was six months after my brother Bobby was killed when I finally bawled my head off.

Bobby, black-haired and handsome, was three years older than I. We grew up in church together. We sang in a quartet together. We played piano and organ together. We rode horseback together cross-country on Saturdays. He was my confidant and best friend, and I adored him.

Then ominously World War II emerged. Bobby finished college and became an Air Force pilot. Eventually he had many bombing missions under his belt and a stronger than ever Christian testimony.

I really didn't grasp the danger. He was God's man. When he came home I was so proud of him. He looked wonderful in his uniform, and he was everybody's hero.

Bobby was a Captain, barely twenty-four, with a beautiful wife and three-week-old twin sons, when his plane went down.

We got the news on Saturday, and on Sunday morning of course I went to church. Where else would I go? All my loving "family" was there. The pastor excused me from my usual post as organist and choir director, although I wasn't sure why. I was perfectly willing. What do private emotions have to do with serving the Lord?

I played for Bobby's funeral—all his favorite hymns and mine. My new boyfriend, Ray Ortlund, in his Navy blues, was one of the pallbearers.

That was August. For the next six months, day and night I dreamed. I pictured Bobby wandering off after the crash into the wilderness; he really wasn't dead. He'd survived. He had amnesia. I dreamed his brain would heal, he'd realize who he was, and with thrill and glory on his face he'd burst through the front door and gather us all in his arms. What joy! What praising the Lord! What a prayer time we'd have!

In February it hit me. Bobby was dead.

He was really dead.

He was DEAD.

I peeled off my clothes and climbed into the shower. Under the pounding water I cried and I cried and I cried and I cried and I cried.

And here I am remembering as I read this lovely *Afterloss* manuscript.

I've known Barbara LesStrang more in her receiving situations than in her times of loss. I remember when I first heard her voice. She phoned to say she and her husband Jacques had read some of our books. Was there a conference anywhere soon in California where Ray and I would be speaking that the two of them could attend?

There would be one almost immediately—at a church in central Orange County. Before we knew it Jacques and Barbara had checked into a motel and at the opening session they were sitting on the front row. And how they received! this tall, handsome couple. Ray and I wished we could know them better.

Next the news came that on their way home from the conference Jacques and Barbara had stopped their car and together they committed their lives to the Lord. They'd received, *really* received!

It was fresh-beginning time for them. And because they'd just moved to California, they had questions for their new mentors. Where should they go to church? We suggested one, and it's been their spiritual home ever since.

Soon after they wondered where their son should go to college. We suggested a school, and Christian graduated from it last year.

Eagerly, lovingly, Barbara and Jacques received.

At that same time they received their dear daughter Diane to California, in the sudden shock of the suicide of her young husband. You'll read Diane's story in this book. She's part of the *Afterloss* ministry now.

Over the years they've received Ray and me so graciously into their beautiful desert home. I got to meet Mrs. Hills, *Maymo,* Barbara's exquisite, classy little mother.

Then one June morning they received our whole Renewal Ministries Board onto their patio for a gorgeous brunch. They warmed our hearts with their testimonies of all God's work in their lives.

Yes, I've witnessed more of Barbara's "receivings" than her losses—but the losses have been there. That's why she can write this book with such authenticity and tenderness. At the same time Barbara has grown and grown in biblical understanding, so that the great underpinning of it all is God's Word and His eternal truth.

Are you in a period of afterloss? As you read the pages that follow, let the Holy Spirit minister to you His comfort and guidance. I commend to you, with love and admiration and thanks to God, the writing of my dear friend, Barbara LesStrang.

Anne Ortlund
Corona del Mar, California

Contents

Preface

And as for me, her devoted daughter, I am going to miss this beautiful lady more than anyone will ever know. There is a small measure of comfort now in knowing that I loved her in every way I knew how to love her. And she always knew it. I believe she knows it still.

She's the one who taught me what love is. She showed me the strength of love when her husband died suddenly thirty years ago. She showed me the courage of love when her son was killed in Vietnam, eight years later. She showed me the beauty of love with her smile, her gardens, the way that she cared for her home. She showed me the wisdom of love in the ways that she loved her husband. I never heard my parents quarrel. They loved instead. She showed me the stewardship of love in the ways that she managed her household. And finally, I learned the gentleness of love when I felt her touch—so soft, so delicate, so filled with care.

Thank you, Mother, for giving me a gentle home to grow in. Thank you for teaching me about Wedgewood and candlelight, for showing me how a husband should be loved, for teaching me how to make something out of nothing when there was the need. Most of all thank you for never making me feel unwanted, unloved, or unlovely.

You showed us the godly woman of Proverbs: the woman of strength and dignity, the woman who had no fear of age, the woman whose children stand and bless her. You taught us how to live, and then you showed us how to die. God gave you to us to love and cherish and now He has called you home. Dear, dear mother of mine, it's time now for your new beginning. Mother, it's His time to care for you.

Two weeks later, the shock subsided and the pain moved in. I was driving my little white convertible down Bob Hope Drive, a palm-lined boulevard in one of the most beautiful towns in the world, the town we call home, when I knew I had lost the battle. Once the great champion of joy and freedom, I had been taken prisoner after all—a prisoner inexorably bound by invisible shackles. I found myself trapped by an all-consuming pain that was unlike anything I had ever experienced before. It not only attacked my body, it drove its ugly, poisonous darts into my mind as well. I had become a prisoner of grief.

As I drove along trying to drown my thoughts in the music of K-PALM, I could feel the warmth of the sun on my face and the wind catching my hair. Flowers were everywhere. It was beautiful. It was springtime in the desert.

Why can't you be happy? I said to myself. *You're in Palm Springs, California. This is the place where presidents play, where stars arrive in their sleek jets to soak up the sun and sample the atmosphere. They market this place as "the pleasure paradise of the world."* But I felt only emptiness and pain. And I was sobbing.

Finally, alone in the privacy of my car, I cried aloud, "How *could* you die? How could you leave me? If you would have tried, you could have lived!"

Get a hold of yourself. You know that's not true. Don't think and don't feel. Then maybe you'll make it. Where's your gratitude? Where's your joy? Where are you? Your husband, your children— they need you. They don't understand what's happened to you. They need you to come back to them. Oh no, here it comes again. Another awful black wave of pain.

"Lord, is it supposed to hurt this much?"

Why didn't anyone ever warn me it could hurt like this? How long does this grief last? Will it ever go away and leave me alone? It follows me everywhere I go. It's even here, right now! I've got to get away—away from this pain, this prison. Hurry. Drive a little faster—maybe right off the mountain top? That would stop the pain. You've got to get a grip on yourself. You've not only lost your mother, now you're losing your mind! Oh, who can help me? I'm all alone in my pain and no one understands.

"Mother, can *you* hear me? How did you do it? How did you make it after Daddy and Russ died? If only I could talk to you, even for a moment. Oh, Mama, where *are* you now?"

My grief seemed like a living, gnawing thing, stalking, preying, entangling my mind, and threatening my sanity. I knew I had better get some help, and get it quickly.

"Oh, Lord, what's happening to me?"

In my mind I heard Him say, "My child, you are grieving. Give Me your pain, and I will give you My peace."

And so it happened.

Book One
Prayer for Recovery

ONE

Turn Out the Light in the Empty Room

She is in His presence now,
experiencing a love that exceeds even yours.

Do you want us to remove her watch and wedding ring?" the director whispered.

I stood there, looking down at the body of my mother.

Take off her watch?

And her little ring—worn so thin from all her years of love and labor?

How could I possibly take her wedding ring?

After all, it was hers. Even she had never taken it off—not once during their thirty-four years of marriage, and not once after. As much as I wanted her wedding ring, I couldn't bear the thought of taking it from her. It seemed wrong somehow, almost as if I would be robbing a defenseless person.

I was still protecting. Even as a child, whenever we played a game together, if it looked like I might win, I would find a way to lose. I always wanted her to have the very best. And now, after her death, the old habit patterns were still in place. No, I could not ask them to remove her wedding ring.

Or that funny watch.

I remembered the day she bought it. Looking up at me with her shy smile she explained, "I like *this* one. You don't have to wind it. And I can see the numbers without my glasses."

"No, please leave them," I answered, still looking down at her. "I would like one of the gardenias, though." I stepped back from her casket and sat down in the nearest chair.

We are gathered here on this May evening to pay tribute to and to show our love for our mother and grandmother and loving friend, Louise Russell Hills—our Maymo.

I watched and listened as once again my beloved husband took charge as the head of his family, holding our torn, ravaged hearts in his strong, capable hands. His words faded in and out as I struggled to assimilate the unbelievable scene that was unfolding before me.

This was my mother's funeral.

This was *her* body lying there before me.

But that body wasn't really her now. It couldn't be her. Not anymore.

But if not, then where was she? *Oh, Mother, is this really happening to us?*

My husband read from Psalms and Romans, and after all the tributes had been heard, he asked our dear friend, Betty Hawkins, to come forward.

Shortly before Mother's death, when I knew I would soon have to face the inevitable funeral arrangements, I asked the Lord for guidance. And each time I prayed, asking how I should handle those arrangements, in my mind I saw Betty's beautiful, loving face. It happened three different times. I knew that I was being guided to ask Betty if she would be willing to speak at Mother's memorial service.

I'm unable to recall many of the inspirational reflections Betty shared with us at the service that night, but I do remember that her words provided our family with much comfort and spiritual healing. Her message was so filled with hope and faith, it lifted me and sustained me throughout the entire evening. She spoke lovingly to the children and even to the grandchildren, saying something especially prepared to comfort each one.

And then she turned her eyes on me.

Barbara, it's time now to turn out the light in the empty room. Don't strive to find your mother here. Her bed of illness no longer binds her to earth. She is in a far more beautiful place now, a place prepared for her by Jesus Himself. She is in His presence, experiencing a love that exceeds even yours. This phase of your ministry of love for your mother is complete. Now, look to the future, as she would want you to do. Turn your attention and energies to finding new ways to honor her as the Lord leads you in the days to come.

Her words were so poignant they lingered in my mind. Days, even months later, I found myself still striving to turn out the light in the empty room as I endeavored to find my way to the other side of grief.

I looked up to see a tall, beautiful woman in the back of the room rise slowly to her feet. I recognized her immediately as Bettymae Rose, co-owner of a little antique shop that Mother and I used to frequent. Like so many others, Bettymae had grown to love Mother too. She affected most everyone that way.

I shall always remember Maymo for carrying such tremendous pebbles of wisdom around with her. My life has been gently touched by that wisdom and also by her love. The day of our last visit, I walked eagerly to her bedside and watched as she pulled her eyes away from the rapt, deep mysteries she had begun to be drawn into. Her hands, delicate and frail, still squeezed gentle, powerful strength, imparting intense love and compassion, and then she turned her loving glance onto me, and I felt transformed. A remarkable sense of my own personal worth seemed to burst alive—almost like a new birth. I told her I was thankful that she had allowed me the very special privilege of looking into the heart and soul of a private and exquisitely rare mother, who loved even me.

Oh, Mother. Could you hear what she said?
Bettymae's words were our benediction.
After the funeral, no one wanted to leave—not even the children. I watched as young and old alike pulled their chairs into a tight semicircle close around her, in one last effort to hold back time and the inevitable goodbyes. We all knew that after that night we would never see her again on earth. I stood there close beside her, looking down at her for my last time, until my husband came. He gently took my arm and led me down the aisle and out into the warm, desert night. As we left, I took the gardenia and held it close to my heart.

"Is you a Hills, or is you a mouse?" my daddy used to ask us teasingly when we were kids. "Being a Hills," he often said, "isn't always easy."
My people have always taken great pride in our name—in being strong, in never losing control, in accepting life as it happens, in always upholding the dignity our name implies—with absolutely no exceptions.
I saw Mother rise to the occasion many times, especially after our men died. "I want Daddy and Russell to always be proud of me," she reminded us many times after their deaths. How I marvelled at our

little Southern belle, who was so tiny but so mighty and strong. There was no doubt about it. Through all those years together, through all her times of trial, she had become a true Hills through and through.

I had always tried to be worthy of our badge of honor too. And, yes, I believe it can be said that on the occasion of my mother's funeral, I was still a Hills.

Back home in bed later that night, and during the myriad of sleepless nights that followed, how I wished I'd taken that watch. I was tormented with non-stop, hideous thoughts of it ticking away under the ground, silently mocking the quiet of the grave. *You imposter! How dare you tick away down there, like you're some living thing!*

I often wondered how many days—or months—would pass before it, too, joined the silence of the tomb. *You should have taken the watch and left just the ring!*

Alone in her bedroom the night after she was buried, I cautiously opened the closet door to look again at her clothes. I shall never forget the sight of them—so small and forlorn.

Look at the order! All her pretty outfits hanging in a row. They're even sorted by color. But who can wear them now? It really doesn't matter anymore. Nothing matters. She's gone. Empty outfits, empty hangers, empty bed, empty room. Gone! It's all gone. All that work to get the money to buy the pretty outfits. All that time to do the work, to get the money, to buy the pretty outfits. It's all gone forever. What a waste.

We had provided her with many beautiful things, and while they had all been used and enjoyed, somehow standing there alone and looking in at them painted a picture of such uselessness and waste that the closet scene has become a permanent part of who I am now. It wasn't that there were too many things; it was that suddenly they had all become so *useless*. I wasn't concerned about the dollars, but the trade-off in time and energy—in life!

And then the spotlight quite naturally focused on my own life. I wondered about the fruits of my labors. What legacy would I leave?

Dropping down to my knees, touching the side of her empty bed for comfort and consolation, I began to pray. "Oh, Lord, have we been doing it all wrong all these years? Father, please show me what's really important in this life. In Your world what can I do for You—for others—something that really matters, something good to leave behind after I'm gone?"

That evening as I closed her door behind me, I knew my life could never again be the same. I had no knowledge, however, of how to prepare myself to face or to survive the torrent of pain and grief that was waiting to ambush me. And I had no concept of how beautifully God would show His love through all those long, lonely days and nights of pain as He faithfully answered each prayer, gently sheltering me and guiding me on as I searched for His purpose for the rest of my life.

I knew it was time to turn out the light in the empty room. But how?

The Parable of the Empty Room

In those first hours after the burial, she went out into the dark night and down the winding road and over to the little empty house. And she opened the door of the empty house and walked down the darkened hall and into the room, and she sat by the bed where last she had seen her mother lie.

And as she gazed around the empty room, she took a deep breath and then slowly opened the closet door and looked within. And she looked at all the pretty dresses hanging in a row. And she looked at all the dainty shoes that were also in a row there beneath. And she saw the bonnets too. And even a tiny purse.

And then she slowly opened the drawer and saw the other things— the cameo, the strand of pearls, the little gold cross, and even a small sachet, everything so neat and dainty, still wearing the fragrance she had come to trust and remember.

But now there was no one left to wear them.

And so, alone there in the little room where they had spent a lifetime—or so it seemed, sharing their last days together, she knew there was something very important for her to gather and carry away in her heart.

And so she sat there, waiting in the empty room. She sat there, trying to understand many things.

And when she finally looked up with eyes of new understanding, she could see a long, white road stretching into the horizon. And she saw that there were yet no footsteps on that road. And in that moment she knew that this must be the road of the rest of her life.

And she saw the road begin, and she also saw it end. Let it be said that she saw an end to the road of her life. And so she came to understand the message she was to gather that night: *She must not in any way waste the steps on the road of her life.*

And so she knelt down and spoke aloud. "Show me, Father," she prayed. "Please, show me the steps for the road of the rest of my life. And I will surely walk therein, for I am but a broken child. I know not how to go out, nor how to come in."

And so He took her in His arms and held her and guided her. He fed her His truth by the silent brook during the long, lonely nights of her deep grief.

And all during her season of sadness, He came and spoke to her many times, teaching and healing, loving and guiding, sharing His promises.

And with obedience and trust she followed His plan that guided her down the long white road of the rest of her life. And so it was written.

And so it was done.

And God shall wipe away all tears from their eyes; and there shall be no more death, neither sorrow, nor crying, neither shall there be any more pain; for the former things are passed away.
                                                    Rev. 21:4 KJV

The Secret Society of the Bereaved

But why are they all sitting in a circle?

Early in the morning I made the call.

Dr. Margie Kennedy-Reeves, crisis counselor and director of her department at the hospital named for President Dwight D. Eisenhower, directed a weekly bereavement class. We had become acquainted by phone the year before, shortly after Jacques' and my daughter's husband committed suicide. Margie and I had discussed forming a Survivors of Suicide group, provided we could locate twelve other participants. Unsuccessful in finding the magic dozen, reluctantly we abandoned the project.

"What has happened?" she asked me.

I replied almost apologetically, "My mother died last week and I'm devastated! When does your next class meet?"

"This afternoon at 4:30. But you need to wait at least a month before attending."

"Wait a month? Why wait a month?"

"You wouldn't be good for the class, Barbara, and the class wouldn't be good for you—at least, not yet!"

I felt almost leprous. I didn't understand. Why wouldn't I be good for the class? For me a month seemed like a year, maybe a lifetime. It wasn't until much later that I fully understood her reasons for making everyone sift through the emotional pain of that awful first month before attending the bereavement class.

We learn a lot during the first month after a loss. The shock dims, ushering in new seasons of pain. Relatives and friends must leave and return to their own lives. The phone, suddenly awkward in a strange new silence, reminds us daily of the changes in our lives. And we come face to face with a new reality: life without our loved one, emptiness, and mind-boggling grief. Our once happy memories are now overcast with shadows. And we are left with the worst pain of all. A pain that we are totally unprepared to deal with, much less heal.

I was beginning to understand just how grief works. How it attacks. Even the stigma of it had become my enemy. Like molten lava, it was beginning to seep into other private areas of my life, further alienating me from the world I had lived in so happily before. In the wake of my loss, it was frightening to suddenly realize that I no longer even fit into my own family. Often embarrassed by sudden, uncontrollable tears (tears that began with no warning), I'd rush away from the dinner table, leaving my husband and son sitting alone in uncomfortable silence, wondering what they could do and when we could again be the way we were as I stood sobbing behind the bathroom door.

Grief takes away the world we knew—our feelings of safety, of belonging—just as death took away the one we belonged to. It robs us of the person we used to be. I had always lived in the center of the wheel, always felt I was a part of the inside circle (not outside, looking in), first as a daughter, then as a wife, and finally as a mother. I felt secure and loved. I felt I belonged. But this grief thing catapults us into a new arena. It throws us on an empty stage, a place of loneliness and pain, a place that somehow robs us of our security. It even robs us of our identity. We are no longer a part of the group. We are suddenly different, misunderstood, and alone. Grief opens the door and throws us out into the cold night.

I kept asking myself, *Where can I go to grieve?* I began to feel a new affinity with a wounded animal who seeks a quiet haven or a hiding place, needing a safe spot where he can lick his wounds and heal, or die. At times the emotional pain was so intense, I thought it would have been easier for everyone if I could silently slip away rather than inflict any more of my pain on those I cherished.

Each day became a struggle for survival, emotionally, physically, mentally. I couldn't even find escape in sleep. Whenever I crawled into our beautiful, canopied bed, the place that had always been such a haven, the memories would gather again, poised for attack.

Her smile, her soft touch, our last day, our last conversation played like a warped tape over and over again, haunting, taunting, tormenting—all the while bringing freshly seasoned pain.

Her softly spoken words had come just before the parting. "You know, the worst part about all of this," she said, "is that I'm going to have to leave you."

"I'll be all right," I whispered guardedly, without looking into her face. "You've taught me how to carry on. Remember after Daddy died and Russell too?"

But mothers always have a way of knowing, don't they? They know when truth is spoken and when it isn't. For this reason, I lowered my eyes as I tried to offer her my consolation.

What a picture! There we were, the devoted mother and her grieving daughter, sharing our last evening together, our last conversation, our last touch. And neither one of us could say the things that were in our hearts, the words we wanted and needed to say. We should have been more open, more honest. But we were still protecting each other. Days, even months, later those parting words, still relentless in their attack, played on, and on, and on in my mind.

"The worst part about all of this is that I'm going to have to leave you."

Leave me? Mother, why did you have to leave me? I could find no escape from the haunting words, nor any answers to my question, "Why, oh why, did you have to leave me? If only you would have tried a little harder. If only you would have tried to eat a little more. . . . If only this. . . . If only that. . . ."

Thoughts of our coming separation had struck terror in my heart. And I'm sure it did in hers too. I really had no idea how I would *ever* get along without her.

We had discussed everything all during our years together. No subject was taboo. Even my friends would come and talk with her, because many of them couldn't speak freely with their own mothers. "We can tell your mom anything," they'd say. Our kitchen was the hangout, where girls could be girls, where we could giggle or cry, where we could tackle any subject. And there was Mother right in the middle of it all. Understanding, advising, sometimes giggling right along with the rest of us. She was always so much fun to be with. She was everyone's confidant.

People would often comment on our special relationship. It was rare—the devotion, the love. It was very special and unique. We both knew that. But in those final hours of wrapping up a lifetime of love, openness, and honesty, knowing that our minutes with each other were numbered, neither of us knew how to begin. We simply didn't know how to say one of the most important things of all. We didn't know how to say goodbye.

Living in our death-denying culture, we pay attention to all kinds of pain. But most of us don't have a clue about how to handle one of the most devastating pains of all. Our society is so focused on winning that we don't know how to think about losing. And death is considered losing. We're so focused on living, we don't understand how to deal with dying. We learn to love and then our loved ones must leave. And no one has ever taught us how to say goodbye and how to cope or survive after our loss.

If I could live those last moments with Mother again, I would cradle her in my arms. Probably I would sob my heartfelt goodbyes all over her shoulder. Maybe we would cry together—good, honest tears, good, honest, comforting, healing, we-have-to-say-goodbye-now tears. Why didn't I make the first move? I was the stronger one. Why didn't I just reach down and take her in my arms and hold her and forget about the words? I don't know. But I do know that I learned a painful, but important, lesson that night. I learned how *not* to say goodbye.

A month later I was on my way to my first bereavement class. I turned and followed the narrow lane past the Betty Ford Center. Even for those of us who live in the desert, it still commands a strange kind of respect as we pass by. Nestled in an inconspicuous corner of the Eisenhower Medical Complex, partially hidden behind rows of tall oleander, it protects the identity of the known as well as the unknown. They come from far and wide, from all walks of life, seeking recovery hidden behind anonymity. I thought of the day I overheard an employee of the Center confide to a store clerk, "Elizabeth Taylor is with us now," obviously proud to be imparting such a delicious piece of gossip.

After repeatedly circling through the parking lot, I finally found a vacant spot where I could park my car. The hot desert breeze tossed me a cooling spray as I walked by the famous Eisenhower fountain and on into the air-conditioned lobby. I noticed the magnificent oil portrait of Mrs. Dwight Eisenhower hanging under a soft light.

Wonder why she always wore those funny little bangs.

Mamie's "Mona Lisa" smile beckoned me on, offering silent encouragement from her place of safety high on the far wall overlooking the lobby below.

Counseling! So, it has finally come down to counseling.

I was curious why I was so embarrassed about my need to attend a bereavement class. Hadn't I managed to survive the challenges of the prescribed month? But I had to admit that, for the first time in my life, I found myself with a problem I could not solve. There was something very unsettling about this. I felt so ashamed that I couldn't cope. I was embarrassed that I couldn't rise above the grief to take control of my life and my emotions again. I felt incomplete. Unsure. Unstable. Unable. Violated and trapped.

Grief isn't something you push under the rug to deal with later when you're "in the mood" or have more time. At least my grief couldn't be handled that way. My grief was dealing with me. It had become the master and I had reluctantly become the slave. I wondered how other people negotiate their way through their grief. Or do they? One graduate of the Betty Ford Center told me, "The greatest underlying reason for drug and alcohol addiction is *unresolved grief.*"

I also found that the pain of grief doesn't just go away, as all the well-intentioned people said it would. But they were wrong! Time *doesn't* heal, because time isn't an action. One woman said to me, "You know, you're lucky it was *only* your mother." How do you respond to that? Maybe that is why we survivors feel so alone, because in truth, no one *can* understand.

Have you heard things just as cruel or heartless? Have you heard: "You're attractive; you can probably marry again," or "You can always have another child," or perhaps "It was God's will"? No wonder grief-stricken people turn their backs on their friends, or their Savior.

The elevator door quietly slid open on "4." I looked out and immediately saw the sign: BEREAVEMENT CLASS.

Now go on in there, sit down in the back row, and just pretend you're auditing the class.

When I opened the door, I wasn't prepared for what I saw. There was no back to sit in! They were all sitting in a circle, waiting. *Why do they have to sit in that circle?* I wondered. It immediately became obvious there would be no opportunity to attend this group incognito. I thought maybe I should just fake a smile, pretending I got the wrong room.

You came down here today because you need help. Why stop now? Go on in there and sit down.

After selecting the chair nearest the door, I moved my eyes hesitantly around the circle surveying each face, analyzing each posture. *Who are all these people? Where have they come from?* I felt I was in the process of slowly being transplanted into another culture.

I couldn't help noticing the impact of emotional pain on posture. Some were sitting with legs crossed in ways I didn't know legs could cross. Others were sitting in a position that somehow brought the term *prenatal* to mind, as if they were hiding or protecting their hearts. I wasn't quite sure which. Many looked down and played nervously with their hands or their purse straps. One lady kept turning a gold wedding band around her finger. The man sitting next to her continually sighed and shifted his position in his chair. A few were talking softly. All of the faces wore varying degrees of pain, but they wore kindness as well. Some looked up as I entered the room, offering stiff smiles. Others did not look up at all. I settled into a chair, my home for the next hour, and waited expectantly for something to happen.

The door opened and she entered the room. This time *all* eyes looked up. They seemed to sense her presence—like tiny birds with open beaks, waiting for the one they've learned to trust for comfort and nourishment.

She was blond, and she was beautiful. She seemed to rustle as she walked. I felt almost like I was in the presence of royalty. I watched the expression on each face; it was apparent that they had all come to love her. She moved quickly into the room, commanding everyone's attention; a white medical jacket partially covered a silk floral dress. She had the bearing of a person who is more than capable of handling any situation that happens to arise.

As I watched her, I recalled the day she told me during a phone conversation how her young husband had been killed tragically in a plane crash when she was seven months pregnant. Her little son, born two months later, is in his twenties now. My respect was immediate. And it was complete.

Thinking I was all settled in the chair of my choice, I was surprised to find that we were all expected to stand up again, while she repositioned each chair with a precision I found difficult to understand. (I learned later that she began each meeting with the same unusual, but oddly therapeutic, procedure.) Once satisfied with the new arrangement, she quickly surveyed the room again, glanced from face to face, nodded her approval, and settled into a chair in the circle. We followed her lead. Evidently the class had begun.

From that moment on, she wasted no time. Out came the gold

Cross pen and the clipboard. Her penetrating blue eyes darted around the room, sharper than a laser, surveying, diagnosing, recording, quickly processing the information she had gathered with calibrated scrutiny. She took roll call like a teacher, remembering every individual's name.

Looking over my way, she noticed me seemingly for the first time. She smiled. "Hello, Barbara. I'm glad you could come." For the first time since Mother's funeral, I became suddenly aware of my appearance. Looking down quickly, I hoped I had remembered to put on something appropriate that morning.

The beeper in her white jacket pocket sounded unexpectedly, suddenly destroying the mood in the room. She quickly reached into her pocket and clicked it off. I felt a momentary surge of relief. Evidently she would be completely ours for the next hour. Then she began her job of extracting the necessary information to do the job she was there to do: help us understand and walk through the grief process and return to the world of the living, whole and complete again.

"For those of you who are with us for the first time, our procedure is to begin with one person and then move on around the circle. Please state only your first name and the nature and date of your loss. If you don't feel like saying anything more, that's all right. You can listen."

She looked over at Dolly, the woman to my right.

"Hello, Dolly," she said.

"Hello. My name is Dolly and my husband, David, passed on two months ago."

"Dolly, please remember we don't use euphemisms in bereavement group."

"I'm sorry. My husband . . . died two months ago."

Watching and hearing her expel the words was heart wrenching. Pain traveled around the circle like an electric current. I found myself suddenly involved with the pain of a woman I had never seen or met before. I was tasting it, feeling it, understanding it, experiencing it.

Will she be able to feel mine? The bonding was beginning to form.

Dr. Kennedy-Reeves moved slowly around the circle, tenderly calling each one of us by name, thereby giving us "the floor." One by one each survivor would open up, sharing moments of failure, moments of pain. As each story unfolded—all during the time it was being slowly and painfully relayed—a hand would often reach over to offer a touch of comfort or a pat of understanding. Some would even quietly cry along, empathizing with each painful event as it was described.

Then she turned her gaze toward me. "Hello, Barbara."

I glanced toward the door and back to her.

"Hello. My name is Barbara. I am here because my mother died a month ago today."

During the next several minutes, I found myself blurting out my deepest feelings as well as my fears, sharing thoughts I had been terrified to own, much less express aloud.

"I've come here today because I need help. I am very concerned about my reaction to my mother's death. I've always been able to deal with problems, but now I find that I can't cope with this one. And it's not that I haven't had to deal with other deaths. My father died when I was twenty-three, and my only brother was shot down and killed in Vietnam eight years later. But when my mother died . . ."

I began to cry. Carol reached over and put her arm across my shoulders. The whole class waited patiently and with manifest understanding as I fought to regain my composure.

"I have a wonderful husband and family who need me, but I just can't seem to be there for them. I try. But I have become so incessantly preoccupied with thoughts of her that I often wonder about myself and my sanity. The other night in an attempt to do something creative to try to help myself, I went to the piano and wrote a song— a love song. And then after writing the music I attempted to put a lyric with it.

> *If I could see your face*
> *If I could touch your hair*
> *If I could call your name*
> *If only you'd be there. . . .*

"And then I thought about her again. I thought about her face and her hair. And when I thought about what was happening to her hair, I started sobbing again. I hate to admit this, but I can't seem to stop thinking about what is happening to her body now that she is dead. I keep thinking about this. And it makes me so terribly sad, and I feel kind of warped inside. I have become haunted by my own mind. I'm trapped inside involuntarily, I should add, and I don't know how to get out, or away. I just don't understand what's happening to me anymore. I hardly recognize who I have become."

She stood up, smiled softly, raised her right hand and said, "Class, how many of you have had similar thoughts about what was happening to the body of your loved one after death?"

I looked out and saw a sea of hands go up. I was stunned. I leaned back in my chair, feeling a soothing wave of relief wash over me. For the first time in a month, I felt hope. I knew that I was exactly where I was supposed to be that last Tuesday afternoon in May—with other broken people, who like me, were trying to learn how to live with their sorrow. We had a common denominator: grief. I had found people who seemed able to acknowledge and relate to this kind of pain. I finally felt "understood." Knowing that made me feel not so alone.

She continued. "A year from now if you should *try* to feel the way you feel right now, it will be physically impossible. The human psyche just can't hold on to intense pain for a prolonged period of time. There are certain things that you can do, however, to help yourself work through the pain of your grief. We call this *grief work*."

She moved on, directing her attention to the lady on my left. "Hello, Carol."

"Hello. My name is Carol and my husband, Bill, died four months ago. Doctor, I'm afraid I'm losing my mind. Does this happen to others. Do other grieving people feel this way?"

"Most everyone I talk to at one time or another during their grief process feels as you do, Carol."

"I've gotten myself into a real mess. I went out day before yesterday and bought myself a new car."

"What's wrong with buying a new car?"

"Nothing, except that I already had a new car! And now I'm trying to take this one back."

There was an unsuccessful attempt by most of us to suppress spontaneous laughter. We actually laughed. And how good it felt. *Well, I'm in good company. So it has happened to her too.* I didn't think I should tell them quite yet that the previous week, a salesgirl talked me into buying a hundred dollars worth of new cosmetics that I really didn't need.

"What made me do such a stupid thing, Doctor? Now I've had to hire an attorney to help me take it back. The dealer doesn't want it back. He said, 'You bought it; it's yours.'"

"Carol, during the time that you were involved with the purchase of the new car, you didn't hurt, did you? You had a healing moment, or moments. Every moment that you are not thinking about your loss is a healing moment. Do you remember when I told you that healing moments are like a string of beads, and that we need to string these moments together? I certainly don't suggest that all of you go out and purchase new cars like Carol did, but, class, can you see what happened that day? Carol was thinking about something other than her loss during the time she was buying that car. She learned that she *can* have moments without pain. Soon all of you will find that you can have moments, even hours, without pain, and then eventually days, and finally weeks. Carol, if I can help you, let me know."

The following Tuesday, I needed no prodding. I didn't think once about sitting in the back or worry about anyone knowing my name. At the appointed hour, just as the large hand passed six, I was there, sitting in my perfectly positioned chair in our circle of recovery, waiting for the door to open and the class to begin.

I was the first one to arrive that week. Following close behind me was a tall, nice-looking man who seemed to be very ill at ease. I took the chair closest to the door again and observed him as he circled the room, pretending to read the posters on the wall. He was very restless, so restless that I felt somewhat uncomfortable being in the same room with him. I was glad when some of the others arrived.

"Hi, Paul, nice to see you again," one lady said, smiling openly. I gathered he must have been one of the regulars. As soon as he sat down, two women followed suit, one sitting at each side of him. *This is going to be interesting*. I watched with the curiosity of a fifth grader.

Another man, who appeared to be in his early fifties, walked in and took a seat on the opposite side of the room. In obvious emotional pain, he assumed one of those strange positions that announced, "Don't *anybody* dare talk to me." We didn't.

But she did.

The door flew open and in she came. She had come directly from the emergency room and was all business. With one broad sweep, she had a bead on everyone in the room. Who was hurting, and who wasn't. Who was faking, and who couldn't. I noticed her observe the scenario of the unsettled widower banked by the two attractive widows. She nodded to me and to several others and then immediately addressed herself to the don't-anybody-dare-talk-to-me man.

"Hello, Ben. Why don't we begin with you today?"

"Hello, Doctor. My name is Ben and my wife, Sarah, died six months ago today."

"Tell us what kind of a week you've had, Ben."

"Terrible! I cried all week. My grandson from up north has been visiting me for two weeks, and it's even worse now that he's here. We always did so many things together when Sarah was alive, just the three of us. And now it's so hard—especially when we have to set three places at dinner time."

"Three places? Who else is here with you?"

"No one. It's just me and my grandson. The other place is for Sarah."

"But, Ben, Sarah is no longer alive. You know that. Why are you still setting a place at the table for her? She died six months ago, Ben."

"But I've always set a place for her. For thirty years I set her place. That was my job. She cooked the supper and I set the table." Then he began to cry. I felt the tears begin to sting at my eyes, and while fighting to see through them, I noticed that several others in the circle were also fishing into pockets or purses for tissues. I wasn't sure if our tears were for Ben or for ourselves. What mattered was the gentle way she helped him understand the new reality of his life—that Sarah was dead, and that it was not healthy grief for him to continue to set a place for her at the table.

"Ben, this kind of activity is what we call *abnormal grief*. You know that Sarah will not be eating with you again. When you go home tonight, I want you to set only two places at the table. One for you and one for your grandson. Will you do that for me, Ben?"

Continuing around the circle, analyzing the progress of each grieving member, she focused her attention on Dorothy. "Hello, Dorothy."

"Hello, Doctor. My name is Dorothy. I lost my husband last month. And I am so angry. It was all their fault. If only they had gotten to us sooner. My husband and I saved for years for this time in our lives. We had just retired. We bought a beautiful motor home. Four couples who have been friends for years started out on an adventure together, each couple in their own motor home.

"We stopped in Arizona to go fishing, and Bill had a heart attack right there in the boat. I couldn't believe my eyes. My husband died right in front of me. I'm a nurse, and I tried to administer CPR. But being in the boat I couldn't do it very well. Someone finally phoned 911, but by the time the paramedics got there, it was too late. Why didn't they come sooner? If only I had done a better job with the CPR, Bill might still be alive. Maybe I killed my own husband. One minute I'm so angry at the paramedics, and the next I'm so angry at myself. I have all of these new emotions that I've never experienced before, and I don't know which way to turn. Someone suggested I come to this group, that maybe you could help me. I'm really desperate. I don't want to live without Bill anymore. I hate my life. I hate everything."

Dr. Kennedy-Reeves moved in quickly to reassure and explain to the tormented widow that there was probably nothing she could have done to save her husband's life. And then she admonished us to beware of the self-defeating "if onlys," the curse that befalls many survivors. She pointed out what a damaging disservice we do to our own recovery by rehashing the moments or days that preceded our loved one's death. She said that guilt or anger often follows closely on the heels of the "if onlys": "If only I had done this; if only I had done that."

I noticed Dorothy's tense body begin to relax as her natural intelligence responded to the doctor's logical explanation of the events surrounding her husband's death.

The interesting thing about being a part of a bereavement group was that the grievers let *everything* hang out. There were no *shoulds* or *should nots*. We stated our feelings in living color. If we hated the paramedics, we said we hated the paramedics. And then Dr. Kennedy-Reeves would talk about the prevalence of anger after loss. If someone broached the subject of suicide and said he or she felt like blowing his brains out, the doctor would offer understanding and sympathy. She would talk about how to combat suicidal feelings, stating repeatedly that many survivors do, indeed, have self-destructive feelings after losing a loved one. It was the perfect environment for healing. We no longer had to pretend that we were getting over "it" if, in fact, we were heading in the opposite direction.

Standing at the door, waiting to say goodbye at the end of each meeting, Dr. Kennedy-Reeves would often reach out and hug each one of us as we left the room. For some, it may have been the only hug of the week. "We all need closeness," Dr. Kennedy-Reeves would tell us. "We can learn to live without love, but we do need closeness." She provided a sanctuary, a haven dedicated to the mending of grief-stricken souls, an atmosphere of safety and understanding where we, the secret society of the bereaved, would gather every Tuesday afternoon at 4:30 sharp. Consequently most of us paced ourselves from Tuesday to Tuesday. *Only three more days until bereavement group.* In those early days of grief, it was the only thing I looked forward to.

As though I were a weary traveler thirsty in the desert, bereavement group became an oasis, my fountain of living, healing water.

Dr. Kennedy-Reeves finally got around to the good-looking widower. "Paul, it's nice to see you again. How have you been getting along?"

"I'm sliding backwards, Doctor. And I thought I was doing so well. I had even begun dating again. Everyone wanted to fix me up with a nice widow or a divorced lady. 'Have I got a gal for you,' they'd say with fat grins on their faces. Well, I tried spending some time with some of those women, and now I feel worse than ever. No one can begin to compare with Lori.

"Doctor, those women weren't interested in me. They just wanted to see where I live or to know what clubs I belong to. I felt like a commodity. I just want Lori back. Everything I look at shows her touch: the floral arrangements, our room, the beauty of our home."

Dr. Kennedy-Reeves stood up before she began to speak.

"Class, do you see what has happened to Paul? He began to socialize *before* he had completed his grief process. His friends didn't understand his needs. They thought they were helping him, and you can't blame them for that. But Paul is still in the middle of his grief process and is still terribly vulnerable. He doesn't need a woman; he needs to find himself. When we begin to get involved in a new relationship, our grieving process stops. Please remember that.

"Paul, how long has it been now since your loss?"

"Three months."

"I'm glad you got yourself back to group. Eight to twelve weeks after our loss is often our most difficult time."

"I do fairly well during the day, Doctor, but at home again at night, I feel like I'm going crazy. And I feel so guilty. Lori was afraid of the surgery. I'm the one who talked her into having it. I probably killed her."

"No, Paul. You did not kill her.

"Class, let's take a good hard look at this word *guilt*." Then she went on to tell us that guilt and grief—the two "G" words, as she called them—are often interchangeable. She explained how most survivors feel guilty about one thing or another, real or imagined, after our loss and that we think if only we had done this or that, our loved one would still be alive. But this is usually not the case.

She told us that guilt can be one of the most self-defeating and self-disparaging responses in the grieving process and that guilt is a very normal part of grief. "Realizing this," she said, "we can then give ourselves permission to stop running the 'you're guilty' tape in our minds and learn to replace that message with more positive thoughts. Guilt, like any powerful emotion, can be effectively resolved."

I watched with great admiration as she gently removed the thorn from the paw of this broken lion of a man. She carefully relieved his guilt, explaining that he was as normal as the rest of us in his battle against the grief/guilt twins.

When he stood up at the end of the class, I noticed that he seemed more relaxed. He stopped and hugged Dr. Kennedy-Reeves as he left the room. I noticed, too, that the two widows who had been sitting beside him had found someone else to talk to.

The third week the door opened and in she came looking as beautiful as ever, but I noticed an unfamiliar sadness in her eyes. She seemed pensive and somewhat preoccupied. Later I learned that she had just come from helping a couple make the decision to donate the organs of their son who was killed when the car he was driving hit a tree. *What a job she has.*

The same ritual began as she began her visual walk around the circle, looking into each face, gently smiling, debriefing, and arming herself with the information she needed to help guide each griever through the recovery process.

I noticed a newcomer in the group, a stunning woman. She was sitting directly across the room from me. Dressed in an exotic tunic, she had pulled her long, blond hair tightly into a chignon. When it was her turn to speak she began to cry. "I am afraid to live alone."

"Carol, please remember our procedure: state your name and the nature of your loss."

"Oh, I'm sorry. My name is Carol. My husband, Marshall, died three months ago. Doctor, I'm terrified of living alone. Because of my fear, I rented out a room in my lovely home to a woman, a stranger to me, and now I don't want her there. But I'm afraid to ask her to leave."

"Class, do you see what has happened here?" She went on to explain that Carol had acted too precipitously after her husband's death. She had taken a stranger into her home and now was faced with the problem of getting her to leave. She urged us not to make any major decisions until our emotions have stabilized, acknowledging, however, that some of us may find it necessary to move for financial reasons. In those cases, we would have to proceed accordingly.

"But we must learn to explore all of our options before rushing into something that may prove unsettling to us later," she said. She suggested that Carol simply tell her roomer that she needed the privacy of her home now. "You might want to ask a friend to be present when you tell her she'll need to make other arrangements," she advised.

Bobbie, the beautiful woman sitting at my left, was also a newcomer that day. She was totally distraught and had every reason to be. A month before her husband, Scotty, had gone into the hospital for some corrective surgery, suffered a heart attack, and died. She was in a state of total shock. To complicate matters both her parents were very ill, and she had the responsibility of their care. Her father had Alzheimer's and was totally incompetent. Her mother was bedridden with heart problems.

"I didn't think my life could get any worse, but it did. How will I ever deal with all of these things? There is so much to do—papers to sign, legal matters, insurance, wills. I feel so incompetent. I've never had to do things like this before. How can I ever do all of this without Scotty?"

"Do you have any brothers or sisters?" Dr. Kennedy-Reeves asked.

"Yes, one sister living in Carlsbad."

"And what is she doing to help with the care of your parents?"

"Nothing."

"Then why don't you phone her and tell her you must have her help?" (By the following week, the sister had become involved in the responsibility and care of her parents.)

Dr. Kennedy-Reeves did a very interesting thing that day. She went to the board and began to write. With pink chalk in her hand, she wrote numbers from 1 to 20. And then she asked each of us to tell her the most difficult problem we'd had to face since our loss. Everyone began speaking at once. Comments were tossed out into the room faster than she could record them, each one more devastating than the one before it.

I saw the class melt like butter; I saw smiles leave and tears begin. I saw people begin to sag and droop and cry and lament and touch and support each other for comfort. I watched as the circle of recovery became a circle of despair. As each comment was hurled into the group she wrote it next to one of the numbers:

1. I miss having someone in the house when I come home at the end of the day.
2. I miss someone to eat with. I hate eating alone.

3. I miss being able to tell Bill something cute that one of the kids said. Now, nobody cares what our kids said.
4. I hate the loneliness. I hate my life now.

As she was writing, she purposely misspelled the word *loneliness*. Three people immediately corrected her. That planned intrusion eased the tension and pain a bit.

5. The forms, insurance, the will, the medical bills, Medicare. I don't know how to fill out any of these forms.
6. Seems all I see are couples. I never used to notice this before, but it's all I see now. I hate going out anymore.
7. I miss having someone compliment me. I've lost all my self-esteem.
8. Touching, loving, the physical contact. I miss feeling that I was special to someone.

She spun around, looking everyone in the eye and said, "OK, what else?"

9. I can't stand to look at her clothes, but I'm afraid to give them away. It's like as long as her clothes are still there, maybe she will be coming back.
10. It's so different now. When our kids come home, they have no parents to come home to. It's just me, a widow. We're not a family anymore. I'm afraid they might stop coming.
11. I'm sick and tired of my friends treating me like I'm after their husbands now. I'm not interested in anyone's husband but my own, and now he's dead. But they watch me like I'm a predator. I just don't enjoy being with my old friends anymore.

By this time I had totally lost track of any pain that I had brought with me that day. My concern had focused entirely on Margie. *How will she ever be able to deal with all of this pain?* But she knew exactly where she was going. With one quick motion, she drew a long pink line right down the middle of the board. And then she wrote the numbers from 1 through 20 again. This time to the right of the line.

"All right, class, let's look at number one. Someone in the house at the end of the day. What can Mary do to help herself with this problem?"

"Leave a radio on when you go out," one suggested.

"Get a dog," from another. (There were a few verbal pros and cons from the group in response to that one.)

"As soon as you get home, call a friend," said another.

One widow said, "I used to feel that way, but each time I would go out and come home, it got a little easier."

"Let's look at number two. How can Ted deal with eating alone?"

"Fix a tray and eat in front of the TV," one said.

"Call me and I'll come over and eat with you," wised off a widower. Quickly someone else said, "Come on over to my house. I'm a good cook, and I hate to eat alone too." (Last I heard, he was still going over there.)

She moved right down the list not only making suggestions of her own but gathering data from her circle of grievers, both novice and intermediate, allowing one widow to share with another—one who was midway through the process to help one who was just beginning. At the end of the class, all of us sitting in her circle were all back together again. Once again, she had made it happen. I nodded at the word *Lonliness,* written in beautiful pink script, as I walked past the white chalkboard on my way out of the room.

Riding down the elevator after class, I noticed that several of the members of the group were beginning to make new friendships. I heard them discussing a suitable place to congregate for dinner that night. I watched, too, as the man who hated to eat alone walked out alongside the widow who liked to cook. I walked out alone and got in my car.

When I got home, the house was empty. I didn't know where my husband was, or our son either for that matter. I felt uneasy. I had seen the growing distress and sadness in my husband's eyes, and I knew he missed his wife. He didn't know how to relate to me as a grieving spouse. And I didn't know how to act myself, because my emotions were so unstable and I was filled with such pain.

When will all this be over? When can I be me again? I looked up to see my husband slowly walking up the long drive. He'd been out for a walk. He was trying too.

May brought Mother's Day, less than two weeks after Mother died, and her birthday on the twenty-fourth, two weeks later. I wanted to hide in bed and sleep through Mother's Day. But I don't do things like that. I only think about doing them. And so I forced myself to attend church and sit there right alongside all of the other people, many with their mothers sitting beside them as they celebrated Mother's Day. I hated that day. How can you celebrate Mother's Day when you have a dead mother? June brought with it a sudden trip to the emergency room at Eisenhower Medical Center for my husband, and a subsequent week-long hospitalization. July brought minor cancer surgery (is there such a thing?) on my forehead and an ugly scar. And August almost finished me off, as our youngest child, Christian, left home to begin his first year of college.

That's when the dam broke.

I managed to make it through the final stages of packing by slipping out to the mall "to look for a few last minute things." I could see I was headed for big trouble watching him dismantle his room and carry the pieces of his life out to his car—the posters, the football jersey (#80), and even the big old teddy bear.

Watching as the seventh and last child packed up and prepared to leave home, I remembered a pattern I had witnessed six times before. When they leave for college is when things really begin to change. From that point on, they're pretty much gone. I've never been a clinging mother. It was just that so many changes were coming so close together—loss after loss, loss upon loss. I didn't know how to deal with so much loss.

The night before he was to leave, he came into the living room and sat down. "Mama, I don't want to go to college. I don't want to leave my room, my girl, my life—and you guys."

How tempting to say, "Good boy. I was hoping you'd say that," or "No problem. You can stay home and go to junior college." But as parents we are committed to unselfishly guide our young in ways that best promote their growth and development (and not our own selfish wishes).

"You must go and try," I said. "I do believe this is God's plan for your life for this year. If after a couple of weeks, you feel this is not what you want, then call and you and Daddy and I can talk about it then." (He loved Westmont and has graduated as a business major.)

Well, I made it through helping him move his clothes, posters, football jersey, and, yes, even the old bear (who was by now wearing the football jersey) into the dorm room. I made it through meeting the roommate and his dad and watched as many other parents and their children prepared for this important transition. I made it through the picnic on the lawn and the dinner with the other parents and, finally, on Saturday night, I made it through the big dinner with the president of the college. Somehow I kept it all together all during those four difficult days.

But on the last night, after the president's dinner, just before they were to wean the kids away from their parents, we were all sitting out under the stars for the final program. The parents and their children were all sitting side by side on a beautiful summer evening in a spot overlooking the ocean. Then the chaplain rose, walked forward, and said, "I'd like to offer a special closing prayer. Why don't you take your child's hand in yours as we pray."

Uh-oh. I knew immediately that I was in big trouble, and I swallowed hard trying to forestall the inevitable. I hadn't held his hand in mine since he was a little boy. We'd had lots of hugs and 'I love yous' over the years, but for some reason, I hadn't held his hand. Looking up into his face I saw the solemn expression in his dark eyes. I reached out and put that big hand of his in mine and at the same time felt the gentle protective touch of my husband's strong hand as he reached over to cover both of ours.

Simultaneously I felt a sob forming somewhere down in my toes. And I felt it make its way up through my chest and then sit like a clump of lead on my heart, waiting for an opportunity to escape. I kept swallowing. I felt the tears begin to form in the corners of my eyes, roll into them, fill them, and then slide down my cheeks. I kept blinking.

I could feel the warmth and security of both hands, my son's and my husband's. And I remembered all the years of love and happiness and the fun we'd had with all our kids—with mothers and daughters and fathers and sons and formals and weddings and giggles and horses and picnics and puppies—and I felt that it was all ending that night, that it was all being ripped away, that from that night forward, *we would no longer even be a family.* (We don't think clearly when we're grieving.)

I could feel that sob getting restless, and I knew it wanted out. I was suddenly totally helpless to suppress or hold it in any longer. I was terrified with the thought of embarrassing our son, or my husband (or myself), and so I just sat there and shook uncontrollably. I shook with long, silent, racking sobs, as the tears of a thousand years, it seemed, came forward that night and dripped quietly into my lap.

As we walked across the field later that evening one woman walking alongside me said gently, "Well, I'm glad I wasn't the only one crying tonight."

Fortunately during the time of the many challenges that occurred that summer, I had the support of Margie and the bereavement group to help me through those forays through change and uncharted waters. The ebb and flow of grief. Wave after wave. What a devastating and difficult process. But, it *is* a *process*. Margie told us, over and over again, "Grief is a *process,* not an event. Remember, class," she would emphasize, "a process always has a beginning *and an end.*"

The bereavement class gave me the opportunity not only to understand the grief process, but to learn how to deal with the practical, day-to-day aspects of recovery after my loss. I shall be indebted forever to my friend, teacher, and associate, Dr. Margie Kennedy-Reeves, for her understanding support, her wise counsel, and the many kindnesses she extended to me during the weeks that I sat in her wonderful circle of recovery.

We drove up to Carmel the week after we took Christian to college in Santa Barbara, and the experience of being out in nature together was very healing for both of us. We were away from home, permitting a temporary leave of absence from some of the consuming sad memories. But contrary to what some people say, *you do have to go home again*. Soon it was time to prepare for the trip back down the coast to the desert, past the gates and up the hill and into the empty house. I walked down the long hall and hesitantly tiptoed into the semi-bare room where our son and his old bear used to live, fell across the bed, and buried my face in his pillow.

But God was waiting for me when we got home that night. And the next morning, He took over.

THREE

The *Afterloss* Story

And the name shall be known across the land.

I t's time to get back to work."

I was shocked, even a bit dismayed on that bright, autumn day when I heard the gentle command. But hadn't I prayed, "Show me what I can do for You, Lord"? Hadn't I asked Him for guidance, that He show me what was important in His world? How, then, could I ignore this simple request? It was time to decide: I was either going to follow Him—or I wasn't. I was either going to be obedient—or I was not.

Lord, I don't think I'm ready for this yet. How can I begin again? What if I break down? What if I fail!

I seriously wondered if I was ready to resume the demands of the career I had put on hold. And I also wondered if I would be able to achieve the same level of success in my work again. I felt unsure. I was afraid. But I resolved that dilemma by thinking, *Well, you can always try.*

That evening I told my husband I would be returning to work the following day. He lowered his eyes for a moment and then looked up and said quietly, "You've been missed."

For the first time in months, I set the alarm clock and early the next morning, dressed in something resembling a working person's attire, walked to my office; the office with the barren desk and the empty In and Out boxes; the office with the idle WATS line and the unopened calendar.

Well, Lord, I'm here.

My responsibilities at work had always revolved around sales and marketing for our midwest publishing company, Harbor House Publishers. And that meant talking to people, lots of them. *Lord, how can I ever talk to all these people now? I'm just not ready for this yet.*

But His command rang loud and clear. I had no doubt that it was the Holy Spirit urging me forward. And so, each morning from that day on, obediently I walked to my office, patiently I waited for His direction for the day, and then I did the work I was guided to do.

In those early days, I began by picking up the threads of my former business activities and half-heartedly (half a heart was all I had to work with) went about trying to re-establish contact with former clients and trying to remember how I used to work. Press releases went out saying, "She's back!" Yes, I was back—sort of. As much as I could gather of myself was back (talk about "the shadow of a smile"). But I could speak, and I was beginning to remember how to think, and soon I became effective in my work again. Like an old rusty ship, with some paint, a little patience, and some grease and oil, my gears slowly began to turn.

Even though my heart was heavy, I felt a strange new peace as I went about my work and began to resume my role as an active participant in the world of commerce. I realized I had missed it after all—the excitement, the challenge—and it was very comforting settling back into my office right next to my husband's. He had been very understanding and supportive during the time I had been away, and he seemed genuinely glad to have his old sidekick back at it again. We had always worked well together, and a new kind of happiness began to emerge and reign in my heart. It was that special kind of joy that comes when we know we are doing what we are supposed to do. It's called *obedience*.

I felt a strong sense of God's presence in my office each day, and I talked openly with Him. Since I heard no more commands for awhile, I kept on with the only program I knew. I was doing what I didn't *want* to do. But I was giving it my best. At the same time, I was trying to maintain a positive attitude and keep an open mind and a listening ear. I was trying hard. And I trusted my Lord.

I knew that I didn't have the answers I was seeking. I also knew that I didn't want to waste the rest of my life. I had abandoned myself totally to Him. I had such complete trust that I didn't question where He was taking me. I was just happy that I had the strength and the ability to follow. A strange new kind of serenity began to form as I slowly put all former agendas away, determined to follow only Him, to "abide in Him."

The following Tuesday afternoon at 4:30, I happened to glance over at the clock. *Oh, no! How could I have missed bereavement class?* Then I thought, *Well, you must be getting better.*

Flipping over to the last month of the calendar, my eyes fell to the square marked 25. *Somehow now you've got to find a way to make it through Christmas without her.*

They came from far and near, the children and the grandchildren. The highlight of the LesStrang family tradition is celebrating Christmas Eve by attending church services and then gathering together for my husband's Bible reading from Luke 2. I made it fairly well through the days preceding Christmas by turning off the music, by selecting many of our gifts in Carmel when we were there in September, and by exchanging emerging thoughts of sadness with *don't think* and *don't feel.*

Each time I wondered how we'd get through that first Christmas without Mother, I would go into the *don't think and don't feel* routine. This self-imposed swindle worked fairly well until Christmas Eve. The family had gathered, the kitchen was swarming with children, grandchildren, and dogs. Carols were playing and the room was filled with the aromas of Christmas and the gentle banter that typifies a family gathering. As I stood by the stove stirring the oyster stew, I felt it coming. I kept blinking and swallowing. I tried *don't think and don't feel* but my heart would have none of it this time. I could no longer hold back my feelings. They were all there waiting. And I had to let them out.

I stood and stirred and shook and sobbed as a tall son gently put his arms around my shoulders. I knew then I had better find some way to excuse myself from attending Christmas Eve church services with the beautiful music and the candles and the people. I did not want to sit in a pew shaking and sobbing, as I had earlier in the year at Westmont College. I decided that it would be better for me to remain at home. Of course, my husband, being who he is, said he preferred to stay at home too, but we insisted the children go. Reluctantly they obeyed, only to return thirty minutes later with the excuse, "We couldn't get in. You know, there were just too many people this year."

Yes, we knew. We knew better.

We took that first Christmas on as a family. Sure there were tears and moments of deep sadness, but we comforted each other. We all grew in strength and wisdom, and we all learned that it is OK to cry on Christmas Eve.

The New Year came, ushering in January and thoughts of my first birthday without her. That month I headed back to bereavement class for some needed fortification. There were a lot of us whose attendance had tapered off but, after surviving the holidays, wanted to get back into the circle for some necessary comfort. "You've got to plan ahead for those special days or anniversaries," the doctor told us. "Don't just expect them to work out automatically. Get out of the house! Or do something special with a friend! Take control of your day! Plan!" And so I planned, got out of the house, and did something special with a friend. And it worked!

And right around the corner after January was the month that was! That's when the *Afterloss* story really began.

I recall vividly that I wasn't very excited about the work I was doing that fall, but only that I was able to do it again. And I have to smile with love and gratitude as I recognize God's supreme wisdom. He gently guided me back into a familiar setting where I was able, slowly, to pick up the reins of routine procedures, which helped me to regain my confidence. I was so broken at first, and so unsure. How could He have sent me forward into something new until I'd had time to heal and restore, and become acquainted with the new person emerging from my grief? He took me back to an environment of safety where later the concept and birth of the *Afterloss* program could follow.

That fall and early the following year, sitting in my office each day waiting for His direction, I found myself reminiscing and reviewing many of the things I'd learned in bereavement class, not only from the doctor, but the other people in group as well. As we confided our innermost fears and shared each small victory, we all grew in strength and confidence and understanding. With Margie gently looking on, protecting like a mother, teaching, encouraging and guiding her baby grievers, and offering wise counsel to those who were midway through their process, she'd smile and say, "One of these days, I'm going to invite some 'graduate grievers' to come in, just so you can look at them! Then you will believe me when I tell you this grief process actually will end for those of you who are willing to do your grief work." I realized how fortunate I was to have had the opportunity to walk through those doors on that first day and to be a member of the circle of recovery. And then my heart went out to all of the other suffering people who had no class to go to (or who were unable to share their personal feelings with strangers), those who quietly suffer at home behind closed doors, alone in their pain, with little hope or knowledge of how to help themselves find their way again without their loved ones.

I thought of all of the people who have been told, "Time will heal," when it doesn't, and "Come on, pull yourself together; it's time to get on with your life now," when they can't. And then I thought of the night after Mother's burial when I knelt on her bedroom floor and prayed, "Show me what I can do for you, Lord, something to help others, something to leave behind after I'm gone."

Slowly a new feeling came over me—a feeling unlike anything I had ever experienced before. I felt the presence of the Lord right there in my office. And then I heard, "Now take what you've learned and share it with the world."

I was beginning to understand God's plan. He was going to take this once broken vessel (me) and use the new energy He was nurturing to help create something to provide comfort and healing for His people. I was to be one of the vessels through which He would pour His healing waters: "He that believeth in Me out of him shall flow rivers of living water."

But how, Lord?

"Do it and I will help you."

We have no tools here for this kind of work. We'll need to produce a publication of some kind, something not too lengthy, nor too hard to read or understand. You know how hard it is to concentrate when we're grieving. It should be something that could be sent right to the home of the grieving person each month.

We'll need a computer, and someone to set type, and some kind of desktop publishing capability. We'll need mailing lists, a printer, a designer, and an artist.

Oh, Lord, how should we do all of this?

I was beginning to get a feel for what was needed, and I was also beginning to experience a surge of excitement, a sense of new purpose, and a strong spiritual commitment. We had the capability and more to produce a publication at our Harbor House facility in Michigan, but not in California at that time. And the Michigan staff was already swamped with new work and new projects. So I did what I often do: I hurried around the corner into my husband's office and told him what God was asking me to do.

"Don't you want to research the market first to see what else is out there?" he asked.

"No, darling, if something like this were out there, I would have found it."

"Well, if you feel this strongly about it, we'll find a way to make it happen. Why don't you give Margie (Dr. Kennedy-Reeves) a call and see if she would like to serve as editor."

A few days later Margie and I met for lunch. After I told her the plan, she was just as excited about the project as I was and immediately agreed to serve as the editor. And we were underway, well, sort of.

We still needed a name, of course, and the copy, and a way to translate it from legal pad to print, and a way to set it in type, and a way to print it, and then a way to distribute it. We needed all of those things. But I knew that I no longer had to worry about the details. I just had to stay focused and keep listening.

And then I saw the most interesting picture in my mind. I saw a vineyard with many laborers bending over, working together harvesting. The women were all dressed in old fashioned garments, wearing long skirts and large billed bonnets to protect them from the scorching sun. Then I realized *I* was one of those laborers. And immediately I recognized another. I saw the face of our beautiful widowed daughter working diligently alongside me.

The name Beverlee Kelley seemed to jump out at me one morning as I thumbed through my address book. I recalled that Beverlee used to sell computers, and that I had heard she also taught people how to use them. "Do you suppose I could ever learn to work a computer?" I asked hesitantly. "I'm in my fifties, a grandmother with seven grandchildren. Maybe I'm too old now? What do you think?"

"Well, I'm in my fifties too. And I'm dyslexic. I learned, and I would be delighted to teach you."

That did it. Within two weeks we had a new computer. Beverlee offered us the use of her laser printer for our final copy and said that when we were ready she would teach me how to use the desktop publishing program. Margie got right to work writing copy. I took on the job of learning how to work the new computer and went scouting for a printing company.

All we needed was our name. The perfect name.

In her book, *Disciplines of the Beautiful Woman,* one of the things that Anne Ortlund talks about is the importance of writing our prayers. To be honest, I'd never done it, because I can't write fast enough or legibly enough. But the new computer opened up a new way of doing many things. I began writing my prayers. One day I sat there with my eyes closed and wrote:

"Lord, we've followed you this far. Now we need our name. What do you want us to call the newsletter? And, Lord, please help me keep my ego out of Your project."

It happened in the shower! The name *Afterloss* dropped right into my mind. And I knew immediately what it was for and where it had come from. I jumped out of the shower, grabbed a towel, and headed for the nearest pen and paper to see what the title would look like in print. It looked wonderful! Standing there with tears in my eyes, alone in our kitchen, dripping wet, and wrapped in a towel, I heard, "And the name shall be known across the land."

The articles began to roll in: "The Message and the Mission of *Afterloss*"; "Grief Work: Introduction to a Ten-Part Series"; "Your Own Special Grief—What Makes It So?"; "Grief: Your Unwanted Journey"; "Loss and Recovery"; and "Answers to Questions Asked during Bereavement Class." Like the rest of us, Margie was also working long hours to keep the pipeline filled.

My husband, a Book-of-the-Month-Club author as well as an editor and a publisher, began refining and editing as I wrestled to understand and master the intricacies and capabilities of our new Mac. The following day my husband finished the layout of our first issue of *Afterloss* with all copy perfectly positioned. He brought it into my office and dropped it down on my desk. I'll never forget the feelings I had as I looked at each page. We were almost ready to go to press. The only remaining task was to get the material into a computer publishing program.

It was time to call Beverlee again. I'd never been to her home and had no idea where she lived, but when she gave me her address, my heart began to ache. She lived five doors down from Mother's, in the condo on the end. *Oh, Lord, not in there.* My knees suddenly felt weak. I sat for a minute, realizing I was going to have to drive right past Mother's little place to get to Beverlee's. There was no other way.

Is you a Hills or is you a mouse? I asked myself. *Well, by golly, there are no mice around here.*

With a new determination, I picked up the layout, walked through the door and got in our car. When I arrived at the entry gate, the entry I had driven through on a thousand occasions, my mind went blank. I could not remember the security code. Sitting there, entering one code and then another—with a string of honking cars and impatient drivers behind me, I fumbled around, trying to remember the four numbers that would open the gate. Finally I got out of my car, walked back to the car behind me, apologized to the very impatient driver and explained that it had been almost a year since I'd used the gate and that I had simply forgotten the code. He really didn't care why I'd forgotten the code. He was hot, tired, and mad.

All he wanted was to get home. "Wimmin!" he muttered under his breath after he barked the code.

The gate finally opened and I drove quickly past the place where she had lived and died. The old feelings of pain and grief came flooding back. Tears stung my eyes and I felt the fingers of pain reach out as I drove on by. *Out of all the homes in this desert, why does Beverlee have to live in here?* When I walked into her home, I found it had a floor plan identical to Mother's. And the room where I had spent so much time, the room where Mother died, was the room in Beverlee's house that housed her computer and laser printer. I was to retrace those same steps many times in the ensuing months. But I found that each time I drove by Mother's house, the trip became a little easier. And I never forgot the gate code again, ever.

That first issue was proofread, and proofed again, and looked over, and prayed over like no publication we've ever produced. "Stop picking at it!" I heard. "Are you proofing *Afterloss* again?" The day the paper was delivered, I drove out and watched with tears in my eyes as it was unloaded and hauled in the back door of The Print Shop. At last we were ready to take our message of hope and healing to the world. After four months of non-stop work and many hours of prayer, everything had finally fallen into place. We had 2,000 newly printed copies of our first issue of *Afterloss,* and three subscriptions! *Lord, is this a step of faith or an act of insanity?*

In the weeks and months ahead there was little time to do much but work. Press releases had to be written, ads needed to be written, designed, and placed, copy was entered, edited, and proofed, strategic and marketing plans conceived and implemented. All of the myriad of labor-intensive tasks relevant to the production and subsequent marketing of a new publication had to be executed. At about that time, my husband told me he had been thinking about asking Diane, our widowed daughter, if she would like to join Harbor House (West) and begin to learn the many facets of the publishing business. My thoughts went immediately to the mental picture I'd had some time before of the laborers working in the vineyard and the women working side by side harvesting. I had a feeling that soon Diane too would be helping with the *Afterloss* project.

More and more people were hearing about *Afterloss* and as soon as they did, they wrote or called. Our editor had done such a superb job that soon we began to hear from people from all over the country. Funeral homes began to subscribe for their families, pastors, and school counselors. We made up personalized portfolios containing every issue of *Afterloss* for pastors, senior centers, retirement homes, hospices, libraries, and high school counselors.

I remember checking the FAX early one morning and discovering a long roll of paper spread all over the office floor. I thought the machine had broken. Instead, Memory Garden Memorial Park in Brea, California, wanted to provide every clergy member in their county with a gift subscription to *Afterloss*. They had just faxed us over one hundred names. One funeral director in Tennessee told us they conducted a survey of all of the clergy members in their state and found that 94 percent had received no instruction in grief recovery during their pastoral training. As a result of these gift subscriptions, grief recovery networking began to form between members of the clergy and the funeral homes, two very logical resources for grief assistance. New friendships developed as directors and pastors began working together to bring helpful assistance to the people they serve.

We began meeting and talking with funeral directors all over the country and became acutely aware of the unfair image the members of this caring industry have struggled with for so long. These are some of the finest, most caring, dedicated people you'll ever meet.

We received letters from pastors, thanking us for *Afterloss,* sometimes asking us to send gift subscriptions to needy members of their congregation. We heard from hospice workers, bereavement counselors, care-givers. We heard from grieving parents, kids, husbands, and wives. We heard from the hurting people in America.

"We've needed something like this for so long," they said. "Finally, a publication that speaks the truth about grief recovery." "I've been grieving for nine years. Reading *Afterloss* was the turning point for me." "Where have you all been all my life?"

It was beginning to look like *Afterloss* would be around for a while.

That December, in conjunction with the FitzHenry Funeral Home in Indio, California, we co-sponsored a special seminar, "Hope for the Holidays," designed to provide comfort and valuable information for those who had lost loved ones about how to survive the approaching holiday season. During the evening seminar our editor, Dr. Kennedy-Reeves, spoke to an audience of over one hundred about such matters as the importance of setting limits on their participation in holiday preparations, openly expressing their expectations to others, the importance of planning ahead, not trying to live up to the expectations of others or worrying about breaking down, being open and honest with feelings, and omitting some of the traditions they weren't ready to face quite yet. I spoke briefly to the group too and thought later *what a difference a year makes!* The Christmas before I was sobbing as I stirred the oyster stew. But one year later I was talking to a room full of grief-stricken people. And I had no idea at the time, but the following year I was to be occupied with the writing of this book.

All during that fall and winter and the following spring we lived on the balls of our feet. Each time negative thoughts would arise, I'd chastise myself with *Every moment you spend doubting or thinking of failure, you are keeping God's message from entering your mind and His goodness from touching your life. You either believe in your Lord or you don't. You can't believe and doubt. It doesn't work both ways. You have to trust.*

The work load was immense and there were many times when I secretly wondered if we'd make it or if we would fall on our faces. Actually about that time, I *did* fall, but not on my face. After working late one night, I skipped up onto the tile step (in my nylons,) and felt both legs slip out from under me. I attempted an impossible recovery, but because of my momentum, I was totally helpless to prevent a hard landing right on the garage floor. My leg broke in three places and my knee was injured. This unfortunate accident caused an ambulance trip to the hospital, five days of hospitalization, and the beginning of almost a year of pain, frustration, inconvenience, casts, grueling physical therapy (I had to learn how to walk again), and humiliation. Then six months later came the final insult: knee surgery. But on the positive side, I did learn how to do wheelies off the front porch in my electric cart, negotiate the sharp turn around the corner into the bedroom, bounce myself into the high canopy bed, and capsule my complex emotions so that I didn't go stark raving mad. I also got a lot of work accomplished. It was just about the only thing I could do. During this recovery period, *Afterloss* truly saved my sanity.

My poor husband! After living so long with a grieving wife, now he had a broken one! In my eyes, that year he achieved sainthood. His thoughtfulness, devotion, and dedication were beyond all description. He began writing me little "notes in the night," offering encouragement, new insight, reassurance, humor, and love.

> *We will overcome this.*
> *Cut and paste.*
> *Cut and paste.*

Another challenge! I guess this is the square in which you are standing tonight. And you will be strong enough to survive this one too.

Spring always comes, the sun always rises, God is always there.

You have been so brave and now it is almost over.

You will recover. Someday soon this will be part of your history.

It won't be much longer now.

We grow through the adversity we have gone through or go through and surely there will be more up ahead.

Let's plan not to push, not to expect more of ourselves than we should, and let health and strength and energy find their way back into our lives without feeling we should do more or do better. It'll come. Just you watch.

Wounded, I think we have to admit that is what we are now, each in our own way. We never really admit adversity, you and I, we look the other way. Take another breath. Press on.

And we will come through this strife too. And live each day for as many days as we have with the same characteristic strength.

It is a privilege to be able to help you when you are unable to do for yourself. Helping you is my joy.

We don't have to like it to walk through it. Pain is no stranger to either of us but its end is out there to see, and there's no defeat in any of this.

A time for tenacity. You can be under siege and survive. You will emerge victorious, stronger than ever.

What a remarkable concept. What a remarkable man.

With his help and the incredible dedication and medical skills of Dr. Robert Murphy and Craig Shouman of the physical therapy department, I learned how to walk again. It's interesting that right in the middle of the leg incident and subsequent recovery period was when I received the call from Ron Haynes about writing this book. In fact, the day after my knee surgery is the day Ron picked up the outline to take it to Nashville. I recall limping and stumbling into the living room to hand it to him personally. Right in the middle of the "sad," something wonderful was about to happen.

And then we heard from *The New York Times!* Sometime in the early spring of the following year I picked up the phone and this time the voice at the other end said, "Hello, this is Trish Hall from *The New York Times,* and I would like to speak with you about *Afterloss.*"

Lord, it's The New York Times!

Trish went on to describe a feature she was planning about assistance for the bereaved. She had heard about *Afterloss* from a funeral home in New York state and wanted to know just what we were all about. She asked many questions, and we spoke at great length about the urgent need for information and grief support in our fragmented, fast-food society.

"Unlike so many things in our society today, there is no quick fix for grief," I told her. "Recovering from grief takes time, and a lot of energy, and tears, and then more tears, and a patience you never believed you had or would ever need.

"People who are grieving need to understand the grief process. And those who are trying to help them through it also need to understand. But who wants to go out and read up on grief? We've been taught that it's the enemy.

"Well, we're taking on grief," I explained, "and we are going to show people how to walk through it and come out on the other side, whole people again."

I also said that for years, we've hidden grief in the closet, right along with sex. Well, obviously, sex got out. Now we are going to let grief out too.

"Death is a natural part of life. And after death comes grief. I believe the time will come when people will begin to see the grief process more as a friend and less an enemy. This is a vital link, a necessary part of the ultimate goal: recovery."

"Have people been afraid of grief all of these years?" Trish asked.

"I don't honestly know," I said. "But this I do know: When I needed help, I didn't have a clue where to go to find it. Now we are finding that the world is filled with people who are in the same sad situation. Like labor pains before a birth, we've got to go through our labor to get our baby. But we've learned that there are many things we can do to expedite delivery—proper breathing, relaxation exercises, knowledge of the process. And now there are classes all over the country to help make this experience less painful and of shorter duration.

"There are some strong analogies between the two processes. There are also many things we can do to expedite our grief, to make it less painful and of shorter duration. Fully experiencing grief is the only way to recovery. And how can we experience it properly if we don't understand how it affects our minds or bodies?"

Several weeks later there it was—a very lengthy article, entitled "Solace After Bereavement: Counseling Services Grow," right on page one of *The New York Times*. The wire services picked up on it right away, and soon both our Michigan and California offices were receiving letters and calls from all over the country. Even a few came from out of the country.

A page one story in one of the finest newspapers in the world. A story that later went out on the wire services to newspapers all over the country, who then reprinted the article in their own papers or called for interviews and did their own feature stories. Imagine that.

Lord, I know You're somewhere in the middle of this.

We moved on, delving deeper into recovery, taking on subjects such as "The Way Children Grieve," "Sexuality and the Survivor," "Abnormal Grief," "Marriage at Risk," "The Effects of Grief on Your Health," "AIDS," "Suicide," and "The Differences Between 'His' and 'Her' Grief." We did five special-focus issues: "The Lament of Child-Loss," "You and the Holidays," "Adolescent Grief," "Widowed," and "Stigmatized and Traumatic Death."

We published booklets containing questions asked during bereavement classes and their answers, a coloring book to help kids learn about grief, and an on-going series of *Afterloss* question and answer newspaper articles and radio announcements, each one providing answers to specific questions about the many different aspects of grief and its recovery. These *Afterloss* articles, sponsored by local funeral homes, are now appearing in newspapers all across the United States, Canada, and Australia, bringing information about grief recovery to millions of readers.

Finally the truth about grief was getting out where people could take a good hard look at it. Jack Smith, a nationally known columnist, did a feature about us which ran in many newspapers all over America. A nationally distributed health magazine, *In Health,* did a feature story on grief and health and listed *Afterloss* as a resource for recovery. We were deluged with calls from people all over the country who were still imprisoned by their grief. One woman had been struggling for sixteen years. We had calls from adult children who are desperately trying to find ways to help a widowed parent, from widows trying to help themselves, from devastated parents who had lost children, from one friend simply trying to help another. And they called *Afterloss* twenty-four hours a day. They still call twenty-four hours a day. And we answer every call. People are searching for information about this mysterious subject that is adversely affecting so many lives.

What are these calls like? Here are a few that are typical of the calls that come in daily now. A Los Angeles woman, widowed eighteen months before, said, "It seems like my husband died yesterday. We used to visit Palm Springs quite often, but I was afraid to go back alone. Over Labor Day I decided to try doing it without him. It was very difficult and I didn't stay long, but while I was there I saw the *Afterloss* question and answer feature in the newspaper. I called the FitzHenry Funeral Home and they sent me a copy of your publication. It is the first thing I have read in the eighteen months since my husband died that has made any sense to me and I want to subscribe. I've gone to libraries and rented books. I've gone to stores and bought books. Nothing helped me until *Afterloss*."

Another call came from a man in New York. "I am ready to kill myself. I have been so devastated since my loss that yesterday I almost threw myself in front of a car. A friend of mine read about your publication and suggested I call."

"Promise us you won't do anything for twenty-four hours," we said, and then we sent him copies of *Afterloss* by overnight express mail. We've spoken to him several times since, and his gratitude and new awareness of life are very evident. He has read every word we sent him. We suggested that he seek some professional help as well.

There was a call from a young woman whose parents died three months apart: "My religion is the only thing that keeps me from committing suicide. I know that if I do, I will never see my parents again. Otherwise, I'd be dead by now."

One of the saddest calls came from a woman who was looking for a way to help her friend, a mother whose two-year-old twin daughters drowned in their swimming pool. We were told the father was so devastated he couldn't attend the funeral.

Moments like these send me right to my knees.

As of this writing, over one hundred thousand issues of *Afterloss* are circulating and I've lost count of the number of newspapers that are running our *Afterloss* articles. Both are taking information about loss and recovery to readers all over this country and other countries. Having outgrown our original space, we have just moved into our new *Afterloss* Fulfillment Center and opened an office in Santa Barbara, California. God is gracious in His provision for our growth once again.

People still smile and say, *"Afterloss!* What a perfect name! Where did you ever find a name like *Afterloss?"*

And we aren't a bit shy about telling them.

FOUR

Afterloss Meets the Press

It's one heck of a leap from international commerce to grief and bereavement. But there's a drama in that leap, a drama that defines our commitment and our dedication to bring the subject of grief out into the open where we can take a good look at it.

Had I heard her correctly? "You want me to what?"

"Be our guest speaker at the Palm Springs Women's Press Club meeting next February. We want you to tell the *Afterloss* story."

V. J. Hume, a radio talk show host I'd met soon after her fiance's sudden death, was on the phone. She was my new friend and had just asked me to do something I had never done before. It was something I'd never wanted to do. It was something I'd never had any intention of doing, ever. She wanted me to make a speech! Not only did she want me to write it, she wanted me to deliver it before a professional organization: the Women's Press Club. I really couldn't believe any of it.

Lord, now what do I do? I don't know a thing about making speeches.

"Come, be my guest next month. Nancy Culp will be our speaker. You'll love her! She's one of the stars from "The Beverly Hillbillies." Funny, bright and witty, she's one of the most entertaining speakers around. I'll introduce you to everyone, and then you can get an idea of what we're like."

I didn't need to get the idea. I already had it. They were used to listening to film stars and television personalities, to professional entertainers and public speakers. How could I possibly follow acts like those?

That night, feeling somewhat apprehensive about the unexpected invitation to speak and looking for a quick escape, I picked up the current issue of the *Reader's Digest* and began to read. There, waiting to be discovered, right on the page where the magazine opened was:

Speaking Easy
Seven steps to panic-free public speaking
by Charles Osgood

OK, Lord, I'll accept. But I'm going to tell it exactly as it happened—sharing You all the way. Two months later, as I stood to face the members of the Women's Press Club, my opening remarks were hot off the pages of the January edition of the *Reader's Digest*.

Looking out into the room, I paused for several seconds after the introduction until V. J. got seated. She took a chair at the table directly in front of me. Looking up, she smiled briefly. Her face, filled with expectation, had a hint of sadness. In every sense she was a true professional. But I knew her grief was fresh. Six months before, Peter, the man she was about to marry, suffered a fatal heart attack, right in the middle of a beautiful autumn morning. She, too, had met grief. She had felt the stigma and the pain. She knew the heartache, the mindache. She knew it all.

Undoubtedly her grief was the reason I had been asked to be a guest on her radio talk show the previous November. Later she had said to me, "You should have seen the switchboard light up! The station was flooded with calls after we went off the air." And my deep belief was confirmed: People everywhere are searching for ways to understand and deal with grief, all kinds of grief. That December, radio station KWXY, along with "V. J.'s Corner," awarded "The *Afterloss* Story Interview" their Interview of the Year award. But I knew that the honor had been bestowed, not because of the guest speaker, but because of the impact and timeliness of the subject.

As my eyes circled the room, pausing momentarily on each face, I wondered how many other members of the Press Club were struggling with new griefs or had secreted away old ones. Yes, I remembered well, and I understood much about the ubiquitous, secret world of the bereaved.

Taking a step toward the mike, I swallowed and began.

Well, this won't be a speech as speeches generally go. I can't begin to tell you about rides in Rolls Royces with Cary Grant, or conversa-

tions with Clark Gable the way Nancy Culp did when she enter-
tained us so royally last month. Instead of giving a speech, I want to
tell you a story—a true story. It's a story about a relationship be-
tween a mother and her daughter and the love they shared. I am the
daughter, and this story describes what happened in my life after my
mother died and what led to the creation of the Afterloss *Recovery*
Program.

I told them about the losses in my life, about my father, my
brother, and, finally, my mother. I told them what it was like watching her die, about our last conversations—even about the clothes in
her closet hanging in color order. And then I told them about how I
asked the Lord to show me what was important in His world and
how I asked Him to guide me so I could use my life for something
that really mattered, something that would make a difference in
other people's lives for whatever time I had left.

And I told them a little about my mother. She was sweet and gentle, sensitive and pretty, and was always thinking of ways to help
others. Orphaned in her teens, she had to make her way alone when
she was just sixteen. She often spoke about the insecurity she felt
after her parents died. "I can remember walking along the streets as a
young girl and looking in the windows and seeing all the other
people—the happy families, the ones that had homes, and belonged!" Maybe that is why she always provided such a beautiful
sense of home for us. This was a part of her legacy to me.

During my growing up years, every night before Daddy arrived
home, no matter what kind of a mess she'd gotten herself into during
the day, she was bathed and wearing fresh make-up and a pretty
"afternoon dress." As far as I know Daddy never saw her with her
hair in curlers. I never heard a cross word between them.

My parents were hit hard financially during the Depression and
they never fully recovered. When Daddy died suddenly at fifty-seven,
Mother was left with her little house paid for, but not much else. She
managed by working for $3.25 an hour at the neighborhood drug
store. Eight years later, her only son was killed in Vietnam.

We loved, and cared, and watched out for each other for the next
twenty years. Our bond grew even stronger when we were carrying
on without the wonderful men in our family.

My husband said that during her final days it was really like
watching two people die instead of one. Our family physician said to
me, "Your mother is going to die. You shouldn't spend all of your

time with her. You need to take care of your own health." But, knowing that she would soon be gone, I could not stay away.

My mother left me with a rich and beautiful heritage of lovingness. She taught me well. I learned how to love and how to care for
others by watching the way she lived her life. But after she died, I
knew that I had to go on, using those things she had taught me and
parlaying them into something more. I had many questions, but at
the time, I was too distraught to think, much less take on the larger
lessons in life, the deeper things of God. Maybe this is part of the
reason I moved so quickly and so completely toward God's guidance.

*I used to think that I was pretty resourceful, that I could usually
find an effective way to deal with my problems. I thought I was up to
most challenges in life, and, like most of you, I considered myself a
survivor.*

*But when we're grieving, our minds don't work the way they used
to work. They not only don't work, they go on the attack, and we
end up convinced that we no longer even have a mind. We have a
live-in enemy.*

*My husband and I have an incredible marriage, but we began
bumping heads soon after Mother's death. He thought that after the
funeral our life together would begin to return to the way it had been
before she died. He needed me back again. I wanted to be back
again. And, sensing those needs, I tried to go back again and be the
person I had been. But it just wasn't working. I kept tripping over
my broken heart. I didn't fit into myself anymore. Sadly, I discovered
that I couldn't go back. I had been changed. I had become a different
person, a person I no longer knew (or cared to know). We didn't
understand what was happening to us. We simply didn't know how
to treat each other anymore. This was the main reason I decided to
attend the bereavement class. And that led to my friendship with Dr.
Kennedy-Reeves and the beginning of the incredible* Afterloss *story.*

I told them the whole *Afterloss* story, and about how it was born.
And then I shared with them many of the things we teach our bereaved survivors. I want to excerpt a little from that part of the
speech for you.

So what is Afterloss *all about?*
*In a nutshell, we take what is taught in bereavement class and
share it with the world. We spoon-feed grieving survivors a little bit*

of help each month. Since it is often so difficult to concentrate when we are grieving, we limit each edition to just eight pages. We let survivors know what to expect in the course of the grief process, and then we show them how to deal with each phase as it arrives.

Grief is a powerful emotion. Afterloss tells our readers they must not underestimate or try to avoid their grief. But there are many things that the bereaved can do to help resolve and ultimately shorten their grief process. Most people don't know this. I certainly didn't. This is known as grief work.

Some of the things we tell our readers that we can do to help ourselves are: Learn to let go. Begin to loosen the bonds that keep us tied to the past. Begin to accept ourselves as separate entities. Each of us is valuable in our own right. Learn to express emotions freely. Write about them, cry, talk about them (if we're comfortable doing that). Start making readjustments to our new lifestyle. Start searching for creative ways to give to others. Reach out to make new friends and build a network of new acquaintances that will lead to new friendships. Create and maintain a balanced routine with time for work, rest, relaxation, exercise, and mental stimulation. Give ourselves time and space to learn to be alone before becoming involved in new relationships. Begin to accept the return of joy and happiness in our lives and learn to identify special moments. Know that it's okay to look forward rather than to the past, and begin to do this without guilt or the fear of forgetting our loved ones. We will never forget our loved ones.

Afterloss has a very popular feature called "Loss and Recovery." We ask people who have recovered from loss to share their stories, to tell what happened, how they felt, where they are now, and how they got from "there" to "here." This is not meant to be an instructional page, although it sometimes is, but real-life honesty. It is those who are recovering saying, "This is what worked for me. Maybe it will help you too."

We also have a "Question and Answer" page. Here our editor answers the questions most frequently asked in her bereavement class, questions like: Why doesn't anyone mention my dead son anymore? Why do all my women friends treat me funny when I'm around their husbands now? How do I deal with the holidays? My brother doesn't seem to be grieving, but he also won't allow anyone to talk about the death of his wife. Is this normal?

The question and answer format is easy to read and easy to under-

stand. It's concise and simple, and very popular with our readers. We also take a look at the effects of grief on health. Our readers learn that it takes a lot of energy to grieve and that grief causes great stress. We teach them that it's good to pour out feelings to a friend. Our editor warns our readers to pay attention to proper diet, to get regular rest, keep a regular schedule, and to exercise even if they don't feel like it, to force themselves to take walks. This trains the body to welcome sleep again. Many who are grieving turn to medications and alcohol, but that's not a good solution. Taking care of health is an individual responsibility, even though at times the bereaved may not feel like it or care about health.

Afterloss *talks about the differences between "his" and "her" grief, saying that most of us don't realize that men have feelings of pain and grief equal to those of women, but simply have different styles of coping. It is only in their outward responses that they are different because these responses have been dictated by our society. These are a few of the differences our editor identifies.*

Women aren't afraid to cry. They usually have a social support system to tap into and are used to sharing needs and feelings with family and friends. They have less tendency to become isolated, because they have been used to making social arrangements with family and friends and they are more willing to seek out a support group. All of these things aid in their recovery process.

Men fear breaking down and crying and consider it a weakness to do so. They fear losing control of their emotions. They think they must endure pain alone and think they should always be self-sufficient. They're accustomed to accepting difficulties with controlled responses and often don't have a confidant to talk with. They often don't know how to express emotional pain and resist seeking outside support. They also retreat and become isolated after a death, because over the years their wives took the initiative and made most of the social plans with family and friends.

Afterloss *covers special days, holidays, anniversaries, and birthdays by suggesting that survivors plan ahead to get out of the house and be with friends. Tell others how you need to be treated; they can't read your mind. Don't apologize for tears. Omit traditions you are not yet ready to face, and let someone else cook the turkey or special holiday meal that first holiday.*

Afterloss *also suggests ways to learn how to handle the loneliness. Talk about your feelings to another person. Give yourself away.*

Take control of your life. Create new situations for yourself. Make a strong commitment to help others. Develop a hands-on cause. Make an effort to make new friends.

Our editor wrote a powerful article, entitled "I Never Know What To Say," suggesting different things we can do to help someone who has had a loss. Most of all, listen to your friend's fears and concerns. Risk your own feelings by expressing your emotion honestly. Don't pretend. Don't hide or swallow your emotions. Be real. Say, "I'm here and I want to help," or "I came as soon as I heard," or "I love you." You aren't expected to have all the answers or know how to say everything perfectly. Just be there for your friend; touch or hug them. And listen. Think of ways to help. If you are dealing with a terminal case, offer to bring food or to read or listen to music together. It's usually more important to be there than to do something.

One day we all have to face loss. It's going to happen to each of us. I hope that by my sharing this story with you you'll have some understanding of the grief process and won't have to walk the tortured path I have walked.

Someone once said that all love leads to loss. And loss leads to pain. But when it does happen to you, I hope you will remember this day and the things we've talked about and learned together. I hope you'll remember about "grief work" and how important it is. And about the waves. And the stages of grief. I hope you'll remember that grief has a beginning and also an end and about the importance of attending a bereavement group.

It seems that for a long time we've been dealing with a cultural oversight in our society. We pay a lot of attention to many kinds of pain but we don't pay much attention to one of the most debilitating pains of all, the pain of grief. Well, we've taken on grief. We've established a subsidiary company for the purpose of producing publications to bring hope, help, and healing to those who are grieving. It's an interesting counterpoint to our parent corporation.

Well, it's one heck of a leap from international commerce to grief and bereavement. But there's a drama in that leap—a drama that defines our commitment and our dedication to bring the subject of grief out into the open where we can take a good look at it. We want to show the people of the world how to deal with the pain of grief and loss.

I used to tell my husband that if I ever connected with the thing I really believed in, to watch out. And yet I know that Afterloss *isn't me, and it isn't Dr. Kennedy-Reeves. It's* Afterloss! *It has a life and a mission all its own. And it's here now for you, and for all those who walk the painful road of grief.*

In the words of our masthead, "we comfort those who mourn." This is our mission, and this is our song.

I ended by turning the attention of the Press Club members and friends to a six-minute memorial video. I invited them "to meet the lady who was, and still is, the inspiration for *Afterloss,* my wonderful mother, Louise (Maymo) Hills."

As the words of the Lord's Prayer began to fill the room, sung with such strong emotion and meaning by the well-known tenor Merrill Womach, a beautiful memorial tribute to my mother's life that had been prepared by his company began to move across the video screen.

Gathering my notes, I stepped down from the stage and headed toward the Harbor House table where my husband and daughter and a few friends were waiting.

A woman in her sixties, her eyes brimming with tears, caught my hand. "My husband died three months ago," she said. "I didn't feel like coming at all today—I don't go out much anymore, but when I read that you would be speaking about grief, I knew I had to come. How can I ever thank you for sharing your inspiring story?"

And another very regal woman, her face bandaged from recent surgery, walked over, reached out, and took me in her arms and held me for a moment. She explained softly, "I almost didn't come. I lost my husband a year ago today, and I honestly didn't know if I was physically up to this or not, as you can probably tell just from looking at me. But I want you to know that I have been receiving your publication for the last six months, thanks to our funeral home. And I want to tell you how very much it has done to help me."

Later that day someone asked, "Did you hear the applause? Did you see the standing ovation? There wasn't a dry eye in that room!" But I heard no applause. And I saw no standing ovation. I could only recall the tears on the cheeks of the widow who caught my hand. And the courage on the face of the bandaged woman. And the expression in V. J.'s eyes as I passed by her table.

And of course the hug.

FIVE

The *Afterloss* Forum

I don't know how to do this yet nor do I know exactly what it means, but I do know that I have to take responsibility for my life in a way that I've never had to before.

Knowing how each person responds so differently to the grieving process, we decided to ask a group of people from all walks of life and in different stages of their recovery if they would be willing to come together and share some of the things they did to recover from their grief. Under the umbrella of The *Afterloss* Forum, we focused on some of the most challenging problems faced by survivors.

This wasn't meant to be an instructional series of discussions, but rather an opportunity to provide insight into how others have felt, acted, and dealt with their lives following their loss. We felt that by sharing some of the very basic problems, or identifying ways in which others dealt with the routine day-to-day affairs of living, perhaps those who are presently going through the grief process can gain some helpful insights from others who have already traveled a similar path.

Our *Afterloss* Forum consisted of these participants:

Hope: sudden loss of husband 6 months ago
Irelene: loss of husband 11 months ago
Pat: loss of husband 12 months ago
Rolly: loss of wife 12 months ago
Betty: sudden loss of husband 17 months ago
Jackie: loss of husband 19 months ago
June: sudden loss of husband 21 months ago
Mary Anne: loss of husband 22 months ago
Diane: loss of husband by suicide 34 months ago

Barbara: loss of mother 18 months ago

Dr. Margie Kennedy-Reeves, thanatologist and leader of bereavement group: sudden losses of spouse, father, and child

Dr. Kennedy-Reeves offered to sit in on our discussion to make necessary clarifications, identify steps in the recovery process, and offer comments on answers from participants. We selected questions that we felt dealt with some of the most difficult challenges we all face after loss, put a tape recorder in the middle of the table, and then asked the participants to respond to any question they felt comfortable answering.

Afterloss: *Please share some of the most helpful things that friends said to you or did for you following your loss.*

Pat: After my husband died, one of the nicest things for me was the friends who were comfortable letting me talk about him. And at that time, I *needed* to talk about him. A lot of friends are very uncomfortable after a death and don't want to talk about the deceased person. They seem to like to pretend. They don't want to upset you. But it is so important to talk. I had a network of friends and relatives who called me regularly and gave me the chance to do that.

Betty: My family was all there, of course, all twelve of us. Two of our neighbors called early in the morning and said, "Please don't cook." Two nights in a row they brought over an entire gourmet dinner and served it, which I thought was really special. I really did appreciate that.

Hope: One of the things that helped me a great deal after the funeral was to be invited to a friend's house for about ten days. This gave me a perspective on what had happened and was a real comfort. It also helped me a great deal to be able to talk about my husband. The very fact that I was removed from the scene where he died and where all of that emotional trauma took place was a great comfort to me.

Jackie: One thing that was important in addition to the friends and family and all the people who called, was people who didn't mind if I cried and even encouraged it. I felt it was okay to cry, and sometimes we would all cry together. I didn't feel that I had to put on a show.

Mary Anne: I found it very helpful when my close friend and neighbor had me come to her house four or five nights a week for dinner for probably the first six months. Being with a family and kids and around other things that were going on in real life made it so I didn't just sit with my loneliness and hurt.

Diane: One thing that was helpful to me was that some people were willing to open up and talk about my husband's suicide, like it wasn't a secret or something that no one wanted to talk about. A lot of times people aren't willing to talk about death because they're afraid of your reaction. In my situation close friends being willing to talk about it gave me the openness to talk about it too. And this helped me start to work through the grief. Another thing I also appreciated was this: I went through a time when I would stutter a lot and cried constantly. The fact that some of my friends didn't act like I was colored green or something when that happened created a bond of unconditional love. They just loved me for who I was.

Rolly: I had a number of friends from out of town who couldn't be with me personally but called me constantly. Two or three men friends called me sometimes two or three times a day. They would ask me how I was doing and remind me of some nice things. That helped and I knew they cared a lot.

Afterloss: *What emotions were, or still are, the most difficult for you to handle?*

Hope: The most difficult emotion for me right after my husband's death was guilt. It was because in all the years I knew him, my husband wouldn't go to a doctor. I felt that perhaps we could have dealt with his illness—that he might not have died—if we had looked into it sooner. So I have that guilt.

June: I had a lot of anger directed at the hospital, the doctors, and the paramedics. I also had to deal with many irrational fears that I developed immediately, which did clear up later. The other significant emotion was that there were so many things I hadn't discussed with my husband. He wouldn't discuss his health or that maybe someday he would be gone. I wasn't prepared for this, and I felt guilty that I hadn't insisted upon getting everything out in the open. So many things were unsaid, things I missed being able to say to him.

Jackie: I had feelings of realizing my inadequacies and I hadn't really thought of that before. I had to deal with things that Bob had always taken care of and an overwhelming feeling of *Oh God, I'm all alone and I don't know how to do this*. It was so frightening. I had a lot of trouble figuring out who I was and if I was really capable of going on alone. I had depended on him so much, not only for physical things but also for emotional feedback that had helped me feel important and secure. I miss that terribly.

Mary Anne: My most difficult thing was—and, really, I think still is—the loneliness and the hurt and the aching and the missing of the person who was a part of my life seven days a week, twenty-four hours a day.

Afterloss: *What are the most positive steps you've found to speed up your recovery process?*

Betty: Instead of focusing on the depressing situation of not being able to say goodbye because Bill's death was so sudden, I have turned it around and focused my thinking on our lives the week before his death. That way I wasn't continually depressed about the reality of what actually happened. Thinking of the things that were good between Bill and me just before he died, rather than focusing upon his death, was helpful to me.

Barbara: The most positive thing for me has been attending the bereavement class. Another positive was that I felt an obligation to try to be the person my mother raised. I saw the way she handled the death of my dad, and then the way she dealt with the loss of her only son eight years later. I can still remember her strength—for example, how she presided at her dinner table that first night after she'd gotten the news of my brother's death. She set a beautiful example for me to follow and I really turn to that. I knew that I had a responsibility to her to pull myself together and try to get control of myself and my life. It wasn't always easy to do, and I did a rotten job some days, but I kept trying because I wanted to honor her and the example she set for me.

Rolly: Two or three things were positive steps for me. One was right after the funeral and memorial services. I said to my kids, who were with me, "I'm getting in the car and will be gone for three or four hours. When I get back, I'd like to see not one thing of Sue's in the closet. I don't want to see her shoes, her blouses—her beautiful blouses—or her skirts. I don't want to see them. They're gone." I got in the car and drove for three hours, and when I went home it was all gone, just as I had asked. I think that helped me a lot. The only problem with it is that some of the beautiful clothes were taken by some of her friends and now this one gal wears them once in awhile and I see them. Some of the things she uses I bought for Sue. But this woman doesn't think about that, I guess.

Another step I had to take was because I was here at the hospital so much, day and night, during three different times with my wife. After she died I had trouble coming through the hospital doors for my bereavement classes. Somehow I just forced myself to walk through those doors and finally that problem has dissipated. That's been a positive step for me.

June: I think the most positive thing I did was decide that I was not going to allow my life to be ruined. I decided I would not be a victim or a loser. I began going to a church that had a positive approach. I read every book I could get my hands on about being a widow and living alone. At first my bereavement group was really all I had to look forward to. I was in touch by phone with new friends from the group and also with my family. I reached out one step at a time, and I'm still doing that.

Hope: Realizing that you can't keep more than one thought going in your mind when you're grieving, I tried to divert my thinking by making a list of things that I needed to do to go on with my life. One thing was that I needed to take forty-five units to renew my real estate license. So I kept my mind busy doing that. When I was quiet I would read religious books or philosophical books that I had already read. I reinforced myself with them and I started going to church a little more so I could expand my thinking about life on earth and life in the hereafter and that has been comforting to me.

Jackie: I agree with all these approaches and have tried to do them too. Bereavement group has helped me tremendously. The friends I've made—the people who are going through the same things I am—there's something so comforting about that. I've also taken some classes at our local community college. I've always been active doing things outside the home, and I've continued that. And I've involved myself in some happy times—little pursuits that I enjoy—and that keeps my mind off worry and keeps me from feeling sorry for myself and from missing Bob so badly.

Mary Anne: Several days ago I had a call from a dear friend who just lost her husband. She says she can't cope, feels she can't handle it. My immediate response was that the best thing for her to do is to get in a bereavement group. So I realize my bereavement group must mean a lot to me.

Diane: There are a couple of things I've learned and I agree with everything the others are saying. Because my loss was a suicide, it was a little different in certain ways. We all have ideas about the ways someone should act because of or in reaction to a suicide. But those ideas aren't always right or appropriate. So one of my most positive steps was learning to just be real. One of the emotions I had to deal with, as well as the sorrow, was anger. And I felt abandoned and rejected, although I never felt angry with God. When things were really bothering me, I learned to say, "This is really bothering me." And instead of trying to skim over it, I learned to take the time to deal with the issues that were there.

It takes time for all of us to make the pieces lie down. I learned to say, "I'm going to learn how to deal with this so that it doesn't always grab me and won't hook me for the rest of my life." I remember that when the guilt would come in, I would draw a line on the floor with my foot and say, "You can't come in. You can't come at me and ruin my life." It sounds kind of funny now, but I wasn't real good at making choices to begin with, so I had to learn how to fight some of this stuff. If I hadn't that suicide would have destroyed me in one way or another.

I had three little girls to raise and we all had lives to live. We just couldn't be destroyed and devastated and go and live in a corner of the world for the rest of our lives. Being real and learning that I did have choices, positive choices, that I could choose to be terribly afraid or I could make the choice to say, "What is it that I am really afraid of?" and then learn piece by piece to deal with that fear—that's what I had to do. And I had to do it one step at a time, sometimes going minute by minute. And I still do that. At times when situations get overwhelming, I deal with one thing at a time.

Rolly: Really the most positive thing is joining the bereavement group and getting in touch here. That is the most important thing.

Barbara: I think we all agree on that. This wonderful lady at the end of the table has been so important to all of us in our recovery.

Dr. Kennedy-Reeves: I think it's important though, that when we give our friends in other areas the advice "just get yourself into a bereavement group," to remember that it's not always out there and available to a vast number of people. Our experience in this bereavement group is unique to us. There are bereavement groups here and there. Some are small groups that often are not run by professionals. It's hard to connect if you are not in a big city area. Even in San Diego, with eight hospitals, there isn't a bereavement group that meets regularly. A lot of peer groups spring up and that is one kind of therapeutic support, but it isn't learning, it isn't teaching, it isn't education about what you are doing. So there is a lot of fragmented information getting out.

Rolly: As a matter of fact, my daughter is in the same situation that Barbara is in. She misses her mother. I told her to go to the local hospital and see what kind of support group they have. So she is going to do that.

June: I'd like to comment on one thing about this bereavement group, because it meant so much to me that I've never forgotten it. Occasionally I tell people about my first time at bereavement group. I was upset. I didn't know what it was about. And I didn't know what I was doing. What I remember now is seeing all those faces and how warm I felt to have these people to look at. I'll never forget it. I couldn't see my husband in my memory as he was before. All I could see was when he was unconscious. Our counselor explained to me that this was a physical thing and that after a certain amount of time it would pass. You'll never know the relief that comment gave me. I relaxed. I knew that I wasn't going crazy.

Barbara: I had the same reaction. I thought I was really "losing it" too. But when Dr. Kennedy-Reeves told our class, "Even if you tried to feel the way you are feeling now a year from now, it would be physically impossible," that gave me hope for the first time that things would get better for me.

Dr. Kennedy-Reeves: It's so interesting from my point of view. Even though each of you has a very distinctly different set of circumstances going on with your bereavement, when I talk to newly bereaved persons and they tell me their stories, it's almost like a tape recording that I've heard many times before. I know what they're leading up to. They tell me all of these things that are happening to them, and they want me to say, "You're not crazy." Not too many of them will actually say, "Am I losing my mind?" Some of them will, and they say it in many different ways, but it's the same message.

"Am I losing it?" And that is one of the biggest and most fearsome and awesome things that happens in that acute phase of grief.

Irelene: About two months after Paul's death, I just didn't think I could handle going in front of strangers and speaking of my hurt and my grief. I didn't go to a bereavement group until four months after Paul died. I finally decided that I had to do something because I thought I was losing my mind. I would walk from one room to another and not only cry, but sometimes *wail*. I thought, *I'm going to end up in an institution*. So I came and was greeted very warmly. After the first meeting I went home feeling worse than when I came, but I said that I would come three times. The second meeting I started to feel the benefit, and it's been the one thing that's saved me.

Afterloss: *The holidays are coming and this can be a difficult time. How do you plan for them? How do you deal with special times such as holidays, birthdays, and anniversaries?*

Pat: Last year the thought of Christmas really was an awful thing to look forward to. I kept thinking, *How will I get through this?* I knew I was going to go up to Washington where my daughter lives and spend Christmas with her and her children. But that is where my husband died. I thought, *Oh, this is going to be tough*. But I got there and got very involved with the baking and the things of Christmas. I did cry when I heard certain Christmas carols, which are touching to begin with. It was a different Christmas, but I wouldn't say it was a completely unhappy Christmas. I think part of it was that I was very busy doing the things I'd always done like baking, shopping, looking after little grandchildren tagging around me. That tremendous activity took my mind away from the terrible sadness of not having him to share it with us. We did remember my husband, of course, and we talked about him a great deal. I think having a lot of people and love around you can be joyous even though you have a loss. On the other days, like birthdays and anniversaries, I have to get out of the house. I make sure I have something planned to do or otherwise I'd be home moping. That's how I get through them.

Mary Anne: I try to keep very busy.

Irelene: Last Christmas I also went to Washington where my son lives and had Christmas with them. I held up. Paul died shortly after Thanksgiving, so it had only been a month. I went up there determined that I wasn't going to spoil their Christmas with a lot of weeping and I didn't. I did the weeping when I came home. Before Paul died we were signed up for a cruise with a group of friends. When we found out about his condition and that he would have to have surgery, we weren't able to go. And then when he knew he was terminal, one day he asked me to bring a pad and pencil to the hospital. He wanted to clue me in on everything that I should know. He went through everything with me and then at the very last he said, "Now this is the most important. I want you to take the cruise and I'll be depending on you to do that." I wasn't very enthusiastic about going on a cruise by myself. So when my son was down I said, "I have an offer to make," as the Godfather would say. "Instead of spending all the money on me, I'd like to take you and your family to Hawaii for Christmas." So that's where we are going. It's all set.

Dr. Kennedy-Reeves: I want to comment on the difference between one Christmas and the next. Even if you wanted to feel as bad this year as you did last year, it's not possible.

June: I was afraid to meet my daughters when I got off the airplane, but once I got off that plane and they met me, everything was fine and I overcame another fear.

Afterloss: *What was the most difficult obstacle for you to overcome following your loss?*

Hope: The most difficult for me was making decisions. Although I like to think I'm very independent, my husband and I used each other as sounding boards for many decisions we needed to make. We would sift through all the thoughts that each of us had. Now I don't have that. I'm out there on my own and have to make decisions on many things alone, like selling property, about employment, and about so many things—such as what to do with the rest of my life. But I'm trying. I think I'm going to make it.

Diane: I think the most difficult obstacle for me to overcome was a lack of confidence. You know, the whole self-esteem thing and the confidence that I can raise up my three kids as a single parent and make decisions, good decisions, and be out there on my own. It's the same type of thing you were talking about, Hope. It seems that all of a sudden you feel very vulnerable and alone. Even if your somebody doesn't give you feedback, just the fact that there is somebody you can share things with gives you confidence. And then all of a sudden, you're by yourself.

June: It was the same with me: decision-making and the fear of being alone. I can be alone at home and feel thoroughly happy a good part of the time now. I'm over a lot of the loss, but the biggest thing is learning how to live again and be independent and on my own. Making decisions, taking responsibility, having to get out in the world again—I compare it all now to back when I was eighteen.

Rolly: The one thing that has been so hard for me is eating alone and being alone. But I think I'm overcoming it now. I have real good friends and that's really helped. Another thing is that it was such a long period of time when we had our problem that I lost a lot of weight. And I couldn't seem to get my emotions under control so I could gain it back. But now it's beginning to turn.

Pat: I think one of the things, too, is that we look inward during this time. One of the nice things in recovery is learning to look outward and forward again.

Jackie: My biggest problem was—and sometimes still is—knowing that I was special to him and that now I don't have anyone who finds me a really important person in their life. That is still hard for me to accept—that I'm not really somebody special to anyone anymore.

Afterloss: *One recent widow called* Afterloss *and asked this question: "Now that my husband is gone, there's no one to tell me that I look attractive or to compliment me when I do something well. I have a hard time with my self-esteem now. Also, as I age, I feel more sensitive about my looks." Can you offer any suggestions on how to deal with these new feelings of insecurity?*

Hope: I'm wondering if this is a physiological change, or if it is in my mind. About a week after my husband died I felt that I had aged about twenty years. Maybe I always looked as bad as I do now, but the fact that he was always around—the fact that I had a man to begin with—and that I had someone who complimented me (even though he may have been lying in later years!) gave me confidence. I've also noticed the way I am treated when I'm out now, even in the business world. When my husband stood next to me, the reaction was much more affirmative. Is it our imagination that we're treated differently?

Dr. Kennedy-Reeves: It's not your imagination at all, but every slight that occurs to you now, when you're in such a vulnerable state, is so much more intense. A lot of these things happened to you before, but you were not so isolated and alone, and you didn't feel so vulnerable. Now you feel, "I have to deal with this too, along with everything else that has happened to me. This isn't right. This isn't fair." So it happens all the time. You're sensitive to it. And that's never going to change whether it's after you've had major surgery, after a move, or certainly after a loss.

Afterloss: *What do you do to overcome the loneliness?*

June: Keep busy. I am going to New Beginnings, which is a social group here at the hospital. I went before, but it was too soon after my loss. Now I have a different attitude. I feel the need to be with people now more than ever. And I feel I need a cause. I haven't had a cause since my husband died. I need people to be with and things to do. I feel that now I want to put my energies toward helping others.

Barbara: Then what you're saying is that you are going to give. Do you remember that in the last issue of *Afterloss* Dr. Kennedy-Reeves talked about giving ourselves away?

Betty: I entertain a lot. I have the girls for coffee, for lunch, and for dinner. I love to entertain and the excitement of planning and looking forward to it helps me. I also visit with friends and family. I find that as long as I have someone, a person with whom I can look forward to doing something, I am content.

Jackie: I don't entertain now because my home is so small, but I have friends I can contact at any time and we do things together. Things that I might have been concerned about doing alone, I don't mind doing, if I have one girlfriend to do them with. I do a lot of things with other widows since we do have so much in common. With another widow, you don't have to worry if you feel like crying one minute and laughing the next. I have made a network of wonderful friends whom I can call on at any time. And, of course, my family is close by.

Mary Anne: I have decided I'm going to take my free time and do new things, like learning to play tennis. I want to make new friends. I want to start anew, to begin my life over. I still hurt like the devil, so in some ways I'm slow and in other ways I'm going forward. I just got back from Hawaii and I was so lonely there. It's the first time that I noticed the couples. Now that I'm home, I'm going to keep busy.

Afterloss: *Finally, are there any additional thoughts, ideas, or suggestions that you would like to pass along for our* Afterloss *readers?*

Mary Anne: Yes, make new friends, keep busy, and help others.

Hope: My advice is to join a bereavement group and get yourself occupied with things to do and with other people.

Diane: I think my advice is to begin training yourself to look for the positive, to look for the love and grace that's out there, because there is a lot of it available. It's like learning to see again. When things get real tough and you get real lonely, you have to go back to those first moments when people brought meals. Dwell on the moments of love.

Irelene: Remember your loved one not in terms of the loss, but all the happy times you shared. That's what I've been doing.

Jackie: When I start feeling sad and thinking *Poor me,* I have to tell myself that I'm not the only one that's sad and blue. Others are feeling the way I am. I make the effort to help them and then that brings me out of myself.

June: I think self-pity is the biggest bugaboo for me. If I get into that, it's my downfall. Then I must get out of it. I get out of the house or on the phone or something.

Barbara: After getting through the first stages of grief, when I was able to think clearly again, I focused myself in a new direction: a project that I felt would help to comfort others who were also grieving. That is how *Afterloss* was born—to help comfort the bereaved. While it wasn't my intent to relieve my own suffering with this work, it certainly has been very instrumental in my own recovery. I would encourage others to force themselves to move into new directions. Try to remember that your loved one would not want you to spend the rest of your days in deep sorrow. Rather, cherish the time you shared in each other's lives and let those memories guide you to find new ways to make the rest of your life a blessing for others.

Dr. Kennedy-Reeves: I think that if we could say it in one statement it would go something like this:

I don't know how to do this yet nor do I know exactly what it means, but I do know that I have to take the responsibility now for my life in a way that I've never had to before. Maybe I've never truly been alone before. I will choose not to be the victim here. I will choose to create happiness and positivity in my life.

To me, this means accepting the opportunities offered and taking full responsibility for everything you do. That means giving yourself away; it means finding a cause; it means filling up the lonely hours; it means creating a new life; it means becoming that new person that sees through new eyes. And all of that is inherent in the statement: "I must accept my own responsibility for my life." That is one of the hardest things that we, as humans, have to do.

When we are forced to exist under the worst of circumstances, we can say, "Look at the horrible thing that's happened to me. I'm a victim of it. I can't rise above it. There's nothing I can ever do to make my life good again." And if we think that, chances are we're right. We see it in the drug culture, in alcoholics, in abused children, in cancer patients—in every area of life. Once you put that thought in your head, you're going to get exactly that.

But when you choose, as Diane said, "to see things through new eyes," and you rise above your circumstances and know that you are strong and valuable, you can make everything else happen. But you've got to start with that one premise. And if you don't know how, that's fine. You can learn.

Book Two
Decisions for Recovery

Book Two, "Decisions for Recovery," contains twenty-two chapters written by brave men and women who have suffered loss and are willing to share their painful stories with you. Most of the writers are people I've met through my work as founder of the Afterloss Recovery Program and as publisher of Afterloss.

Reading these stories is an indescribable experience. Nearly all of the survivors told me that writing about their losses was an experience filled with deep emotional pain, and that often they wrote through blinding tears as each traumatic event was recalled. But these caring people have shared their personal stories because they want to reach out and help you! In chapter 30 we'll take a brief look into the lives of these writers to see where they are today.

I have included these stories of tragedy and triumph because all of the survivors made the decision to seek recovery after their loss. Each one valiantly fought the way to freedom. Each one has found it.

My prayer is that you will learn from them.

Phyllis's Story

*I realize Ralph will not be coming back and that
life will never be the same. Neither will I.*

My husband died two months ago. I stood by his hospital bed, helpless and forlorn, and watched him go. He had been the core of my life for thirty-five years, and I began to feel the absence of his physical presence immediately and acutely.

Following the doctor's softly spoken "He's gone," the doctor, the nurse, and my grieving, true-blue sister left the room, discreetly granting me one last time alone with my beloved. The door closed quietly behind them.

Ralph was comatose and on morphine for the last few days of his life. But even prior to that, because of a tube inserted into his trachea, he'd been unable to talk. I had not heard him speak since the morning the ambulance took him to the hospital. I ached for the sound of his voice. I still do.

Before the coma we hadn't expected Ralph's death so soon. He had overcome pneumonia, only to fall prey to hospital-acquired infections. Even if we'd known then, we wouldn't have been able to discuss death or to say our goodbyes. I will always regret that.

I studied his dear, familiar face and marveled at its serenity. The peace that came after the morphine crowded out the pain had carried over into death. I twined my fingers through his, stroked his strong hands, smoothed his hair, and kissed his eyelids and the tip of his nose. When I kissed his lips I thought I felt a response. I glanced quickly at the monitor, but the heart line remained still, straight, and resolute. I supposed I was willing him to live, trying to summon him back to life with my own heartbeat.

The truth is I'd worked arduously at willing him to live during the three months he had been bedfast in the hospital. I was in his room all day and much of the night during those months, intent on keeping his morale up and his thinking positive. I filled in for busy nurses and spoke to the doctors for Ralph since, hampered by the tube in his trachea, he could not speak for himself. One of Ralph's many notes to me said, "Thanks, mouthpiece."

Most relatives and friends have been extremely supportive during these trying weeks of mourning. Their loyalty has touched me deeply. I've found that such devotion gives me strength. Most of these caring individuals have the insight to understand that grievers must be encouraged to speak about their feelings if they are to get any relief from the pain inside. But, trying to help, several of my sympathetic mainstays, who happen to have not yet experienced grief firsthand, have suggested that I should interrupt my period of mourning by getting out more. They say, quite seriously, "What you must do is get out among people. Go on a cruise. Take a bus trip. Then you won't feel so lonely."

But I am not lonely for *people*. I am lonely for *my husband*. I might add that I don't feel whole enough to resume routine social activities. But how can I expect these innocents to understand that I feel as though my body has been torn apart, that my soul has been mutilated? How could they understand that to me, at this particular stage of grief, life is simply a matter of survival?

For the most part, it's my married friends and acquaintances who have been least able to rally around me as a grieving widow. I think what seems to be indifference is, in truth, a self-protecting mechanism provided by nature. My loss has given them a stark preview of a similar loss they will experience some day, and they prefer not to watch me.

I yearn for Ralph. I miss our love rites: my kiss planted on his balding head; his fingers gently caressing the back of my neck; his soft, warm "I love you too," spoken in response to the love light in my eyes.

Thirty-five years of compatible togetherness allows a lot of time for establishing love rites. It comforts me now to know that the memory of those rites will be with me long after the memory of the death rites is forgotten.

We continued our love rites in Ralph's hospital room. They helped to lighten the load during those stress-filled months. Lowering the bedrail so I could reach him for a good-morning or a good-night kiss became a ritual. Intertwining our fingers and letting them linger became a ritual. Touching was a comfort.

SIX

He wrote many notes to me. Some were practical: "Remember to buy gasoline?" "How are the neighbors?" "Are you getting enough rest?" "How soon will I be going home?"

But the messages I cherished most were the ones that said simply, "I love you. XXOOXX."

I have survived the immediate shock of Ralph's death only to find that grief opens the door to many strange emotions: guilt, self-reproach, longing, anger at having to go it alone. The mind never seems to shut up. It constantly dispatches flashbacks of distressful moments that are better not dwelled on. I am helping myself through this stage of grief by attending a grievers' support group that meets each week. The longer term grievers in the group have helped me to accept my strange emotions as normal in my particular stage of the grief process. It helps me, too, to be able to reach out and comfort another griever.

In the past few weeks I've gone through piles of reading material focused on grief and coping. I'm doing my homework by following the writers' unanimous recommendations that, in order to survive, the griever needs to set up schedules and routines that include daily chores, yard work, eating regular meals, reading the daily paper, personal grooming, and exercise. All of these appointments with myself are helping me regain my sense of being in control.

Grief is more shattering than I ever imagined. Never could I have anticipated the emotional upheaval that has taken over my life. And even the grief itself is not a stable thing. It is an ongoing debate, with the body saying one thing and the mind another. Grief is like an illness—a physical ache. But even so, we mourners cling to it. After all, grief is love hanging in there. Ideally someday I will reach the stage where my mind can let go of my grief while my heart remembers bittersweet memories of the love I lost.

Right now I'm at the point in grief where I realize Ralph will not be coming back and that life will never be the same. Neither will I. I can only hope to discover that it's possible to live with such a major loss and, at the same time, function as a level-headed, well-balanced individual.

Occasionally I give myself a little congratulatory pat on the back for having come this far into survival. Although I'm light-years away from being whole again, I am beginning to believe what I read in the "self-help for grievers" books, that we grow through crisis, step-by-step, and gradually come to a sort of rebirth—the same person, yet different.

To me that means the part of me that remains the same, my heart, will always remember and cherish my beloved husband, will always mourn my loss, will never forget the sweetness of our uniquely precious relationship or our love rites. The different me, my mind, made stronger by my struggle through the dark days of grief, will develop into a better me, a wiser me, a more spiritual me, perhaps even a doer of good deeds.

SEVEN

Sharon's Story

Death the Invader . . .
Steals our most precious possession.

My husband died February 28, 1986.

In November 1987, I took a creative writing class. Feelings had been rolling around in my heart and my brain for many months, straining to erupt. When the professor instructed our class to write a short story or set of poems as our final exam, I decided I would—I must—voice these feelings and get them out of my system.

I locked myself in my bedroom one entire weekend and wrote, and cried, and paced, and cried, and wrote. The words, the feelings, spewed out onto the pages almost automatically. The next weekend I rewrote, adding and subtracting, until the total result said exactly what I had been feeling and what I felt then. I felt grief, pain, loneliness, and many emotions shared by those who lose a spouse.

I also felt, deeply, a lack of understanding. Nobody really understands how a widow or widower feels, do they? Perhaps it is impossible to really understand until experienced. But I wanted *somebody* to understand!

The few poems I share with you here constitute a catharsis for my grief. They also are love songs to my husband.

After Jim died, I finally realized that if I was ever again to be a functioning human being and a mother to my children, I needed more help in dealing with grief than I was getting. And I decided I must help myself.

I learned (barely) to play golf and played it (badly) with my sons and in company golf tournaments. I walked, took Yoga classes, volunteered, read books about grief. I prayed and tried to concentrate on gratitude for twenty-eight Jim-packed years. And finally, I went back to school, which I loved, where I wrote "Eulogy of Grief."

Several of the books I read searching for help and answers say that it is valuable to write down your feelings. It doesn't matter how we write or what we write. No one else has to see it. The writing process helps us focus on how we really feel. Transferring these feelings to paper may release some of them. Writing, even when painful, can be a great purging experience.

I think you can see me healing in my poems. If sharing a few of them helps just a few others through their own grief, or helps someone to better understand another's grief, even half as much as writing them helped me, all the tears and pain will have been repaid in silver and gold.

INVINCIBLE FOES

Death the Invader
Quietly advances upon our territory,
Runs our ramparts,
Attacks our citadel,
Violates our person,
And hand-in-hand
With Death the Conqueror,
In the darkness of our night
Steals our most precious possession.

FUNEREAL FEELINGS

Numb . . .
    Gladiola
    Chrysanthemums
    Pick the flowers for the coffin

        Dazed . . .
            Select the suit
                the songs
                the pallbearers
                the cemetery plot
                Make it through the days
                    . . . Dazed

Lifeless . . .
    Insurance policies

        Paralyzed . . .
            Shake hands
            Hug
            Kiss
            Smile
            Don't cry
                . . . Stupefied

Frozen . . .
    Ground
    Assets

        Anesthetized . . .
            The smell of disinfectant
                formaldehyde
            Mixed with gladiola and
                chrysanthemums
                . . . Benumbed

Shocked . . .
    Raining
    Cold
    What are you doing
        there in the cold, black ground
        with dirt all over you?

SCREAMING

Monday
I screamed and shrieked,
Struck the walls
With shaking fists,
And cursed God.

Tuesday
I screamed at Jim.
Asked why
Did he leave me
Alone and unloved?

Wednesday
I raced,
Late at night,
On the by-pass—
Car windows down,
Wind blowing in my face—
And screamed.

Thursday
I screamed at my sons,
Said I wished
I could die, too.

Friday
Crying,
Chastising myself
For screaming
At my children,
My God, and my Jim,
I screamed at myself.

Saturday
I was silent,
All screamed out.

Sunday
I wept at Mass,
Screaming inside.

They tell me screaming
Won't help me.
Nothing will,
Except time.
Yes, in about 100 years,
No one will remember him,
Or me,
Screaming.

GUILT

I'm sorry.
I regret every ugly word
I ever said to him,
Every unkind look
Or deed committed,
Every act of love
Omitted.

I'm sorry.
I wade through
Waves of remorse,
Trudge over
Mountains of "If onlys."

If only I had realized
The pain in his back
Was a heart attack.
If only I hadn't
Hurried off to work.
If only I'd called.

I'm sorry.
If wishes were wings,
I would soar
Out of the valley of grief,
Over the dead end of too late.

Guilt is
A one-way trip
To nowhere.

DO SOMETHING

Some people
Won't look me in the eye.
Why?
Are they afraid I might hex them?
Is my pain so terrible to see?
Or do they hide the relief in their own eyes
That it was not them, but me?
        Look at me!

Some people
Say nothing. Ignoring my loss.
Why?
Do they hope it will go away?
Are they afraid of my tears? Shy?
Or do they simply feel inadequate,
Not knowing what to say?
        Say something!

Some people
Don't listen when I speak.
Why?
Are they afraid of the truth?
Of the grief they hear in my voice?
By sharing my sorrow, do they come too close
For comfort, to their own?
        Hear me!

Some people
Stand distant from me, not touching.
Why?
Is death contagious?
Sorrow slimy?
Is a widow a touch-me-not?
Or are they afraid of being touched themselves,
Of coming in touch with their feelings?
        Hug me!

Have I suddenly joined the league of
Untouchables?
Non-persons
Incapable of intelligent conversation
Or human feeling?
Unloved and alone?
Look at us.
Speak to us.
Listen to us.
        Love us.

I THINK I'M GETTING BETTER

Hi, my honey,
I think I'm getting better.
Grief still hits me in the stomach sometimes,
Doubling me over.
I still cry for you in the night.
But some days I feel happy for a while.
I can laugh again.
      I think I'm getting better.

What would I do without our families and friends?
My sisters are beautiful,
Always there for me.
Dalarna and Bob are having Thanksgiving this year.
They understand I can't.
Camilla is taking off from work to be with me
During the operation.
Since you can't.
My friends at work help to cheer me up.
A bridge friend dined with me on our anniversary.
But I don't want to be a widow!
Nobody really understands.
I wish I could talk to you.
      But I think I'm getting better.

The boys and I will spend Christmas
With Tina and Jarrett.
But what will I do January first on your birthday?
Or on mine?
Or on the day you died?
I love you, my honey.
The oven is broken again.
So is the washing machine.
And the lawnmower.
Some things never change.
Aren't you glad
You don't have to worry about them anymore?
I miss you, my honey.
      But I think I'm getting better.

It has been painful
To write about your death and my feelings.
But helpful.
Better than a psychiatrist.
And cheaper.
My professor said I made you sound perfect.
Didn't you have any faults?
You know what they are, don't you?
I told you often enough.
I'm sorry, my honey.

I started smoking.
Then quit again.
Now I eat.
I've gained ten pounds.
But neither smoking nor sweets
Satisfy my craving.
They don't take your place.
        But I think I'm getting better.

October leaves are here.
Remember last year
When we camped at Rough River?
I sold the camper.
Every time I see a red or yellow leaf
Or a brown and white camper
I miss you, my honey.
I'm crying again.
        But I think I'm getting better.

Your Jonathan is his old happy self again,
Making A's and B's.
He quit worrying every time I cough,
Has learned to juggle.
I wish you could have been here
For Brett's graduation.
I think he's settled down some.
He's going to the Community College,
But all he really wants to do is play his guitar.
My old car is holding together long enough
To get Tracy back and forth to Western
For his last semester.
I will miss having him to talk to.
Tina called.
We miss you, my honey.
        But I think we're getting better.

Do you know all this?
        Do you see us?
          Hear us?

I took off my wedding ring today
And put it on my right hand.
I hope you don't mind, my honey,
I will always love you.
Someday we will be together again.
In the meantime,
I have this life
And this world
To get through.
I'm lonely, my honey,
        But I think I'm getting better.

EIGHT

Terry's Story

You have to want to get over this grief and then work at it.

Life was wonderful. I felt the excitement of spring. The air was filled with the sweetness of flowers and the songs of the birds. I thought I had everything I'd ever dreamed of—a husband, a home, and a career, and soon a daughter.

My husband, Denny, and I had waited anxiously for our baby all during my pregnancy. Would it be a boy or a girl? Have brown eyes or blue? Be meek or mischievous? And what would it be like to actually hold and love our own baby—to guide this new person into adulthood?

Finally on August 4, 1984, Anne Jolene Bogard was born. She was a real beauty. She immediately found a special place in our hearts as she laughed and cuddled, grew and blossomed.

By June she was just cautiously beginning to take those first steps as we coached her on. I had great plans for our summer: We would take walks in the stroller, go for rides on the bike, and go to the beach. She'd wear that new pink swimsuit with the ruffles.

The phone call came on a Friday morning while I was at work. "Something has happened to Anne. She's in the emergency room at the hospital. And she's stopped breathing."

Denny picked me up, and we drove wildly across town, not knowing what to expect when we arrived. Was it a false alarm or was it for real? I imagined she would be sitting in a room playing with a tongue depressor, charming the doctors and nurses.

Walking into the emergency room was like a nightmare. At first we weren't allowed to see Anne. Jenny, our baby-sitter, was there pale and distressed, clutching her own son. From somewhere our minister appeared. We cried, and waited, and prayed, and pleaded. Finally a nurse reported that there was a heartbeat. I was shocked to see my tiny little sweetheart lying still and lifeless on the stretcher. I wanted to awaken her. She looked peaceful, and I knew that she was already with Jesus. When I looked into her eyes, both pupils were dilated. I felt helpless. I am a nurse. I thought I should be able to do something to heal, but medical technology could only keep Anne breathing, not really living.

The next two days were black. Family and friends came to the hospital, but I was consumed with a pain deep down inside that I had never before experienced. As I sat by Anne's bedside, in my heart I hoped she would start breathing on her own, but in my mind I knew she wouldn't. I prayed and bargained with God to let her live.

Early Sunday morning, with the sun just making the world all bright, we went to the hospital to say our last goodbyes to Anne. It was comforting that it was the Lord's day. I was reminded of Easter morning when Jesus conquered death. How significant that was now.

We turned off the ventilator. And then, for one last time, we held our little Anne, touching her face with our fingers—tracing forever in our minds her tiny, beautiful face. We left the hospital feeling exhausted, numb, and empty. We drove home in silence—each lost in our own thoughts.

The funeral was two days later on a rainy, dreary day. The church was packed. Denny and I held each other for comfort and strength. I heard portions of the message.

"I do not urge you to hold it in, but to let it out. I am your God and Anne's God. The children of believers are holy; that is, they are set apart for God. The Christ, the only Son of God, was crucified so the Annes of this world can live in joy and die in certainty."

The most painful time for me was at the cemetery when the casket was closed and my child was put into the ground. It was so final, so cruel.

Let go?

How could I pick up the toys we were just getting used to stepping on? How could I put away all those sweet-smelling pink clothes, most of them unworn? How could I close the book on all those plans we had made as a family? All those dreams snuffed out—just like that.

I touched and smelled everything Anne had played with—trying once more to experience some closeness with her. But the emptiness remained. The pain that I had begun to feel at the hospital had not gone away. My heart felt like it had been torn out, leaving me with a bleeding hole. I didn't know how to deal with this new emotion, so I just cried and cried until my head throbbed.

I thought I was supposed to feel better with time, but I didn't. The numbness had worn off, and Anne was dead. Never to return to me. I wanted the grief to be over. I wanted the ache to be gone. I wanted life to get back to normal.

I returned to work, but my emotions were like a roller coaster. I never knew how I would react to anything. Some days I wasn't bothered much, but on other days even a small remark would send me to tears. Often I was angry with friends who tried to comfort me because they couldn't really understand my feelings. It was *my* baby who was dead, not theirs. Mostly I tried to avoid conversations about Anne. I didn't know how I would explain to anyone how I felt because I couldn't put it into words. I didn't want others to feel uncomfortable around me.

A subtle wall began to build between my husband and me. At first we had been so close, holding and comforting each other through the hospital stay, the funeral, and the first few weeks. Denny loved Anne as much as I did. He had always been involved in her life, from distracting her while I fed her, to being part of the bath and bedtime routine.

We shared the same feelings about Anne's death. We did not blame anyone or each other. We felt we had been the best possible parents to Anne. We both believed she was in heaven with Jesus.

Still, the wall began to grow. Denny seemed to be getting back to a normal life of working and socializing, but I was too embarrassed to let him know I still cried daily. I felt I couldn't share with him that I still missed Anne and was not enjoying life. I was afraid he would think I was being morbid.

The one night when I was feeling especially sad and depressed, I told Denny I didn't think I could ever be happy again, and I was angry. I had been going through the motions of being busy, but I felt empty and isolated. I felt as if I was waiting for something, but I didn't know what. I knew Anne wasn't coming back and I would have to adjust to life without her, but I couldn't.

Denny told me that I had to *want* to get over the grief and had to *work* at it. He said it was not easy for him either, but he was trying to get on with life.

How can you ever fully recover from an event that is so powerful it consumes all your senses, your whole being? Maybe we never do completely.

My life has been irreversibly changed. I am very different inside. I hope for the better. I am more serious and more sympathetic to those who have lost a loved one. I am also more open in showing affection and in telling others I love them.

I finally realized that crying and isolating myself were not going to bring Anne back, but would only turn away those who loved me. I had to admit to myself that I still had a life. I was not dead, and I needed to enjoy living again. It comforted me to think that Anne was in heaven with Jesus and that someday I would see her again. She would never have to experience any unhappiness, or anger, or frustration, or hatred. I imagined she was everyone's favorite because she was so small and charming—our little angel.

Denny's words hit hard, "You have to want to get over the grief and you have to work at it."

Of course, I wanted to stop feeling so miserable. So I began writing a journal of my feelings. That helped me realize that I was afraid to feel joy again because I thought I would be a bad mother and somehow untrue to Anne if I did. In my journal I wrote things about her life that I wanted to remember, her personality traits, and anecdotes that I was afraid would be forgotten. I was keeping her memory alive. My journal also provided me with something tangible and helped me to put my emotions into words. Then I was able to share with others how I was feeling.

One day Denny and I saw a beautiful rainbow. Anne had a mobile of a rainbow and stars in her room that she would reach out to touch every night after her bath. When we saw the rainbow in the sky we decided that it must be a sign from God that Anne was all right and didn't want us to be sad anymore.

For a long time we left Anne's hand-print on our mirror. It reminded us that her hand had also touched our hearts and made us happy. The things we say and do now are a reflection of the love we shared. She will always be a part of us. We decided to have more children—not to replace Anne—but so that we could again experience the happiness and fulfillment of nurturing another life. We were good parents. All these things have helped us overcome our grief.

NINE

Georgann's Story

*A terrorist bomb exploded. . . . In an instant
my husband of twenty-one years was gone.*

The chilly gray morning of December 21, 1988, was filled with the promise of the upcoming holidays and a reunion with my husband, Jim. He was flying home that day from a business trip to Wolfsburg, West Germany. He would board Pan Am's Flight 103 at London's Heathrow Airport to fly to New York City's JFK Airport and continue on, arriving in Detroit after midnight. The next day would be our son's eighteenth birthday. Jim, a British Airways regular, had decided to take this Pan Am flight in order to be home with Chip on his birthday.

It had been a hectic fall for our family. In fact I had seen Jim only six days that month, but we were looking forward to being home for the holidays and enjoying Jim's ten-day vacation. We would spend time with our family and friends.

The telephone rang, and as I picked it up, I heard a friend ask, "Is Jim flying from London to New York this afternoon?"

"Yes," I answered.

"Is he taking Pan Am?" she asked hesitantly.

I scrambled through some papers on my kitchen counter and located Jim's itinerary. It said, "December 21, Pan Am 103." My mind seemed to drift. Why is she asking these questions? A jab of pain seemed to explode inside me. I gasped for breath.

"Why?" I asked.

"Because, Georgann, a Pan Am flight from London to New York just crashed in Scotland."

My mind went blank; then I heard a voice in my head say, "Jim was on that plane, and he is dead."

Thirty-five minutes into the flight a terrorist bomb exploded, ripping apart the jumbo jet, killing 270 people, and scattering debris across the tiny Scottish village of Lockerbie. In an instant my husband of twenty-one years was gone. Gone was his wonderful sense of humor, the gourmet meals, the incredible energy, the unconditional love—and the hugs.

For the next fifteen days my house was filled with people, and I was a gracious hostess—comforting them and accepting comfort from them. At Jim's services—a memorial five days after, and then a funeral fifteen days after—people marveled at my poise and composure. But I remember feeling I was outside myself, watching me. When I think about it now, that is the way I have always handled crises, both professionally and personally, and this was the most demanding crisis I had ever encountered.

Then the day after the funeral my friends and family all went back to work and to their homes in various parts of the country. Stacey, my daughter, returned to college, and Chip, my son, was concentrating on his high school semester finals. The cold, gray, starkly-empty January day was welcome. It matched how I was feeling inside.

For a moment I broke my promise to myself not to look ahead. "OK, Georgann, what are you going to do with the rest of your life?" I had no idea what I would do or even how I would continue living. "How can I live the rest of my life without Jim?" My feelings were so intense and overwhelming, eventually I became physically ill.

One day, an FBI agent called. He wanted to come over to my house to ask a few questions. Reluctantly I said yes, and then I began to think about the frustrations I'd had with Pan Am, the State Department, and the Scottish authorities in getting information and having Jim's body returned home. The anger flared. I had not felt anger before. How dare these bureaucracies treat my dead husband and my family with disrespect. That call plunged me into a new stage of grief.

For the relatives of the bombing victims, the months after the terrorist attack brought many frustrating, demeaning, and anger-provoking situations. As it became clearer that this tragedy could have been prevented if the bureaucracies had been doing their jobs, ironically these same bureaucracies made our lives more difficult. They withheld death certificates and our loved ones' personal effects and treated the memories of our loved ones and us as though we were all criminals. Woven through our sadness were times of intense anger. Once, unable to contain my anger, I yelled into the telephone,

"What does a criminal investigation have to do with my husband's wedding ring? I demand you send it to me."

I remember little about the next five months. My thinking was fragmented, my memory and concentration poor. I felt exhausted most of the time, and I had fleeting thoughts of suicide. My appetite was poor and I had trouble going to sleep and trouble staying asleep. A stressful situation, being overly tired, or consuming too much caffeine would trigger catastrophic-like sadness. Much of the time I felt overwhelmed.

Gradually the shock lessened and I was more aware of reality. Sometimes the awareness would come in such enormous waves, I would be consumed with anxiety and sadness. I would have little jabs of reality, of what the loss meant to me, and the pressure would build. If I allowed myself to cry, it would pass. If I didn't cry, I would get a headache and feel restless and anxious.

I decided to make friends with my grief. Because I am a mental health professional, I knew intense grief would be with me for a long time. I decided to respect it and to experience it. It represented my love for Jim and my commitment to him, our family, and our life together. But, I also knew about pathological grief. I had seen it in clients. I could not allow myself to grieve indefinitely. Jim would not want me to do that. He would want the children and me to have happy, productive lives.

Besides allowing myself to cry when appropriate, I decided to go to a therapist to talk out my grief. Also several family members of others who have died on the plane lived nearby. These people were a natural support group and became wonderful, understanding friends. We were able to talk about our experience and share our grief, frustrations, and anger—the horror of what had happened to us and our families.

I still had not experienced the full impact of the loss of my husband, but my shock was lessening. I felt increasingly angry and an almost constant sadness. I began to think about the circumstances surrounding Jim's death.

I had a growing sense of a lack of control over my life and I felt vulnerable, as though there was no longer anyone to protect me. I decided to do something productive each day. I took several weekend trips, began tackling business matters, decided to move and put my house on the market.

Still I lived in a fog.

I began to question what happened to Jim as he died and after. I focused on his dying. Did Jim know he was going to die? Did he suffer? What were his last thoughts? When he died, what happened? Where was he now? Was he happier or unhappier? Was God taking care of him and loving him as I did?

I had to have answers. In desperation, I began to read the Bible, to talk to ministers, to read about near-death experiences, after-life, reincarnation. I went to psychics and mediums. I questioned, talked, and read, questioned, talked and read. I was obsessed with gathering information. I didn't decide what I believed until over a year later.

I also had intense feelings of loneliness and aloneness. I did not have a strong religious background, yet my faith had been fairly steady. In my aloneness I prayed for strength and peace, and immediately I would feel them descend on me. I knew the only thing that would be with me—guaranteed to never leave me, was my faith.

I made a commitment to work on making my faith stronger through prayer, by reading and learning more about the Bible, and by attending church regularly. I did not blame God for Jim's death. I know that God gives us free will. The evil people who murdered my husband and 269 others took him from me, not God. I know my belief in God and His power to comfort and sustain me has helped my recovery and has strengthened my faith.

And I made another important decision. I decided I had no unfinished business with Jim. I would not allow myself to feel guilty about not giving him an extra hug when we said goodbye the last time or about the many times I was a bitchy wife. I went to the cemetery and I told him I was sorry. I said that I loved him and I had done the best I could. I knew I couldn't change the negative things I had done and said during our relationship, but I could highlight the positives. This decision allowed me, I think, to let go of any guilt I had and opened the way to more positive memories.

Until that time in my journey through grief, I had not been able to handle memories. It was too painful to think about Jim, look at pictures and videos, or read his letters. I even had difficulty finding comfort in the condolence letters I received from family, friends, and business colleagues. I had decided to handle the memories later.

All my family and Jim's live away from Michigan. I don't know if their not being nearby was a hindrance or a help, but I was spared their grieving. My children, with their youth and independent spirits, seemed to think they could handle their own loss. Eventually, though, they isolated themselves from me and from each other.

Sometimes, when they were angry, they would both direct their anger at me, threatening what was the very heart of our family.

It took Stacey and Chip almost two years to be able to talk openly about their father and to reminisce about the fun times they'd had with him.

About six months after Jim died, I became more concerned about the injustice of his death and the circumstances that surrounded it. Frequent news releases alleging neglect by Pan Am, the State Department, FAA, FBI, CIA, and German government only added salt to my wounds.

As my anger surfaced more, I looked to place blame. I became unraveled by the true realization that my husband had been murdered. I was outraged that someone had stepped into a peaceful, hardworking, middle class life and violated my husband and my family as well as 269 other loved ones and their family members. I thought the world was no longer a safe place to live. I began to realize that our government does not always protect its citizens as I had thought it should and did. I felt vulnerable in every area of my life. I felt the loss of predictability. I felt disillusioned and alone.

I had difficulty managing everything—people, tasks, business affairs, my job. When dealing with business affairs, I was reminded that the person I trusted the most was no longer here to protect me or to help me. I felt a tremendous void. I also realized I was no longer special to someone and I no longer had someone special in my life. I had a difficult time watching couples holding hands. I wanted to scream, "It's not fair. You have the person you love; mine is gone."

Some of my friends expected me to date. They said, "You have to let go of Jim. It's been long enough. Get on with your life." And so I accepted several invitations. But being with another man brought feelings of guilt and sadness. I felt emotionally and physically vulnerable. Even though Jim had not rejected me, a part of me felt abandoned. The sense of who I was and what I believed had been intensely assaulted. I felt incomplete. My thoughts and daily endeavors were still consumed by Jim's death.

"How can I let go?" I thought. He had been a very important part of my life. We had children together. The thought of letting go of him produced new and stronger feelings of anxiety and outrage. I was afraid that if I let go I might forget.

On the first anniversary of the bombing, memorial services were held in Lockerbie, Scotland; New York City; Boston; Washington, D.C.; Syracuse, New York; and Detroit. Here in Detroit my children, some friends and I, and the family members and friends of the other thirteen people from Michigan who died on the plane attended the service that I had helped plan. We lit candles and read the names and ages of the 270 who had died. We held hands and sang "Let There Be Peace." Afterward, friends joined my children and me at our home for an open house. We reminisced about Jim. We laughed and cried. We talked about the present and the future. It was a wonderfully therapeutic day and evening. It was one of those steps forward a griever makes just before slipping backward.

The next six months was the most devastating time. The reality of both my primary losses and secondary losses became very clear. The shock had worn away completely and I was left with an identity crisis. Everything I felt I was and everything I believed in was in question.

I began to feel some of my friends moving away from me. It was as though they were saying, "I'm done grieving and you should be too." Some of them continued to tell me, "You need to get on with your life." I tried to assure them that I was, but I had to do it in my own way. Sometimes, though, I just nodded my head. In truth, I was surprised that so many of my friends had been supportive for as long as they had. But I was not through grieving. I needed to talk about Jim. I was still quite self-consumed and I had little to give others emotionally. I was not a very good friend.

I continued to be disorganized and to feel emotionally overwhelmed and vulnerable. I began to have real doubts about myself.

I picked myself apart physically, socially, and intellectually. It was as though I had regressed to the unsure school-age child I used to be who felt she had little control in her life and few assets to gain control of. The intervening years and my accomplishments meant little to me. It was as though the first year I had grieved for the loss of my husband and in the second I was grieving for the loss of myself—the person I had thought I was. I was no longer married, yet I didn't feel single. Most of all, I didn't want to be single. I was no longer a wife. I had thought I was fairly independent; after all I had a career of my own. But the career had little meaning now that Jim wasn't in my life. All these secondary losses began to seep into my consciousness. I felt like I was on a train speeding to rock bottom. Everything I believed in, everything I was, came into question.

To relieve my pain, finally I retreated into my memories. I watched videos of Jim, looked at family pictures, read letters, and daydreamed about our life together. I cried about the loss of the present and the future I had thought belonged to the children, Jim, and me, and then I cried some more. I thought I would never stop hurting or crying.

Over a year after he died, the full force of the loss of my husband had finally reached me. No one, except God, could have gone with me on this journey through the valley of the shadow of death. My mind seemed to go into fast-forward as I worked to create a different vision of myself; a different vision of my relationship with my husband now that he was no longer with me; a different vision of myself as a parent; a different vision of my world and what I valued in that world; a different view of the future. My mind was never quiet. It was an exhausting task!

As I moved into the second half of the second year, I began to reorganize my life. A window opened and I began to see new possibilities. I realized that life would never be the same again, that it would be understandably different, but that it could possibly be good again.

On June 30, 1990, eighteen months after the bombing, my children and I joined more than one hundred other American relatives in Lockerbie. Many were there for the first time, including the three of us. We gathered for a special dedication at Thundergarth Church, located five miles outside Lockerbie where the nose cone of the plane came to rest.

Jim's body was found in the nose cone.

The people of Lockerbie treated us with loving care and respect and we Americans formally expressed our gratitude to them at a reception. We gave them special pins to thank them for their kindness and sensitivity. Some of the Scottish women had washed and ironed my husband's clothing before it was returned to me.

The beauty of the Scottish countryside and the loving kindness the children and I received from these gentle, loving people stood in stark contrast to the visions of horror, hate, and disrespect for human life that had brought that plane down. I felt I had experienced the best in people and the worst, and I knew I could no longer hold onto the anger and hate I felt for the terrorists. I asked God to help me forgive—to release my anger so I could fully give and receive His love.

The visit to Lockerbie was a turning point for me. I had some very bad times for several weeks afterward, but in general, I am no longer sad most of the time. Jim is not in my thoughts so much. When I do think of him, I usually smile, having recalled a memory of some silly thing he did or said. Sometimes I hear his voice in my head telling me, "Slow down; prioritize what you want to do," but most of the time, it's me speaking to me. I no longer feel his presence; but I do feel his love. It is a part of me and it is always with me.

It has been a long, painful journey, but I am beginning to see some real possibilities for my life based on me—on my talents and my accomplishments. I like the person I am becoming, and I am feeling more empowered.

When I look back over my life since that fateful day, December 21, 1988, I am amazed at what our group, known as "The Victims of Pan Am 103," has accomplished in making the public and our lawmakers aware of the need for new airline and airport security measures. And I am amazed at how much my children and I have come through. I am learning a lot and am changing. I am learning to be alone without feeling lonely.

Also some of my values have changed. Now I appreciate small things. My faith has grown and provided me with a great deal of comfort. I take time to see the best in people, and I am more positive and optimistic. I have less tolerance for phoniness. I am a more loving and less critical parent. I am not afraid of death. I like and am nurturing my creative side. I am more grateful. I can forgive more easily.

In May 1990 the Presidential Commission on Aviation Security and Terrorism presented its findings and recommendations to President Bush. The report contained sixty-four recommendations designed to dramatically upgrade aviation security procedures as well as options for handling terrorist threats and the treatment of families of victims of terrorist acts. It also identified defects in the systems that allowed the bomb to go on the plane.

From the Commission's report, our group worked with Congress in sculpting the Aviation Security Improvement Act of 1990, which was passed into law in November 1990. We had worked hard to get the President to appoint the Commission. The passage of the law was a major achievement and gave comfort to all of us. It won't bring our loved ones back, but hopefully it will go a long way toward sparing others the kind of pain we have had to endure. As victims, we banded together and turned our powerlessness into positive change. By helping others these efforts boosted my healing.

Since Jim's death, I have deliberately selected memories which comfort and inspire me and highlight his personality. It is important to me that they are based on reality. My husband had a number of traits that were very special to me, such as his sense of humor, his optimism, and his lovingness. In my memories of him, he models these traits for me and now I work on making them more my own and sharing them with others.

It has been an arduous journey, and it is not over. I will probably grieve the loss of my husband at times for the rest of my life—especially on holidays and anniversaries, or when I hear a special song. I'll feel the loss strongly at special times—the children's college graduations, their weddings, the birth of each grandchild. I am learning more and more to focus my memories on the best of the four of us together, on his love for us and our special life together.

His memory deserves it.

And we deserve it.

TEN

Susie's Story

She prayed to the Lord to water the wilted flower in me.

We moved out while he was at work. My mom had called his parents to come pick us up. And when they came, his father took his gun. But later, he talked to him and gave back the gun. We moved into a new place.

Then we heard the news—"Greg is dead! He shot himself in the head."

When I heard the news, I smiled. I don't know why, but something inside me felt extremely happy. I felt like a five-hundred-pound weight had been lifted off my shoulders. I felt free of guilt and pain.

When I say *free of guilt,* I am referring to when I was about five years old. I woke up one morning to find I had wet my bed. I begged my sister not to tell Daddy. "Please, Sarah!" I wailed. "Don't tell Daddy!"

But she got up and told him.

I got a really big spanking for not wanting to tell him and for not making it up to the bathroom. In our house it was sometimes hard for a little kid to make it to the bathroom. It was upstairs, and most of the rooms were downstairs. The light switch was a round knob that was practically bigger than my hand and not very easy to turn. Just the same I got spanked because I didn't make it to the bathroom. And soon I got more and more spankings for other small things like that. Slowly I lost my self-confidence.

When I say *free of pain,* I mean free of going upstairs to see horrible things going on. When I was coming up the stairs one day, I saw him hurting my mother. No, not just hurting. He was punching her face, slapping her so hard, she fell back from the blow. She cried a scream, but it seemed as though nothing could hold back his anger. I sat on the steps, horrified, unable to speak or run to get help for fear he would beat me too.

But my smile didn't last. During the month after Greg died I felt sad and depressed. When I went back to school, all the kids wanted to know what it really felt like. One girl was a very understanding friend. And she told me "it" was called *suicide*.

We read things in the paper that say, "Father Abuses Mother, Children," and we think, "That can't ever happen to me." Well, it does happen. I felt it happen. Sometimes even now I get overwhelming anger when I think about it, about him and what he did, and the scar he left on our family.

One of the most difficult things though was that it seemed to me that my family was feeling less grief than I was. I felt angry at God. I was angry that He let my mom marry this guy, angry that He seemed to be rejecting me. I struggled with all of that for a few years, and then at our new church I heard a song. It says, "Let me love You again, Jesus, bring me closer to Your heart."

That was neat.

I had felt God say, "Come to me, Susie. I'm waiting. I love you."

And I wanted to. I hungered for His word and His loving touch. But I felt that no matter what I did, it just wasn't good enough. It seemed like there was a giant wall between us. But after that song, I poured out tears of pain and tears of anger.

Some friends and adults came to talk and pray with me. I said God was doing things. Then we went on an all-girls' retreat while I was still new to the church. And we had a revival meeting. Everybody started lifting their hands. I had seen my mom do that in our old church, but she was the only one and it was weird and embarrassing. But at the new church everyone did it without being embarrassed. All of a sudden, I did it, too. I just threw up my hands in praise. Nobody looked at me funny or anything, so I kept my hands up to see what would happen.

Well, something happened.

I felt a tear on my cheek, then another, and another. I was crying to the Lord. Soon my teacher was right by my side crying with me. We sat down and she started to rock me in her arms while she prayed to the Lord to water the wilted flower in me. I cried so much, but knew it was not in vain, because I sincerely loved Him. After that I didn't feel so dry, but something inside me wanted more. That's when I wrote this piece.

This pain is real. It seems no one cares whether you live or die. You are a reject, a loser. You're not worthy of love. Your mother stays in her room and cries while your sisters are out playing. They hide their hurt deep down in their hearts. You are a small person down in a cave. No one helps you out. You can't understand what you did, but it hurts. Finally, after what seems years, a big rough hand touches your shoulder, and you are slowly being pulled out of this black nothingness.

Slowly, very slowly, you realize what is happening. You are being relieved. Slowly, very slowly, you gradually become more alive than you have ever been. You still have memories and pain, but you are relieved. A weight is being lifted off your shoulders. You are like a butterfly as it grows into a beautiful creature. It soars high with its graceful body. You feel protected by an invisible shield only you know is there.

I went to camp and re-dedicated my life to Jesus. So, if something like this should happen to you, and you feel there is no hope, I'm living proof that there is. But only if you believe in yourself and God enough to fight and never give up.

ELEVEN

Diane's Story

*Nineteen eighty-seven would have been
an easy year for me to go insane.*

My husband, Greg, committed suicide on January 18, 1987. He was successful. He is dead.

I was thirty-three years old. I was left devastated. And I have not been the same since. That would have been an easy year for me to go insane. It was a struggle not to. But I always had the choice to hang on and choose life.

Greg was troubled. We lived in a household of constant emotional upheaval. I asked him if we could go for counseling, but he chose not to go. Then the violence began, followed by the blanket-blame that everything was my fault. His drinking, his fits of rage, and his depression were because of me, he said. Over and over again he tried to prove himself as blameless.

"It's all your fault. If only you would submit to God and be a better wife, our home would be normal. My reactions are caused by *you*."

I didn't know how I could be "in rebellion" the way he said. I loved Jesus. I loved my husband. *Lord, please show me,* I prayed.

Greg didn't allow me to talk to anyone about this. When I did, the cost was very painful. He watched me like a hawk. I was a prisoner in my own home.

Then the beatings, and mimicking, and unpredictable mood swings moved at a much faster pace. His brilliant, "logical" reasoning confused me. Greg knew the Bible well, and used Scripture in an artful, manipulative way. I felt tired and worn. I felt like earth eroding over a steep cliff. I prayed that God would help me understand.

I begged Greg to go for counseling so we could get our family back together. Months passed. I continued to suggest counseling for both of us. Still he refused.

So I went alone.

I took my children and ran away. I sought out counseling by myself.

"Please help me to get better. I am so confused. I must be the cause of my husband's drinking. He hits me and says I'm not good enough. Last week he flew into a rage because I left baby powder on the couch. He . . ."

The therapist did something that I'll always remember. He got tears in his eyes. He looked sad. Then he looked troubled.

"He is very dangerous," the counselor said.

"I love him, but I am afraid of him."

"Listen to that fear. Don't go near him. Even if he begs and says he will change, don't go near him."

I found a job. I moved into my own apartment. I went to Meijers Thrifty Acres and bought a wastebasket, a hair dryer, and an iron. As I paid for them, I thought, *Why am I buying these? By tomorrow I will have two of each.* I paid the cashier with a check and dismissed my strange thought.

That night Greg shot himself in the head. By the time the police arrived he was dead. By morning I had two hair dryers and two irons. I threw the extra wastebasket away.

I sat at the antique oak table with four friends. It was 1:00 A.M. I looked out the picture window and noticed how heavily it was snowing. These friends of ours (now mine alone), wanted to stay. We had so many pieces to try to put together. We needed to make sense of something that made no sense. I drifted in and out of the conversation. I tried to figure out what Terry was talking about. What did hell have to do with life now? Gradually, it dawned on me.

Some people say those who kill themselves go to hell.

I knew suicide is not a permissible option to pain. How could it be? My Lord promises there will always be a way of escape. Yet, why didn't God intervene? He is capable of miracles. The gun could have jammed. Then Greg would still be alive now.

So now what, God? One more endless round of "I don't know" in a life of I don't knows.

I didn't sleep at all that night. I prowled the house again, staring, crying, looking for clues. I tried to pray, but prayer was like dry cotton in my heart.

Was I angry at God?

No. God didn't shoot Greg. Greg did.

But I was reduced to nothing, beyond nothing, negative nothing.

In my mind, I was broken beyond repair. *God, you will have to scrape me up and put me together again. I don't know how.* And then I remembered that little song, "Jesus Loves Me." I listened to it in my mind because there was no music in my heart. It was dark and lifeless, like me. The song didn't make any sense. But I listened anyway.

Outside my torment I was vaguely aware that God's grace must have been very present, but it didn't penetrate—at least, not that I could tell. Somewhere close to dawn I fell asleep and I dreamed.

I was in a place I felt I should know but couldn't identify. A man in a white, linen robe walked carefully over jagged rocks. He was carrying someone in his arms—a full-sized man. His face was kind, yet concerned. He was not angry but very pained.

I looked at the one he was carrying. It was Greg. He was bleeding, but the blood was not in this dream. He had been in intense pain, but the pain also was not in this dream. He was fragile and broken. He was man-sized, yet he seemed like a very small child. The man carried him tenderly.

He moved toward a rock, massive and solid—like rock should be, but this stone seemed to be alive. At its base was a clear, deep pool of water. It flowed down from the boulders above. I knew these were healing waters.

The man placed Greg—my fragile, broken Greg—beside the pool and gently sat down beside him and began to undress him. And then he put Greg into the healing waters.

I knew that the Greg I loved was there with Jesus. The angry, violent, confused blackness was not there. It was gone, and left behind was a shattered man who was immersed in the healing waters by his Lord.

"So You did win after all, didn't You, Lord?"

I didn't speak aloud but I knew He heard me. He who is always faithful had answered my prayers. He had healed my husband.

Dreams can be a blessing. If your dream is a nightmare—you get to wake up. But I woke to the awful reality that I had been dreaming. And my waking nightmare loomed before me. My husband was still dead.

Everything seemed distant. Life had become too painful and my God was too small. I began to understand how people sometimes discard God in the midst of torment, as if the Creator of all the universe is an outgrown, worn-out coat. Was this all there is to the power of God? Was this the depth, and width, and breadth, and length of His unspeakable love that my Bible promises?

I met Jesus on a country road at seventeen. I was radically changed and "on fire for God." A revival swept the country in the early 70s, and I was a part of it. I witnessed many miracles. But now at thirty-three, life was reduced to a bleak minute-by-minute, choices-to-make-to-continue-to-go-on existence. There was only grueling anguish.

My clothes hung on me and I smoked a lot of cigarettes. My hair fell out in clumps. I realized one day why I didn't eat anymore—I couldn't taste. Food was like straw in my mouth.

Grief following a suicide is different. It is two-sided. The one I loved had the last word. Then he took his life. His suicide not only destroyed him but it also sought to destroy me. But I here remain. I am hanging on.

I loved him and I hated him.

I have never been an angry person, but I experienced a rage within. I was so angry I couldn't sleep. I paced and stormed and wailed instead. I was working a job that required my full, physical strength. I was so full of rage, I worked all day and still was not exhausted.

Then I would fall. A part of me wondered how I could hate so. He was ill. How could I be angry at one who was ill?

Then I was no longer angry. I began to weep. My energy was gone. Despair surrounded me. If only I had loved him better. If only I had known. If only I had been able to stop him in time. If only . . . if only . . . until all the guilt and blame were on *me* like a semi-truck, as if I were the one who shot him, instead of the one who loved him. The weight was incredible. I did not know how to move it. Sometimes I felt that crazy insanity come in so close. *Yes, it is true. You killed him. You are to blame.*

Did I? Did I kill him?

I was jerked, and tossed, and thrown against so many walls. Some people did blame me. Logically I knew that really they also were dealing with guilt, their own guilt, and the false guilt that always accompanies suicide. But it's always easier to have a scapegoat.

I began to attend a Survivors of Suicide group. I wasn't the only one who thought she was going insane. We told our stories and re-told them in a circle of gut-honest pain. People blamed us and shunned us, but we were doing that to ourselves already. That made it even worse. We were angry and distraught. We all felt so vulnerable. We crawled, step by wounded step, together and alone. We all went out and bought answering machines.

Slowly I began to learn that the answers of men in God's name are not always God's answers. Pat answers, offered by well-meaning Christians, brought me no comfort. These "counselors of Job" often brought more pain than relief, leaving me bruised and shaken.

I learned to accept what I could not change. It was true honesty of heart—the genuine love of friends and the deeper unfolding of the nature of a truly awesome God, that ministered to my broken heart. I stepped onto a new land. The old one could no longer hold me. And I began to draw the line.

It happened one morning as I looked into the closet. My mind was fuzzy, and I didn't know, didn't care, what I would wear. I heard Greg's voice on one of those memory tapes that echoed in my mind. He came up behind me and said, "You have such bad taste. I guess I should pick out your clothes so you'll look halfway decent."

I whirled around. "Shut-up!" I screamed. "Shut-up!"

Then I took my right foot and drew a line right in front of me with my toe. I didn't know much about boundaries, but this made sense.

"Don't you step over that line. You are dead, and you can no longer hurt me. Don't you dare step over that line."

I began to get dressed for what lay ahead.

The weapons for war are as varied and creative as the flowers of the fields. I learned to use truth as my shield, speaking aloud to the accusing voices thundering in my head. I taught myself to forcibly "change the channel" when terrorizing images attacked me. I began slowly to identify nameless reactions that seemed to come from nowhere and catch me, pull me, drag me toward depression and futility.

I had to constantly learn patience with myself, to be kind to myself, to love myself. Oh, such a tremendous waste of time, this long process. Why couldn't I be done? But my heart and my mind continued to plod through grief, step by step by sluggish step.

I began to understand about only accepting responsibility for *my* actions. I learned that others are responsible for theirs. Freedom of choice, I would tell myself, is a special gift. You cannot always choose the circumstances, but you can always choose your attitude. Victor Frankyl, imprisoned in a concentration camp, chose life. He chose hope. He found a reason to live. I, too, will live. My life will also have purpose.

One death is enough.

I began to notice changes in myself. There were small ones, but changes nonetheless. I began to become my own friend. I sought to treat myself with patience and kindness in the same way I would treat others. Practicing daily, I moved forward. I learned to offer encouragement to myself, talking, congratulating, consoling, understanding. I was beginning to trust again. But that was and still is a very slow, painful process.

Then I realized I needed to forgive Greg. But first I had to acknowledge that he hurt me, our children, our families, and our friends. Then, I worked to spread forgiveness throughout our lives. It was not a one-day task. Many times I did not feel forgiveness toward him. Sometimes I plain did not want to forgive him. It was always a choice of will.

When the car broke down and I felt afraid and abandoned and betrayed, I acknowledged that fear and abandonment and betrayal, "Greg, I forgive you."

When I finally went for physical therapy and my talk with the doctor recalled much I had wanted to forget, I spoke to both the pain in my heart and the pain in my neck, tears streaming down my cheeks, "Greg, I forgive you."

When that beast called lack of confidence of single parenting ability raised its head, making me feel incompetent and inadequate to rear three daughters alone, "Greg, I forgive you. Even though I don't feel like I forgive you, or want to forgive you, I choose to forgive you! My God! Help me make it so!"

And I pictured myself going to the Cross, dragging a bag holding all my fears and bitterness and tears. It was heavy, but it did not break. I left it at the foot of the Cross, "Greg, I forgive you."

In choosing life, I began to learn to look for things to be thankful for, to see the goodness that is there but so often missed. I asked my God for *new eyes*, eyes to see in ways I have never seen before. I needed eyes that would see God's grace in everyday living. I needed eyes that would look at that which is truly important, and leave the insignificant behind. This restoration of eyesight has continued throughout the years.

Soon after Greg died I began to stutter. I would stutter every time I spoke of him. I still stutter a bit sometimes, but not much anymore. And when I do, it's okay. Sometimes I'm still lonely. Sometimes I don't know how to cover all my family's expenses. I don't remember names very well, and I still have difficulty remembering phone numbers.

But I remember much of what really matters: I remember to take each day one day at a time. That is enough. I remember what is past and what is now, and the healing and new growth that was and is yet to be. I remember that I alone am not able to heal, only God can heal. But I can be a vessel of His truth and compassion.

I try to remember to let myself be all God has created me to be. This doesn't always match other's expectations for me. But my confidence does not come only from the esteem and approval of others. It comes from knowing He loves me, whether I am weak or strong, broken or whole. It comes from knowing myself and being uniquely me, using the gifts He has given me for a life with purpose. Sometimes that's risky; sometimes it's downright scary. Even so, for the first time in years, I am beginning to dream and plan for a future.

I remember that His love is never ending—never, ever, ever.

TWELVE

David's Story

I asked God to relieve me of my romantic love for Lori.
It was time to let her go.

Somewhere in the corner of my basement are boxes of memories—pictures, love letters, perfumed ribbons—reminders of a once meaningful and promising relationship.

Gathering my thoughts about the love I once shared with Lori, the temptation is strong to shuffle through those memories for reminders of what was and what might have been. Looking back now it is surprisingly difficult to recall the intensity of the heartache I once felt. How funny it is to say that. *Once felt.*

Almost three years have passed and, as deeply felt as it was, the heartache did pass. It was a painfully slow process, to be sure, but my heart has been restored. And, in one of life's wonderful ironies, or perhaps as God's reward for patience and perseverance, that process is now leading me to a deeper, even more beautiful love.

My once-intended, a beautiful young lady of twenty-four, did not die—but our relationship did. The loss we each felt, measured by the many things we later wished we had said and those things we're now sorry we did say, was enormous. If the true measure of one's love is the pain experienced when the love dies then we clearly loved each other more deeply than most.

Lori walked into my life about six years ago, on an April day. She was an attractive college student, full of life and enthusiastic about a photo session in Washington, D.C., with her hometown Congressman. I was the Congressman's press secretary, and requests like hers were commonplace. In my first nine months on the job, dozens of similar requests had crossed my desk. This one seemed no different. The necessary preparations were made, and Lori was invited to spend time with her Congressman during a weekly radio interview. It was when I saw her that this request became something more than routine.

The interview went well I think, from the little of it I could remember five minutes later. All I could think of was gathering enough nerve to ask her to lunch. Somewhere between the recording studio and the escalator, an invitation was offered and she accepted.

We spent two hours having lunch and we learned more about each other then than in the following two weeks. We both had families in southern California. We shared a love of literature and music. Each had experienced a family divorce at a young age. We spoke of the hows and whys of our parents' divorces, what it was like growing up separated emotionally from one parent, and the uncertainty we felt about trusting others. During that first time together, her smile was reassuring, her eyes penetrating. And she laughed at my dumb jokes! We left the table having hardly touched our food, our feet barely touching the floor.

Our first six months together are still one of the happiest times of my life. Those days, weeks, and months are magically sewn together into one quilted memory. Each day brought a new appreciation of what we shared as best friends, forging ahead and building a future together. We knew that creating anything of lasting value would require caution and care, love and patience. But we were ready for the long haul.

In those early days, it was all so easy: picnics at sunset along the Potomac River, homemade spaghetti dinners, five-hour phone calls about nothing in particular lasting into the early hours of the morning, time spent just reveling in each other. We spent each moment living, laughing, loving, and learning. Life was giddy, seemingly full of endless possibilities. It was an incredible journey of personal discovery for both of us.

Finishing dinner one evening in December, we were astonished to see a heavy snow falling. With visibility near zero, I insisted on following Lori in my car to see her home safely. At the base of the last hill, her car began to zig-zag across the icy road. Other cars waited cautiously as she rolled her car back to begin another attempt.

Again her tires could not get traction. She rolled down the car window and tears streamed down her face. Even though she was frightened, she was still laughing. Urging only minor corrections, I walked beside her car as she slowly, cautiously made her way up the hill. At the office the next morning, I was greeted with "luv muffins" to share with my co-workers. Of course, the name stuck. I was no longer Dave. I was "Luv Muffin."

We entered a new phase, entrusting each other with our most closely held secrets and fears. It was a new experience for Lori, who had grown up believing men couldn't be trusted, and for me, who believed the same about women. Sitting in my car on a dimly lit street late one night in the rain, she shared the pieces of her past she had never before revealed to anyone else. She hesitated. I reassured her, promising never to tell. Then I held her as she wept, her body convulsing at the painful memories. It was a stirring moment of catharsis. It was the beginning of a healing process needed to let go of years of anger and mistrust. "Hold me, just hold me," she cried, apologizing for the mascara stains her tears were leaving on my shirt. I appealed to God to care for this sensitive soul, this tender, aching heart.

My own emotional walls, carefully constructed and periodically reinforced during twenty-three years of emotional need, came crashing down too. For years I had guarded against letting anyone "in," afraid no one could ever truly love me or know me. It was an insecurity bred by years of questioning and doubt about my mother's misdirected love for her youngest son. Her demonstrations of love for others were limited.

For years, I doubted her every word as she launched into verbal assaults on my dad—my hero and rescuer, the one person who had provided me a second chance at life with his new wife (who became a real mom to me—Mama) and a new family on a farm in the country.

I felt vulnerable to the seduction of my mother's lies, but I continued to resist her.

And I built walls—tall and thick and wide. I determined that no woman claiming to love me would ever penetrate them. It was a matter of survival, of self-preservation. *If my own mother doesn't love me,* I thought, *then how could anyone else?*

On another rainy night, in another place, I let Lori "in" for the first time. My emotional walls, strained by the weight of her love for me, crumbled. After years of resistance, a woman's love had penetrated my defenses. I sobbed and she held me reassuringly. The poetry of A. E. Housman in the final seconds of the film we had just seen had pushed me into the arms of a woman I knew *truly* loved me. *And, I loved her.*

Our spiritual lives played an important role in our developing relationship. As we began praying together in fellowship with a young congregation, Lori was a patient teacher, willingly providing insight into her Catholic faith for her Presbyterian boyfriend. We sang (well, mostly I hummed). We exchanged gentle kisses as a sign of peace. We held hands during the Lord's Prayer.

My fascination with the Catholic church had begun much earlier while I was in college. Many of my close friends were Catholic, and though I wasn't a Catholic, the church was always down the street with its doors open. The day Grandma died, I cried while I knelt in a Catholic church. In early 1984, when I had just moved to Washington, I began trying to develop an active spiritual life, and I spent many lunch hours on my knees in St. Joseph's Church, which was a ten-minute walk from my office. The beauty and symbolism of the church was overwhelming, the love I felt consuming.

I was looking for God. I found Him.

We had entered new, uncharted territory, filled with growing expectations of a life together. After years of building walls and walking in fear, we were two souls walking together, joined as one. We prayed each Sunday for God to love us and keep us in His gentle, loving hands.

During our first Christmas, we exchanged crucifixes on thin gold chains to wear as a sign of our love for each other. The commitment was made to wear them until we died, promising to return them only if we decided to seek separate paths.

The arguments began as verbal sparring and, looking back, were probably part of the healing process we began together—but never finished—while sitting in a car at night in the rain. It's hard now to remember the things we fought about. Perhaps that's a sign of how unimportant they were. At the time though, the arguments were real and divisive, and the most damaging effects were emotional. Lori would raise her voice, and suddenly, there was my mother again, raising her voice. When Lori slammed a door, I saw my mother slamming a door. If Lori cried uncontrollably for no apparent reason, again I had visions of my mother. David, the young man, reacted as David the little boy, scrambling for cover in his emotional shell. Her anger met my silence. We were in an emotional stalemate, and we never learned to deal with the two extremes.

The memorable arguments, the ones we had about commitment and marriage, didn't begin until much later. But they had little to do with our final separation and break-up. In the end, the problem was a matter of trust and making the right decisions for the kind of life each of us wanted to live.

An incident that occurred two years into our relationship caused a hurt from which I could not recover. It was a turning point.

In January 1987, I drove to Michigan to help my sister and her three young children move from their home where a dominant, abusive husband and father had made living dangerous for them. Only hours after I arrived he made threats of suicide over the telephone that created a new sense or urgency in an already tense situation. That morning as I lay on a cold wood floor in a home with no furniture, I slept only during the ten-minute intervals between Greg's phone calls. The three girls—ages nine, seven, and one—in sleeping bags with their stuffed animals, slept upstairs unaware of the horrible situation their mother and I were in. Around 2:00 A.M. a light snow began falling outside. The phone rang again at 7:00 A.M.

Greg had taken his life.

I have never felt death so intently as I did during the next four days. My older brother Paul and I handled many of the immediate details of Greg's death. We spoke with police detectives. We told the children their father was dead. We moved furniture and personal effects. It was grisly, numbing.

Until that Sunday morning my perception of death had been that it is something that happens to old people when the mail stops coming and life is measured by a Sunday evening phone call and reruns of Lawrence Welk.

But this was real. And I felt the impact deeply. My sister needed me. She and her children needed my strength, my love, and my care. And I needed something or someone to help me be for Di and her girls what they needed me to be. Immediately I turned to Lori—my lifeline—for support. She was calm, measured, supportive. "Your place is with your family," she assured me. "Be strong for Di and the girls. I love you."

After the Tuesday evening memorial service, I left my tearful sister and frightened nieces for the solitude of a two-hour drive to Detroit in a cold, freezing rain.

I needed to drive—fast. And I needed to cry.

I went to the home of a close college friend, Anne Marie. When I reached her door around midnight, she was unaware of what had happened. She listened quietly for hours to the details of the previous three days. Exhausted, I fell asleep on her living room floor.

By morning the rain and snow had drifted eastward. The sun shone brightly. At last I was going home. Knowing Lori was at the end of a ten-hour drive would make the day pass quickly, and I called her eagerly with the news.

Then the bottom fell out.

I stood in disbelief as she spoke. The love was gone. There was no warmth, no sense of caring or concern. The understanding, sympathetic voice I'd heard three days before had been replaced by an angry, jealous rage—the result of an evening I had spent talking with my friend, another woman.

Suddenly, the return home took on a whole new meaning. It became a journey of endless miles and unanswered questions. My struggle with the emotions of Greg's death quickly took a back seat to the more immediate concern of appeasing Lori's tangled emotions. It seemed totally unnecessary after the burden of the previous several days, yet it had to be done. Though eventually resolved, the incident exacted a heavy emotional toll. And while we quickly resumed our normal lives, it became a benchmark. I never quite felt the same way about her again. Even months later when, in Lori's arms, I finally, tearfully let go of Greg, there was a difference, a void.

The following summer after Lori had received her undergraduate degree, she readied herself for law school, a dream she'd had since childhood. Her heart was set on returning to California and I offered little resistance, encouraging her to make her own decision. Our commitment, we agreed, if it was meant to continue, would survive the time and distance. Law school—and time for us both to grow professionally—seemed a small price to pay for ultimately being so happy.

We spoke often of marriage, and we met and began to love each other's families. After dating only two months, we had driven fifteen hours to northern Michigan for a weekend visit with my parents at their summer home. Two weeks later, she was exposed to a full family reunion—all six of my brothers and sisters and their spouses, my nieces and nephews, as well as my parents. Everyone was anxious to meet her, and most welcomed her with open arms. I met Lori's parents (whom I came to call "Mom and Pop") at her college graduation. Over the years I came to love and respect them as dear friends and future in-laws. Our families lived in Southern California within two hours of each other and we were able to spend major holidays together. It was almost too perfect.

Though we could not have been more emotionally committed, I still had doubts. Occasional arguments over even the most trivial matters caused me great concern. Foremost in my mind was the desire that I not repeat the mistake my dad had made at an early age. It was something Lori was aware of, and occasionally she reminded me that she wasn't my mother.

Most days, I agreed. But on others, I wasn't so sure.

In spite of that concern, during the several weeks before Christmas 1988, I spent many evenings in various jewelry stores pricing engagement rings. Even with the doubts, I believed a ring would help Lori feel more secure, and perhaps would even alleviate her anger. I convinced myself that buying a ring was the right thing to do.

It didn't take long for me to realize that engagement rings are not only expensive, but at that time one was almost completely out of the question. The two-paycheck rule went out the window as the reality of diamond prices sank in. I risked her accepting a less expensive ring—a small diamond with two sapphires—as a symbol of my love and *eventual* commitment to be married.

But Lori wanted more than my love. She wanted more than a ring. She wanted a definite commitment to be married. The ring and the words accompanying it fell short of what she wanted—and needed.

We spent that Christmas with my family. One night when Lori had fallen asleep on the couch, my dad and I stayed up late talking as we often do when we're together. He spoke, recognizing that I, his young son, was only a matter of days away from proposing to the woman I loved. He spoke of marriage, commitment, fidelity. He was frank, honest. He said, "The decisions you make today will affect you for the rest of your life."

I listened. Even while struggling with my emotions, I could feel Lori beginning to slip away.

Two days later, as I stepped out of the shower to shave, the crucifix I'd worn for two years as a symbol of my love for Lori fell limply into the sink. It seemed to be a visible sign that our love was coming undone. I returned alone to Washington, holding the crucifix and broken gold chain in my hand. It symbolized our relationship. I wanted to fix it. I wanted to make it better.

I saw Lori for the last time a few weeks later when she returned to Washington to attend the President's Inaugural Ball. She was beautiful in her black, strapless evening gown. A little of the earlier magic returned as we had dinner together. But eventually the subject of marriage came up, and the magic seemed to disappear. I promised my continued fidelity. She promised to give us a chance after she completed law school. "If only we had met two years from now," she said, her voice trailing off. I thought it probably wouldn't have made a difference. Still, we agreed that our timing was off.

That night she cried, and we hardly danced. Neither of us was in the mood.

My last memory of Lori is of her tear-stained cheeks as she boarded a plane for Los Angeles. She looked tired. Law school and the burden of our long-distance relationship were taking a toll. We waved goodbye and she blew me a kiss.

I believed God would someday reunite us. But our phone calls became less and less frequent. When we talked we argued about things we could not change, and the arguments became more personal and bitter. Though we never spoke of it, we both felt betrayed. I clung desperately to strands of illusory hope that "true love" would save us by bridging her anger and insecurity with my reservations about our marriage.

For reasons known only to God, it was not meant to be.

Though she was no longer there, I spoke to Lori in private moments: "I lived for you. You were my life. Now I am left with nothing but my memories of the faint sounds of your laughter, the smell of your hair, the gentle touch of your hand. Your love was the only real love I have ever known. And now it is gone. What am I supposed to do with my love for you when you no longer want it?"

I wrote dozens of letters, pouring out page after page of raw emotion. Only a few were mailed, and they were met mostly with silence. I wrote beautiful poetry.

There were moments—days, actually—when I had no desire to continue living. It's hard now to imagine that I ever felt that way. But I did. I could not listen to music. Every station seemed to be playing "our songs." For months, even a year, she remained my last thought when going to bed at night, and my first thought in the morning.

On my dad's birthday a year later, I wrote, "It had my dad's failed marriage written all over it. Still, I wonder if I will ever be happy again."

In the early days of recovery, progress was measured day by day, even hour by hour. It was, in every respect, like learning to walk again: one step at a time; left foot, right foot. Don't stop. Left. Right. Keep on moving. Soon, I resumed jogging with a colleague at work. One afternoon, he shared with me his dream of completing a twenty-six-mile marathon. A casual jogger for twenty years, he was ready to run the race of his life. We spent lunch hours training on the Mall between the Capitol building and the Lincoln Memorial. On

Sunday mornings we ran the sloping and winding roads of rural Maryland, slowly increasing our mileage to prepare for the race in November. By mid-October, we were running eighteen miles with relative ease.

On race day, the temperature was hot, in the high eighties. Relaxed, we crossed the starting line together. Our arms pumping and our legs churning, hitting the pavement stride for stride. Left foot, right foot. At mile four we stopped for water and became separated. We didn't see each other again until the race was over. We both finished. For the first time since the separation, I felt alive again. Even after running twenty-six miles, I was rejuvenated. My friend, at age fifty-two, had completed his first full marathon and unwittingly had guided a broken heart on an even tougher course.

It took me nine months to return to the church Lori and I had attended together. Those first Sundays were tough. Thoughts of her overwhelmed me as cascades of bright sunlight streamed through stained-glass windows, casting shadows on the altar. Lori—my future wife, the mother of my children, my soul mate. There was no singing, no gentle offering of peace. Instinctively I reached out for a familiar hand, and found only stillness. Slowly, I asked God to relieve me of my romantic love for Lori. It was time to let go.

I still miss the part of Lori that was my best friend. I loved her deeply and intensely. She is the first woman I truly loved, the first to truly love me, and I will always carry a part of her with me.

The boxes in my basement have now gathered a thick layer of dust, but the memories will always remain very special, even though they belong to another time, another place.

Lori is no longer the center of my life. My broken heart has healed and slowly, carefully, with God's grace, I am learning to love again.

THIRTEEN

Valerie Jean's Story

I accepted that drowning my feelings in a drink
would not bring Peter back.

It was a glorious, late-September Saturday morning. Peter, my fifty-one-year-old fiancé, was getting dressed to play golf, and I was getting ready to walk my dog, Ziggy. Peter and I had a relationship filled with laughter, wit, and fun—but not that day. Embarrassing as it is to admit, we were having one of those little, mild, dumb squabbles that people have when they're really close to each other. It was about what we would do that night.

I wanted to go to a concert where a friend of mine was performing. He didn't.

I turned my back to him because I was getting angry, and he wasn't giving in. I heard him make a strange sound, and I was sure he was waiting for me to turn around to find him making some ridiculous face to make me laugh. When I did turn around, to my horror, he was lying on the floor. His face was blue.

When I took my CPR course, I wondered if I'd really be able to do it in a crisis. At that moment I found out: It's all you *can* do. I started CPR at once. When there was no response, I grabbed the phone, dialed 911 and screamed for a medic, scarcely able to remember the address. I went back to applying CPR and stopped only to run downstairs to let the medics in. One of them started doing double-CPR with me, and then the rest of them came swarming into the room with their machines and equipment. They took over.

They worked on Peter for forty-five minutes and then took him to the hospital in an ambulance. I followed in the car, because I thought they might have to keep him hospitalized while he recovered.

It never crossed my mind that he was dead. I thought that, because they had worked on him so long, they must have received a response

I hadn't. At the hospital, the doctors worked on him for another whole hour, while I paced the waiting room. At last a nurse came, and asked me to follow her. I remember thinking, "If he has to stay in the hospital, this is really going to mess up his plans. He'll be so mad!"

Peter was a commodities futures broker. In five days he was to leave for China and Hong Kong on business. I was to follow him a week later, and together we were going to explore and travel and buy my engagement ring. He was wildly enthused about the Orient, both for business prospects and the attractive prices on jewelry.

A doctor met me. "The news is not good," he began. We stared at each other.

"He's dead."

I did something I had read about but never seen. I tore my hair. It couldn't *be!* Peter was on the brink of great success. Since his first trip to the Orient two months before, it was all he had thought about, spent sixteen hours a day at the office about, talked in his sleep about.

"I killed him," I blurted.

The doctor stared at me. "How did you do that?" he asked gently.

"We . . . we were having an argument . . ."

He tried not to smile. "And had you ever had an argument before?"

"Well . . . yes."

"And did it ever kill him before?"

I looked at him. "No," I admitted.

"Peter had a heart attack," he said. "You can't *give* someone else a heart attack. Peter was a time bomb waiting to go off."

Then the tears came. It *was* true. Peter had been chain smoking. He ate red meat every day. He was driving himself mercilessly at work. His only exercise was golf once a week. And he belonged to the most notoriously high-stress profession in the world. In addition, his father had died at exactly the same age. (At the cemetery after the funeral, I read the dates on the other gravestones—and found that not one man in Peter's family had *ever* lived past his fifties.)

It added up. But somehow I still felt responsible.

In shock, I drove home and made phone calls to his family, my family, our friends. How lucky I was to have a built-in support group. I had been a member of AA for five and a half years, and I had learned that in this strange and wonderful collection of people there is *always* somebody who has been through your problem be-

fore. I phoned an AA couple whose son had been killed in a motor-
cycle accident a year before.

"What do I *do?*" I pleaded.

"You're not going to like the answer," they warned. "You have to go
to an AA meeting as soon as possible. And you have to share. You
have to tell people what you are going through—without a drink."

Well, that was absolutely the last thing on earth I wanted to do.
But then, I thought: *Do I want to drink over this?* And the answer
was an easy *No.* First, because of all the things that Peter loved about
me, he loved my sobriety best. His first wife had been an unrepent-
ant drunk and he had ended up raising their two children by himself.

The second reason I wasn't going to drink was that I had made a
commitment that *no matter what happened in life, I wasn't going to
drink.* And yet, I knew, who would blame me if I did? In fact they
might sympathize and say, "Who knows. Maybe I would too, under
such circumstances." But I had learned that your circumstances cannot alter your commitment to sobriety.

So I went to AA meetings, and I cried, and I shared the story. In a
numbed state of suspension, I made arrangements at work and with
Peter's children and the coroner and the crematorium. Peter's mother
wanted his ashes brought from California to New Jersey and placed
in the family plot. We worked out plane schedules so that the two
children and I would all arrive on the same flight.

At the radio station, where I hostess an interview show, I had already prepared six weeks of tapes to be aired while I was away with
Peter in the Orient, so I didn't have to think about work. I knew that
as soon as I returned I'd have to move out of our apartment, but I
couldn't worry about that yet. I was living minute by minute.

We buried Peter's ashes on the day he was to have flown to the
Orient.

When I returned from the funeral and had to make arrangements
to move to a new house, then move *again* six weeks later, I guess I
was in a trance. I cried and had weird dreams and thoughts, but I
kept forcing myself to talk and to share at AA meetings, and somehow I got through.

There are many different stages of grief. You can slide from one to
another during the day. And you can spiral down in a tailspin, getting worse and worse, as well. That didn't happen to me for several
months, when the *real* grief came.

I had been given a book, *The Courage to Grieve* by Judy Tatelbaum, by the couple whose son had been killed. And I had been introduced to Barbara LesStrang and the *Afterloss* newsletter by the directors of the crematorium.

Both helped.

Then within ten days three of my friends were diagnosed with terminal illnesses, and I began to lose it. *Is this what the rest of my life is going to be like?* I wondered. *Am I just going to keep watching everyone around me die?*

I had never known death before. I had vague childhood memories of stiff and rather pompous funerals for my grandparents, who had died quietly in their sleep without ever having a sick day. I knew nothing of death. So I read the books and kept trying to verbalize what I was going through. But gradually my friends stopped calling, and I began to see people glaze with boredom as I brought up the topic yet again at AA meetings.

I got the picture. No one wants you to grieve any longer than their level of tolerance. Then it's time for you to recover and be sunny again. I was becoming a bore, an embarrassment, a drag.

I stopped sharing at meetings. I would sit there, a mute lump of pain, appalled at the trivial nature of other people's problems.

I lost weight, too much weight. I tried to write, but it was impossible. I began crying more. I started becoming seriously depressed.

I obsessed, over and over again, about Peter's death. What had our last words been? Had I really done the CPR correctly?

Then there was the shock of learning after his death that some of the things Peter had told me—and his children—weren't true.

But the worst of it was that I lost my music.

I had been a full-time musician and singer before I began the radio show and still performed on a freelance basis. I had *always* found solace in my music—whether I was wailing the blues, or turning to comedy songs, or losing my sorrow in the intellectual demands of singing in foreign languages. But suddenly my music had no feeling. Oh, I still hit the right notes and kept the beat and remembered the lyrics. But the one absolute necessity for my performance was the *feeling* I put into my songs. I had no illusions about my talent; I had an unusual voice and played an unusual instrument. But to hold an audience you need something special. For me, it was the emotion. I knew how to reach down inside my listeners and make them feel things they had forgotten. And that was gone.

That's when I panicked.

I went to a psychiatrist and we talked through five sessions in which I impatiently answered questions about my childhood, wondering when we were going to get to something important.

Then, one morning, I woke up at 4:00 A.M. It wasn't stretch and yawn. I sat bolt-upright with my eyes wide open.

I looked at my little dog, curled up at the foot of the bed. "We're supposed to do something," I told him. Maybe meditate.

Ziggy followed me into the guest bedroom where I closed my eyes in meditation, and then opened them again immediately. "We're supposed to go somewhere," I said.

I dressed and bundled Ziggy into the car, and we headed toward the highway. "It has something to do with *mountains,*" I told him, "and something to do with *light.*" How strange.

I headed north, but inexplicably felt myself pulled toward the east. The dark was giving way to dawn, and I wandered off the highway trying to find a road into the San Bernardino Mountains. I felt pulled like a magnet, but where? "Maybe I've missed it," I thought, heading south.

Suddenly I was there.

A chill went through me as I found myself looking up at Peter's Mountain. That was the name I had jokingly given to the last one of a ridge in the Santa Rosa chain; it was right near Peter's home. I had never actually been to Peter's Mountain, but now I was staring at the very place where it jutted up from the sandy desert floor.

I looked at Ziggy, and he looked at me. We began to climb the mountain. When we were high enough, I sat down and, out loud, began a conversation with Peter. I didn't dare think about what I was doing. I just talked.

I poured out what it had been like since he'd been gone, and about my fears and anger and sorrow. I told him everything. At the end I said, "And if I could change anything since you died, I'd change . . . I'd . . . why, I wouldn't change anything. I'm glad for everything I went through . . . because now I don't have to go through it any more. Peter . . . *goodbye.*"

Ziggy and I climbed down the mountain into the beautiful desert morning.

I didn't feel exhilarated. Or high. Or reborn. But I felt that I had left behind something ugly and angry and old on that mountain, and that I didn't have to carry it around any more.

Soon I was invited to perform at the most beautiful and famous theater I've ever worked in. And when I walked out on the stage, I sang with the old passion once again.

I don't know what that trip to the mountain was all about. It was a healing, and it was a spiritual experience, and I was grateful. I never went back to the psychiatrist except to say thank you. At last I was able to see the *good* in what had happened.

Peter had died at home instead of a week later in China when problems of distance and a foreign language might have created truly insurmountable barriers.

This experience brought new people with a new sensitivity into my life, and I was now able to pass on firsthand words of help to others who were grieving.

Peter had died in full view of that special place in the Santa Rosa Mountains that the Cahuilla Indians believe is the place where your soul goes up to heaven.

A Jewish girlfriend shared that the Talmud lists the seven ways to die. The most blessed is the way Peter went—in a flash, no pain, no suffering, no lingering illness. His feisty spirit could never have tolerated a lengthy, debilitating disease.

I took another CPR course. If I hadn't been able to do CPR, I'd always have felt that my helplessness was the reason he died. In this refresher course, I learned that the reason the medics had worked so long on Peter was *because* I had started CPR at once. The heart can be stopped for a long time, but as long as the brain receives oxygen within the first four minutes, a person can be revived with no brain damage. They hadn't taught me that the first time. Once I knew, instead of feeling guilty, I felt proud.

I look at our photo albums now with very mixed emotions. Was he handsome or wasn't he? What might our relationship have become? What really happened on that mountain?

There will always be unanswered questions. But there are a couple of things I know for sure. One is that I now have over seven years of sobriety instead of "newcomer" status in AA because I accepted that drowning my feelings in a drink would not bring Peter back. You *have* to go through those emotions—sooner, or later.

Also, I know from what everyone says that the time Peter and I spent together was the best time of his life. Although his death was tragic, his last year of life was beautiful. And I am so happy to have been part of that.

I may never replace him. I will never forget him. And what I learned from our conversation on Peter's Mountain will never, ever disappear.

FOURTEEN

Clare's Story

These are true feelings, and if you have read them, please take heart that though they are short, many, many things can be read into them—such a profound love and respect for every member of my family.

—from Jamie Westcott's hidden memoirs

As I move along the grass on my knees, my hands covered with black earth, many thoughts go through my mind.

For over two decades I loved him. I held him when he was a baby, tried as I could to help with his homework, praised him as he succeeded in school and college—the things a father does for a growing son. How could I ever know that one day I would be on my knees hunched over his grave, planting a row of white begonias?

I think back to the afternoon Dr. Low brought us together in Scarborough General Hospital to say a few simple words that we'd hoped never to hear. "I'm sorry, Jamie, we have tried everything and nothing seems to work."

I think back through the short, thirty months before that day when a call came to the house saying the biopsy was positive. Yes, Jamie did have cancer.

The call had come on Christmas Eve 1985.

As I put the green and white flowers in the hard ground I think of that precious boy and the twenty-five years I had with him—to hold him, to love him. And, sadly, I think of all the things I might have done—but didn't. I remind myself of the many, many times I could have hugged him, and I didn't.

Often now when I am on a street or in a shopping mall, and I see a small boy walking with his parents, inside me is the urge to go up and tell them to hug him every day and tell him they love him so very much. One day the Lord may call their precious son to be with Him as He did mine.

So many other thoughts crowd my mind. For many years our large family had been spared the fear and tragedy of losing a loved one. Even though nothing much was ever said, everyone knew that in separate ways family members were quietly asking God to help Jamie. Please make it benign.

And now at Pine Hills Cemetery, on my knees, for a moment I relive those terrible minutes that followed the fateful Christmas Eve message seven years ago. Our prayers were not enough. Jamie had cancer.

So clearly I remember a son who, short years before, graduated with the highest honors from high school and knew in his heart he could make his mark in whatever he set out to do. He became a master of the English language. Winning the highest school honors, he graduated designated an Ontario Scholar by the Minister of Education—and calling me *sir*. So it was not really a surprise when in 1983 he chose journalism. That his sister was a top TV network journalist in both Canada and New Zealand no doubt influenced his decision. Now when I think of him, words like *guts, resolve,* and *courage* flash in my mind like a neon sign.

I am reminded of that day at the hospital in January 1986, when being admitted and briefed on what was in store for him, he buried his fear and despair deep inside, hiding them from his mother. He knew the odds, but he was helping us bear the strain of our feelings of helplessness.

I see him tied upside down to a stryker frame trying to hold up one hand with a Winston Churchill "V" for victory sign. Every move, word, and gesture was designed to send the message to his family: "Don't worry about me, I'll be okay."

Now, as I kneel at his grave, I know what he meant. "I'll be okay either way, I can handle death." Although he did not know that following his operation the surgeon told his mother in a straight-forward, but compassionate, way, "Six months to three years," Jamie surely knew what his chances were with this dreaded form of cancer.

At first the chemotherapy was very tough and the long criss-crossed vaccine scratches to spark the immune system soon covered his back. In the weeks following the operation, Jamie and I talked about his cancer and how it was affecting his life. One of the first things we discussed was the side effects of the treatment, and that all of his treasured, long, wavy hair would fall out. We talked about getting a hairpiece that resembled his own as closely as possible. This was very important, for in a way his hair was his trademark. He must not have reason to stay inside and hide away from his friends because of the change in his appearance.

Rather than waiting for it to fall out, he had it all cut off. He found a hairpiece he liked, almost a perfect match for his own hair, and wore it every day until his own grew in again. But the second he walked into the house, he would quickly pull it off and toss it on a chair.

I remember so well the long talk we had one night about his future. Some decisions had to be made. I suggested that he could live for six months or six years or sixty years—and that only God knew what the future held for him. And now I have to tell myself that God and Jamie knew more than I did. Did he want to finish his journalism course at Centennial College, or did he want to go to work? I knew he had the ability and training needed to be a good reporter, and he had great skill as a photographer.

"I'd rather not go back to college, Dad," he said simply. "I want to go to work."

He started to work in early May at the Toronto Sun as a summer student. His first story appeared with his byline on May 11, 1986.

That fall Jamie was offered a position on the permanent staff of the paper. Some months later, the publisher, Paul Godfrey, told me that Jamie might have been given a job originally because of his condition and the circumstances, but he said emphatically that Jamie was offered a full-time position because he was an excellent writer and a fine reporter. Jamie and I often talked about story leads, and I treasure the memory of this, for in a few cases I was able to help him.

At the start he worked on general assignments, occasionally relieving in the Business Section and at the Police Desk. Finally, he achieved his dream—he became a full-time reporter on the Police Desk. He continued with treatment while at the *Sun,* and it seemed to be working. Life became a wonderful experience for a young man who loved his work and who collected and cherished friends as if they were diamonds. Newspaper awards came his way for his stories, and even though he checked in periodically for brain and liver scans and chest X rays, there had to be some feeling of "Praise God, maybe I've beaten it."

But then it happened. November 30, 1988.

As I look at the freshly planted begonias, I don't really see them, for I have a picture in my mind as clear as a photograph.

Jamie is coming in the front door. He tries to be very matter-of-fact without showing the emotion that you know is there and hidden—but not well.

"Bad news—the X rays show small lesions in my lungs."

Each word weighed a ton, for this meant the dreaded melanotic sarcoma had found its way to yet another part of his body. Remission was over.

Until then there seemed to be reason to hope, but now we were confronted with the hard and tragic fact that he was losing the battle. The lesions in his lungs brought on constant coughing and pain. He tried to work but found it very hard, for breathing was getting more difficult. Most of the time he felt very tired. Sometimes he would sit alone at the end of the kitchen table and bury his head in his hands and cry.

Now as I think of those days, I know he had no fear about where he was going—long before he had made his peace with the Lord. It was what he was leaving behind. It was the sadness of leaving his family—and his friends—and the job he loved so much. And he did not believe he would have time enough to make his mark. He so wanted not to be forgotten.

At Christmas, we were all together again—a short thirty-six months from that fateful Christmas Eve call telling us it was cancer. Although his whole working life as a reporter was only thirty months, he won four awards. His modesty about his work supported his feeling of not having enough time to make his mark. I learned that the *Toronto Sun* was going to establish an award in his memory, to be known as "The Jamie Westcott Award for Police Reporting." It would be given annually for excellence in crime reporting and writing. Although it would be given to honor his memory, the publisher told Jamie about it before he died. Jamie was visibly moved when he heard, and he said, "I'm not afraid anymore." The knowledge of the award comforted me. It meant that Jamie had made his mark. He would be remembered.

Then one day Jamie suffered a seizure and was rushed to the hospital. A scan showed the cancer had again moved, this time to the part of his brain that controls the left arm and right eye. Jamie spent fifteen days in the hospital, with family members at his side around the clock and media and police friends dropping in—all praying for that one miracle Jamie needed so much. Then Dr. Low told us he had tried everything from heavy chemo to interferon, but nothing seemed to stop the cancer. Jamie Westcott's fate moved from the skill of man to the will of God. But he never—ever—complained. He thanked the doctor and said to his mother and me, "Please take me home."

I had a strong desire to talk with Jamie. Because light bothered his right eye, it was always covered. His left arm hung limply at his side. Oxygen tubes with long plastic hoses connected to large tanks all added to the pain and deprivation that wracked his once-strong body. He spent his days and nights in a large chair in the middle of the living room with one or two family members always close by. It was difficult, if not impossible, to be alone with him.

I was terrified that my last chance to talk to Jamie had passed. I needed and wanted so badly to speak to him, as a father to a son, to tell him how I felt and to try to give him some hope. It was very important to me to try to make him less fearful of what he surely knew was slowly and deliberately moving closer to him every day.

For weeks Jamie had been watching and listening to Dr. Bernie Siegal's videos and audio tapes. He had never worn glasses, but now he would try those of family and friends to see the TV screen better with his fading, but still working, left eye. I decided that if I was going to speak to him at all, as a father to a dying son, it would have to be sitting with him in the midst of all the distractions and other things going on, or I would have to find some other way. In my office in the basement, I spoke into a tape recorder as if I were talking directly to Jamie. And that evening, I replaced Dr. Siegal's tape with mine.

I had spent a lot of time thinking about what I would say. I had always been moved by a poem written over one hundred years ago by my grandmother about her little brother who had died, and some letters sent to her forty years later from France about the death of her son, my dad's twin, in the Battle of Bourlon Wood. I tried so hard to think of what a father should say to his son who was dying and, in some way, help to prepare him for what he must face. I wanted to express the great love I have for him, and that of his mother and his eight brothers and sisters. And I wanted to offer a speck of hope, even though I truly knew there was none. These are the things I spoke of.

I will never know what my words meant to Jamie, for he only looked up at me and gently squeezed my fingers with his good hand. I could have asked for nothing more.

Jamie so wanted to be still around for his twenty-fifth birthday on May 30 and for my sixty-fifth birthday on June 17. He made it for his birthday, but not for mine.

Jamie asked that "Amazing Grace" be sung at his funeral. Outside the church Metropolitan Toronto Police Band members played the theme from *Chariots of Fire* on bagpipes and drums. Monsignor Robitaille from St. Michael's Cathedral assisted with the mass and brought with him the St. Michael's Boys Choir. Father Moss read parts from a letter Jamie had written to him, and Father Harper assisted Father McCann with the mass. A *Toronto Sun* reporter read from the Bible. It was a very moving and sad and "great" funeral with all Jamie's friends and a procession to the cemetery. The cars stretched out for over a mile.

The light rain stopped and as a piper played "Amazing Grace," the sun broke through the clouds. Father Moss prayed for Jamie's soul. The boy who was our son was gone to be with God.

As I place the plant in the ground I remember the second part of his wish. He was buried the day before my sixty-fifth birthday on June 17. But he was with us in spirit.

A week earlier he asked "Wally," the nickname he had for his brother Chris, to "get a card for Dad, just in case I don't make his birthday." Jamie asked Wally to print a message on it from Dr. Siegal's book *Love, Medicine and Miracles* and he signed it.

On Saturday afternoon, June 17, all the family gathered at Jamie's sister Kathleen's home for my birthday. I was busy opening presents and cards from my kids, when I picked up a card with "Dad" scrawled on the envelope as if written by one of my grandchildren. I opened it to find it was barely legible, but it said, "Love Jamie."

That was when I came to realize the true depth of my loss. This was pure Jamie.

No amount of love, or care, or medicine could keep Jamie with us. He suffered a very long time, and he died a brave, young man with dignity and heart. As time goes on and all the wonderful memories unfold, we must challenge ourselves to look at our own lives and try to match the legacy of spirit and courage Jamie has left behind. Jamie did not want us to mourn his death. He wanted us to remember his life.

His spirit lives!

FIFTEEN

Toni's Story

It's taking the time to grieve that brings true healing.

On the morning of March 3, 1989, I went to my doctor for my regular monthly maternity checkup. I was in good health and in good spirits. In just four short weeks, I would finally be holding my baby in my arms. I was excited that my job as "Mother" would soon begin.

My doctor came energetically into the exam room, as usual. He asked the same questions he usually asked. "How are you? How's the baby? And how's the Daddy?"

Of course I answered, "We're all fine. And I'm getting fat!"

He turned to me and said, "I've told you before. Pregnant ladies don't 'get fat'; they 'get baby'! Now let's see about finding this baby's heartbeat. How is the baby's kicking activity?" he asked.

"Well, I've haven't noticed any real movements in the past couple of days," I remarked.

The doctor's expression became quizzical.

"No activity? Are you sure?" he questioned.

"I don't remember any kicking or movement since Wednesday," I said.

"So it has been almost two days since you remember feeling movement? Is that right?"

"Yes."

My doctor was searching all over my bulging abdomen with his Doppler, trying to find my baby's heartbeat. "What's wrong?" I asked, suddenly feeling frightened. "Why aren't you letting me listen to the baby's heartbeat?"

The doctor's search for a heartbeat was in vain. There was no heartbeat. After many ultrasounds by a variety of doctors, it was confirmed. My baby had died inside of me.

My grieving began with shock and denial. The shock, a natural response, was very beneficial. It gave me time to absorb the gravity of the tragedy by delaying the impact until later—when I could cope. Denial allowed me a time to protect myself from the pain.

My body was numb. I felt paralyzed. But on the outside, I seemed calm and matter of fact. I was trying desperately to be strong and pretend that everything was going to be just fine. I even tried to convince myself that I wasn't pregnant. But the fact remained that I was—and I was going to have to labor and deliver my baby. At that particular time, and in my frame of mind, that was unthinkable.

Despite the fact that a part of me was trying to convince myself that I wasn't pregnant, another part of me was holding on tightly to the hope that when my baby was born, he would kick and scream just like all babies do when they are delivered. I wanted to believe that somehow—by way of some miracle—all those doctors had been mistaken. But they weren't. On March 4, 1989, at 11:24 P.M., Stuart Bradley Asaro was born. He was dead.

Thank God for the shock and denial stages. They allowed me to be calm and to see my baby, to hold him in my arms as I had dreamed. I saw his small, completely formed four-pound nine-ounce frame, his beautiful little nose and precious little ears. I saw his full head of coal black hair and that the shape of his head and neck were like his father's. I felt his little fingers and wrapped them around my forefinger. I held his body, so nice and warm, next to mine.

Not once did I shed a tear while holding my child. It was as if he weren't dead, as if I hadn't noticed. For those few minutes I didn't care if he was dead or alive. He was just *my baby*. Nothing else mattered. I wasn't even thinking that this was going to be the last time I would ever hold or see my precious baby Stuart. That was the reality, but somehow I didn't believe it.

As the days passed, I remained in shock and denial. That allowed me to take care of the necessary funeral arrangements. If I had not been in shock and denial, I don't think I could have gotten through those days.

In the next stage of my grief, I felt guilt. This was one of the strongest emotions I felt in the grieving process. I began to blame myself for my baby's death. I remembered every single thing I had eaten, had drunk, and had done. I even considered where I had gone and what I wore. There had to be some explanation for this terrible tragedy! It had to be my fault.

The more I blamed myself and others, and the more I searched for a guilty party, the more guilt and anger I felt. All my feelings were turning into anger. I blamed God, myself, my work for not giving me what I wanted—what I deserved—after all those months of waiting. I even blamed my little baby for leaving me.

Anyone and everyone was a target for my anger. I learned later that in the guilt stage of grief men usually express their hostility more easily and quickly than women do, and that women who express no anger may experience greater depression later than those who do. Therefore, my anger was an important step toward eventual resolution and peace of mind.

During the guilt and anger stages, I moved in and out of denial. It was as if I were a turtle, sitting in my shell, poking my head in and out and then always retreating back inside to the safety and sanctuary of my shell. I knew something was different in my life, but I couldn't quite understand what it was. Because of this state of confusion, I would sit and stare out at spring in bloom.

I cried most of the time. I would sit and hold myself and rock back and forth. No one was around. I felt so isolated and alone in my grief. I had no family nearby. A few friends tried to console me, but how could they possibly know and understand my pain? I did nothing each day for weeks. I didn't get dressed, or eat, or drink. I just sat and cried and stared out the window, wondering how the rest of the world could continue as if nothing had happened when my whole world had stopped.

Physically I was always exhausted. I felt a heaviness in my chest and a constant need to take deep sighing breaths. I had heart palpitations, butterflies in my stomach, and aching arms. I tried hard to believe that I had never been pregnant, that my house and my life were the same as before my pregnancy began—that this horrible tragedy had never happened.

But it had happened. I had been pregnant and everything was different. My house had become more than just a house. It was a home, a place where a baby could live inside its sheltering walls. My body and frame of mind were changed and matured as I prepared for motherhood. What had been a ray of sunshine in my life for eight months had been replaced by a hollow, empty feeling. I had no proof of motherhood.

I was a mother with no baby.

Sometimes I felt self-conscious about crying because the tears would come suddenly and without warning, no matter where I was. I thought people might think I was crazy or something—since obviously they wouldn't know why I was crying. But I didn't want to always have to explain myself.

Finally, I began to heal. And the scar began to form. I felt that I would soon be able to face the world again without so much emotion. Although a day never passes that I don't think of my son, now usually I can think of him without crying.

There are no shortcuts in the grieving process. Time, alone, didn't heal my broken heart. I had to help myself by taking the time to do my healing. I didn't bury myself with activity to avoid the pain. And I had to help my partner by being patient with him. After all, grieving is a personal process.

I know that loving our son, Stuart, brought my husband and me closer. I am so grateful that we were able to share this burden and that we have grown from the experience.

I learned that crying is not a measure of how much you loved but is an indication of how completely you have allowed yourself to openly express your feelings. And I learned that time in and of itself would not heal my grief. It's taking the time *to grieve* that brings true healing.

SIXTEEN

Mary's Story

*We never seriously accepted the fact that he might be dying. . . .
The "heroic" measures were stopped and nature was allowed to
"take its course."*

After my husband died, a friend of ours wrote in her consoling
note that she had always thought of Jim as "Gentleman Jim."
Other letters of condolence echoed the thought, speaking of
his goodness, his kindness, his courtesy, his gentleness. I sometimes
wonder if the legacy of loving he left us helped support me far more
than I knew as I struggled to survive his death.

Jim was a good man, quiet, deliberate, slow to anger, slow to
make decisions (an exasperating but salutary counter to my impul-
siveness and impatience). He was introspective, intellectual, well
read in many areas, with a memory for the fascinating that delighted
me. He had a sly, graceful, Irish wit and a sense of self-perception
and proportion that was an antidote to my habit of taking things too
seriously. As a professional engineer, working in both academic and
corporate fields, he enriched and expanded my world, which was
once centered largely on literature, music, and the arts.

We both worked in New York City throughout our forty-four
years of marriage. But we worked to live, not lived to work. All
through those years we looked forward to our retirement. That
would be the time, as Jim put it, when we could do what *we* wanted
to do, not what others wanted us to do. We had planned so much.
We would sail all summer on Candlewood Lake in Connecticut,
where we had a vacation home. We would spend the rest of the year
enjoying the riches of New York, traveling abroad, and basking in
the southern California desert sun in Rancho Mirage, where we had
a tiny condo, given to us by my parents.

A year before his retirement, Jim had a "neurological attack" that none of the dozen or so neurologists in a large New York medical center could diagnose. After many tests he left the hospital with his left arm and leg somewhat impaired. But as the condition stabilized, he found he could still drive a car competently and could still dance, which we loved to do. But at our beloved country home on Candlewood Lake, he found he couldn't sail our boat, use a chain saw and axe to fell and cut our firewood, or easily get about the steep, boulder-strewn woods that shelved sharply down to our lake front. This new situation forced us to change our retirement plans. Sadly we sold the Connecticut house and began to think more seriously about moving permanently to California. We were already spending more winter vacation time in our Rancho Mirage condo.

It was there, during the Christmas week of 1988, a little over three years since the first appearance of his "affliction," that Jim had a second attack. The neurologist diagnosed it as cancer of the spinal cord, and he described to me the logical, inevitable, and fatal course it would probably take.

Jim and I never discussed his illness beyond signing a living will to guide doctors if and when either of us became dependent on life-support systems. We never seriously accepted the fact that he might be dying. We both seemed to assume that his condition would stabilize again. Our minds, our hearts, our hopes, and our total efforts, both in the hospital and in the beautiful nursing home, were on his radiation treatments and physical therapy. In and around my long hours with him every day, I began to look for a larger apartment that we could equip for his use and comfort.

Our time together was intense. On Valentine's Day, only five days before he died, he had managed to get a card for me through the nursing facility concierge. It said that he was falling in love with me all over again, and he had underlined the words heavily.

Six weeks from the onset of the illness, pneumonia sent him from the nursing home back to the hospital's intensive-care unit. He was quickly placed on a life-support system, pinned down by tubes, gauges, gadgets, and pumps. He was unable to speak to me, and we couldn't discuss anything or prepare ourselves for his death. Most of all, we couldn't say goodbye. Guided by kind and wise nurses, I took every chance I could to talk to his doctors, reminding them that Jim did not want to have his life prolonged artificially if he could not recover his former way of life. I couldn't believe then—and still can't believe now—the enormity of what I was asking. The "heroic" measures were stopped and nature was allowed to "take its course." The phone call came at six one Sunday morning. I was so shaken that I didn't dare drive to the hospital, and I was reluctant to bother neighbors so early. I was alone. Helpless. *Alone.*

We had no children. What few relatives or close friends we had lived hundreds, even thousands, of miles away. Jim was Catholic, so, in an hour or so, I phoned a nearby couple who I knew went to early Mass and asked them to take me with them. I dressed in clothes I knew Jim liked. During the Mass I conducted my internal memorial service for him. Since he had always refused to say what he wanted done about his body if I were to survive him, I had made arrangements with the Neptune Society, very quickly and under terrible duress during those last days of his life, to cremate his body and scatter his ashes at sea.

I will never quite assuage the guilt for having made that decision. I'm not even sure why I feel guilty. After all, neither of us had a family hometown or a family burial place. And I knew that without Jim I would be homeless. *He* had always been my home. And I couldn't bear the thought of carrying a box of his ashes about with me until I finally decided what to do.

A few months after Jim died, I was looking for a picture to put on a blank wall at the end of the living room. It had to be predominantly blue; it had to be quiet and soothing. I found it in a discount store. It was just a poster, a large print of a David Jenks' painting called "Illumination." It depicts a wide expanse of calm, dancing, blue sea reaching back to the clear white line of the horizon. The sky above is mottled in shades of gray, blue, and white. Below two spots of light whiten the ocean where the sun has pierced the billowing clouds. It was just right. The blues were the right colors, and under that perfect dancing sea was right where Jim had come to rest. It hangs where I see it many times a day. It eases my remorse. It has become my equivalent of the fulfilling, calming visits to a loved one's grave.

But in those first days and weeks after Jim died, I was anything but calm. The shock of his death and the blessed numbness soon wore off, releasing a flood of excessive feelings that frightened me. I cried a lot, but it brought no relief—just exhausting hangovers the next day. I wept. I bawled, with loud, wracking sobs like a child devastated by anger, fear, and desolation. Was I losing control? Would I go over the edge? I thought more than once of the Hindu custom of "suttee" in which the grief-crazed widow throws herself on the funeral pyre of her dead husband.

In reality a person would have to be insane to do that. In theory, not surviving the death of a beloved husband was not such a bad idea. I felt as if the better part of me had been torn away. If I were to survive, I would have to grow a brand new person on the bloody stump. That realization, that responsibility for my survival, became the hardest part of being left alone. I felt I hadn't the strength, will, or desire to do it. I was in a vacuum, lost in a limbo of not wanting to live, yet not quite wanting to die. Why did others expect me to survive, to "get over it," and get on with my life as if Jim's death were a disease? "You are a survivor," they'd say. "You are such a strong person," they'd go on. "Anyway, time will heal it all," they'd conclude.

So in public I behaved as expected, of course. I even took pride in my performance. There's no room in our culture for shrieking grief. Unknowingly I was putting into practice a slogan I heard only much later when I joined a bereavement group: "Fake it till you make it!" It means pretend to the world, and more importantly to yourself, that you are making it, even though you do not expect you will. Faking it, like whistling in the dark, is a mechanism of sorts to get from one day to the next. For me, it meant acting out the hope that if I could "con" myself into wanting to go on living, and I could keep it up long enough, one day it might become a reality rather than a ruse. That is what keeps a living being struggling to keep on living at such tremendous cost.

In the blur of the following months, the warm and sympathetic community in which we lived sustained me with their attention. Eventually I found what must be one of the finest bereavement groups in the country. The members of that group gave me their kindness and understanding. Over many months, the group's leader gave me the tools to cope with each phase of the grief process. And, by wonderful chance, the newsletter *Afterloss* began about that time. It helped me get a better grip on those tools.

There is a great deal of helpful advice available for those who are in their first years of loss. Possibly the best advice is given often by *Afterloss:* the warning not to make a major geographical or physical move until you feel ready, and not to make any important, and possibly irrevocable, decisions. Perhaps the most important advice is: Try not to do any of it alone.

However, circumstances made it necessary for me to do all of that and to add those high stresses to the already worst stress of my life. During the six weeks that Jim was ill, we had decided to move permanently from New York to Rancho Mirage. We knew that if his condition stabilized, as it had three years before, we could work out some kind of life in a far more pleasant and easier environment than Manhattan. When Jim died, I simply continued the process and began planning how I would wind up our affairs in New York. That caused me to make four different trips to New York during the first year to clean out our large apartment there and to dispose of furniture and other cherished possessions.

The task of discarding most of the possessions we had accumulated during our years together was both necessary and a strange urge for symbolic self-destruction that was first triggered by my mother's death fifteen years earlier and then repeated when my father died. When Mother died, I returned to New York and threw away many of the dolls, toys, and books of my childhood that I had kept for so long. When my father died, scarcely a year before my husband's death, I did it again. Dad had been a very important person in my life. He was my role model, whose aspirations, traits, and achievements I had always tried to assimilate into my life the way he had manifested them in his.

With Jim's death, my need to get rid of the past surfaced again. It was disguised as a need to prepare our apartment to be sold. Hysterically I got rid of the evidence of our years together when I had contentedly indulged my interests. It was almost as if I was being forced to make choices I did not want to make. Out went my extensive collection of carefully pressed specimens of plants and tree leaves of northeastern U.S. flora. Out went all my writing, whether published or not. I threw away records and tapes, and recorder consort sheet music. I gave away dozens of cookbooks and sewing books, my sewing machine, and fancy equipment. Worst of all, I sold hundreds of the books that reflected my changing and ripening tastes and enthusiasms through all those years. I mourn these losses deeply, for they could comfort me today now that I have no comforting companion.

Each visit to New York brought home to me the reality of loss upon loss upon loss. Each visit was gruelling, emotionally as well as physically. I could stand the stress for only a week or two. Then I would flee back to southern California and my bereavement group to gather strength for another assault. On my second visit to New York, I had progressed far enough through this bewildering bereavement to do something constructive and healing. I gave a memorial dinner in a sparkling greenhouse restaurant in the American Museum of Natural History.

I invited a dozen people who had meant the most to Jim. In the guise of a toast to him, I gave a little eulogy using some lines from Rilke's *Duino Elegies* that one of those friends had quoted in a letter to me about Jim's death. I was able to temper the seriousness of my words by reminding our friends of Jim's irrepressible inability to remain solemn about anything pertaining to himself. It was a happy dinner, and for me it was a ritual "Godspeed." It was the farewell I'd been unable to say to him.

At the time I was trying to settle my New York past, I was also working hard—in spite of my blacker moments—to establish a life in the present to fill the painful vacuum. I reached out to others in a way I never had before. I imposed myself (or so I felt) on people and in situations in a way I would never have dreamed of doing before. I never refused an invitation. I went to parties that I didn't want to attend. I was companionable with people who had never really interested me before. I spent a lot of time searching for things to do and places to go and persuading people to accompany me. None of this was what I'd ordinarily call "me."

I was driven.

I pushed hard—perhaps too hard. And I was impatient with what seemed like such a slow recovery in my grief process.

Simultaneously with trying to wind up my past and create a new present, I was also trying to arrange for my future in northern California where my brother and his family live. Between all those trips to New York, this necessitated three or four trips from southern to northern California, each time driving the thousand-mile trip alone, *by myself,* terrified.

During bereavement every emotion is exaggerated, almost out of control. For me, fear was the one to which I was most susceptible and the most destructive. I still think of those journeys with some trepidation. Looking back, I wonder how I did it. But that future life in a retirement community in Sacramento is taking shape.

Like most who are bereaved, I have done a good deal of reading about the grief process. Recently I came across the idea of "a gift in the loss." I was shocked at the thought that there might be some good for me in Jim's death! Or as a result of it! It was abhorrent, yet the idea lingered in my mind. The more I thought about it, the more I realized that I have indeed gained some good things as a result of losing him.

One concerns my brother. Since our teens, we had been separated geographically by schooling, careers, and marriages. When we became adults, we were far from each other. Infrequent visits gave us no real chance to become reacquainted. We knew certain basic things about each other that we had learned in childhood but we knew little about each other as we had grown and matured.

Since Jim's death, however, I have leaned heavily on my brother. Without him, I would not be where I am today. As our relationship has grown, our love has deepened. It has become important to both of us in ways that it always should have been, but perhaps might never have been, if I still had Jim. Now when I need someone, I turn first to my brother, and he is there for me. He is my family. I have no other. His wife has become the sister I never had. His children and grandchildren are like mine. I am deeply grateful for these relationships, in spite of the high price I am paying.

Another gift is friendships with women. Jim and I were content to turn to our own selves and to each other for the kind of nourishment most people find in friendships. Consequently I had very few really close friendships with other women. I never had, nor felt the lack of, a confidante. Yet, for the most part, it was women who came to my rescue when Jim died. It was women to whom I turned to talk, to fill the emptiness, to be my companions. Now everywhere I go, I discover anew the pleasures and richness of friendships with women. How good to find them! How much I was missing!

The third gift is harder to pin down, let alone express. Putting it into words makes it seem suspect. Since my early teens I have been looking for faith, real faith in the existence of a Supreme Entity. I worked hard at it, mostly by reading the mystics, the realists, the believers, and scoffers, the rationalists, no matter their dogma or creed. I desperately wanted to make that "leap of faith," to be able to pray with the certainty of its purpose which others seem to have found. But it always eluded me.

When Jim died, I began praying, asking Someone, Something, each day, often many times a day, for strength to get through that day. And although exhausted and without hope, I would ask for strength to get through the next day. And the next day. And the next. Somewhere along the line I began to wonder what it was—besides desperation—that made me continue to pray. I began to realize that when I stopped trying to find God, something happened to me of its own accord, Zen-like, without my consciously willing it. Something had come to sustain me. Something had begun to take shape within me that might be labeled *belief*. Was it a matter of having hit bottom?

Someone wise noted that when everything has been stripped away, and there is nothing left, there is still God. I'm reminded too of the blues singers who wail, "When you so far down, they ain't no place but up." *Up*. It means anything you want it to, I guess, from a better grip on your life to maybe even a belief in God.

It is the closest I've come, but I hunger for more. I received courage when I had none. And I find that I keep turning to whatever it is that is the source of that strength within me.

With these new discoveries to lean on, I now think that perhaps I can move toward the one more necessary and final goal: the ability to look forward with enthusiasm, even joy. I know now that I will never lose the loss, or the dark depression that lurks close behind it. There is still that destructive undercurrent of pointlessness that surfaces often enough to drag me down into a kind of terrifying purgatory. I still have periods of not wanting to live. And at the same time and equally as strong, I have no desire to die. I am burnt out. I am exhausted from trying so hard to get through the intensive grief work. I am tired of having to invent each day, of pushing myself through it, only to have to start all over the next morning. I feel like Sisyphus, who was condemned to constantly push a huge boulder up a hill, only to have it roll back down again.

What rescues me, time and again, from this slippery pit? What gives me the immediate strength to struggle out again? Largely, it is the gifts of the loss: my brother, the friends who spontaneously reach out to me in the nick of time, and the knowledge that I can pray for courage and more strength. But there is another thing: I also know that the grief process is a growth process. It does not stand still.

As I sit writing this, wrapped in the warmth of Jim's old cashmere cardigan and in the memory of his love and goodness, I look back to the morning he died. I realize, and take comfort in, the distance I've come. I have turned around from the past, and I face forward. I look beyond today and know I still have quite a way to go. But beckoning out there is the possibility of achieving the final goal, achieving the momentum of purpose in living that will carry me forward from day to day toward each tomorrow.

SEVENTEEN

Scott's Story

*The world around me seemed to open up to reveal God
in a way I had not known Him before.*

Growing up as the youngest of six children, the memories I
have of my father are those of a man who had, for decades,
maintained the upper hand in his fight against cancer. When
I was two years old, my father, a Minnesota Supreme Court Justice,
was diagnosed with lymphoma, cancer of the lymph system. Because his battle lasted throughout my life, I never fully accepted and
understood that my dad was fighting daily to survive.

While as a child I knew that Dad was sick, it never struck me that
this illness and its consequences were out of the ordinary. In the first
few years after the cancer was discovered and Dad was undergoing
radiation treatment, I would spend afternoons with him sitting on
his bed watching Mr. Rogers on television. I was too young to think
that Dad being home in the middle of the day, his frequent naps, and
the side effects of radiation and chemotherapy were unusual.

For me, as for every child, my dad and mom were the yardsticks
against which all else was measured. If my dad was sick, it must have
been normal. He did plenty of the things that other fathers did.
When the cancer was in remission, he would frequently feel well
enough to throw the baseball with his sons after work, barbecue
chicken—almost beyond recognition—on Sunday afternoons, and
even make good on his boast of being the "oldest living waterskier on
Sugar Lake."

Because he was like other fathers in so many ways, I thought his
illness could not really be that serious. It never sank in that he confronted death every day for nearly twenty years. After all, Dad went
to the office almost every day, he always made the drive across town
in time for family dinners, he even loaded the family into the station

wagon for our summer trips. Dad's determination and success at pushing forward with the business of living life obscured the specter of death. It just never occurred to me that he might not always be around.

Dad knew though. He often spoke of his "bonus days." In any circumstance, he would be ready to remind someone, "This is the day that the Lord has made; let us rejoice and be glad in it." And I would hear him say, as if to remind himself, "It's a great day to be alive." Around someone so full of life, it would have been hard for anyone, least of all a child, to imagine the battle that he was waging against death.

For my dad and my family, the cancer that weakened his immune system made short stays in the hospital a way of life. Even these seemed routine. He always returned home and life continued.

After a series of tests in October 1987, life began to change. We learned that Dad had developed a rare, degenerative, terminal brain complication called "progressive multifocal leukoencephalopathy," or PML. The PML was just one of the many ways the years of cancer treatment had chipped away at Dad's body.

Over the years my attempts to express my love for my father, due in part to my emotional and his physical limitations, had always centered on responding to his physical needs. However pathetic and superficial my attempts to strengthen our relationship appear in retrospect, I can now understand them from a dramatically different perspective. The abrupt change from semi-independent child to care-giver thrust me into a role for which I was not prepared. It typified my frustration and feelings of powerlessness.

The person who had always been my safest harbor and unfailing protector now needed me in a way in which I was not fully prepared to respond. I felt helpless. I had not yet become fully independent. Now I was challenged to provide support to another human being as he faced death.

At the time PML was discovered, I was completely absorbed in my life as a junior at Georgetown University in Washington, D.C. I had always wanted to go away to college. In fact the thought of going to school in Minnesota never entered my mind. It was out of a sense of adventure that I wanted to leave home and conquer a new city. If I'd had any thought as to what might happen to my family while I was away, I would not have left.

I was leaving home neither to escape unhappiness nor avoid the future. I left home to grow up and to become a man. With Dad's death, I came to realize that one of the most important lessons of being a man, or rather a more complete human being, was still to be learned at home.

During my quest for independence and identity, however, I let more than miles separate me from my family. I missed the day-to-day events that a family shares together, but I did not make enough time in my life for much more than remembrance.

Because I was the only one in the family who did not live in Minneapolis, I had to be called home to face the truth about the seriousness of Dad's condition. While I had always known the facts, I finally had to accept the truth of what they meant. In preparing for this new reality, which I had never honestly confronted, I discovered that the years of presenting myself as independent and self-reliant positioned me to weather this experience alone.

As a family we decided we would care for Dad, ourselves, at home. I wrestled with the question of taking time off from school to be at home with him and my family. Because the doctors told us the decline could take up to a year, I decided to at least try to finish the fall semester, and I returned to school.

But Dad's decline was very rapid. Each time his condition deteriorated, I was called home. Yet each time he summoned his strength and quietly continued his fight. He was unquestionably at peace with death but continued to fight on behalf of his family, trying to assuage our feelings of powerlessness. After half a dozen trips home, I went back to Washington to take my final exams and then return for Christmas. I was not able to finish my exams before I got the call to come home.

When I stepped off the plane early that morning, all of my family except for my mother and oldest sister were there to meet me. I had missed Dad by little more than an hour. No one had to tell me what had happened. I understood.

A numbness took control of my body and allowed me to continue on. My eyes blurred with restrained tears. They were the only visible expression of the emotion in my heart.

That morning I sat alone with my dad in the room where he died. Although there was a hospital bed in this room, it was the room I had known growing up. It still had a familiar and peaceful feel. For the first time, though, I was completely struck by reality. Even though I was surrounded by people and the elements of life I had known for most of my own life, my father's lifeless body was right there before my eyes.

It seemed impossible that my father would not be beside me to take pictures at my graduation, to share the joys and travails of my first job, or to know the person I may someday marry. The thought of passing these milestones without him near me caused me to ache. The pain was not sudden, nor was it especially sharp, but it did not pass quickly. Even though I knew that the people I love and trust were nearby and were reaching out to me, I felt alone.

On that morning, alone in that room, I allowed myself to feel and express more of what was in my mind and heart than I had at any time before or have since. I cried. I talked. I prayed. I hugged. I remembered. I listened. I laughed. And then I was silent. I did all of these things with my dad.

This fundamental event, the kind that at some time will touch the life of every person, began to reshape my life. In a small, but critical way, Dad's death began to release me. Death created a chink in the barriers that I had carefully erected around myself. The elements of my life did not change, but they were reshaped, adjusted, reordered, and then given release.

Caught up in the hectic pace of the holiday season, however, I quickly resumed my stoicism and self-imposed isolation. My family and I seemed to be carried along by the tide of activities. The demands of making arrangements and spending time with visitors seemed to leave little time for mourning. At the time I did not recognize the need to express my needs and feelings, nor did I take the opportunity to reach out to my family to respond to their needs and to share my own.

As we had done for many years, and had decided to do again that year, the family went on a trip over the New Year's holiday. This trip provided as good an opportunity as any during the year for me to spend time with my family. Leaving home, however, also afforded an especially good opportunity for all of us to avoid our grief. This return to routine helped me to continue my life as if little or nothing had changed.

My denial was encouraged by both grief and self-preservation. Death had conquered the present. I refused, however, to grant it any authority over the future by denying that it would follow me. I tried to shut out the reality of death from my mind and heart. I also tried to reverse the physical drain the experience with Dad's death had taken on me. Rather than slowing or diverting the flow of energy that had been sapped from me, I tried to shut it off completely and to provide my grief with no nourishment and no release.

Reclaiming this energy offered me the ideal opportunity to resist death. Because I had turned off the tap, however, I allowed myself no power to grieve. I no longer had any energy to clear my mind and heart of the pain and poison which death brought with it.

When I returned to school, I tried to lead my life as if little or nothing had happened. This was my defense mechanism: Keep a stiff upper lip, no wallowing in self-pity. Bury the emotions and deny the pain. The effort of covering up did not help me to overcome grief, but it let me continue with my life and satisfy the demands I placed on myself and the demands I thought others placed on me. Of course, my emotional expectations and what I believed others were expecting of me were entirely unrealistic. I never allowed myself time to hurt or the time I needed to live my pain. It was as if I expected myself to run a marathon after major surgery. I was my own worst enemy in my recovery. No one would have expected of me what I expected of myself.

Before long, I buried grief beneath my other activities. Removing myself from home made this an easy alternative to expressing my sorrow. I felt guilt and disbelief that my daily life seemed unchanged. Because I was removed from my home and my family and did not daily share the void of death, my grief and my healing were both delayed and prolonged.

Grief does not heal like a physical wound. The measure of recovery from the experience of loss is not how undetectable the wound is, but to what degree and purpose we have incorporated this experience into our lives. The pain we face is from the loss of a relationship. But just as the pain of death is focused on a relationship, so too are the lessons and growth that we carry away from the experience.

When we remember someone we love without remembering their weaknesses, foibles, or other less than ideal human qualities, we risk piling the problems inherent in every relationship upon ourselves. And if we remember a relationship as being either closer, more fulfilling, or more trouble-free than it was, we risk shutting out the people who are reaching out to us.

This emphasis on reality has been important to my relationship with God. Dad's death did not radically and instantaneously change my relationship with God, but it did nurture its growth. I had never had a "mountain-top" experience. For as long as I can remember, I have been a believer. For me, God was a gyroscope who helped to provide the small corrections necessary to keep me on course and headed in the right general direction. I had no sense that God had dramatically entered my life to prop me up either before or after Dad's death. But there was also no question that He was as constant a support during this period as He had been during the rest of my life.

God reached out to me through Dad. The comfort I could find in God was made clearer to me by observing the comfort my dad found in God. Dad's faith had always been evident to me when I was growing up. In the early darkness of school-day mornings, when the two of us would share the breakfast table, it was as common to see Dad quietly reading his old worn out Bible as it was to see him reading the morning paper. The peace with death that Dad demonstrated could only have come from his faith.

On one occasion, after Dad's speech had been largely lost, a visiting minister was reading the Bible aloud when Dad suddenly finished the passage from memory. In all of his physical weakness, he summoned the strength to praise God.

After Dad died, when I tried to turn into myself, God would not leave me alone. My relationship with Him did not change dramatically or suddenly, but it began to grow in new ways and new directions. In the re-evaluation of my life's priorities, I began to see more clearly that the substance of life is in God, not in the world. I started to take a longer view of my life and to re-examine the priorities I had established. And gradually I opened *all* the doors of my life to God— not just the areas I thought He wanted or where I thought He could fit into my designs.

I learned that fully loving God not only permits me to express all my emotions, but that complete love requires honesty in all things. At first, death confused me. I knew that God loved me and I could feel Him supporting me, but I could not understand how He could let me hurt like this. I still don't understand, but I do trust.

I was also angry at God. I continued to hold myself back from Him, because I couldn't permit myself to express my anger to Him or anyone else. I thought it was disrespectful, wrong, or evil. The anger I felt was like the anger a child has toward a parent. He doesn't stop loving the parent, but he wants to beat the chest of his parent. He is frustrated by the inability to understand, even while his parent is trying to comfort his pain by enfolding the child in her arms.

But the pervasive presence of God in my life became more apparent. He reached out to me wherever I was and whenever I needed Him. I began to believe that God really loves all of me, not just the part I bring to church on Sunday.

Early in college, one of my roommates had lost his father just months before starting school. Now I see that as my friend struggled with his grief, I was blind to his suffering. Self-absorbed and lacking skills in interpersonal communication, I could not handle the suffering of someone else. Not having experienced or witnessed a loss through death, I was not even equipped to observe its effects.

After my own dad died, I found myself confronted with the same sense of powerlessness, but then I was on the other side of this experience. Another classmate and dear friend suddenly lost his father. I, of course, had expected that one of the gifts to come from my dad's death was that I would have keen insight and a unique ability to reach out to those of my friends who would also experience the loss of a parent. But it didn't happen that way. It was so important to me to try to reach out and comfort Brian, but I found I couldn't do it in a meaningful way. My frustration was made all the more intense, because Brian, more than any other of those friends who supported me after my dad's death, always seemed to reach out in just the right way.

I now know that death is never made easier by more exposure to it. Unfortunately no one seems to escape the pain, frustration, powerlessness, and isolation that accompany a loss. But I am convinced that it is important for grieving persons to communicate their feelings and to unashamedly incorporate a loss into their lives.

As a part of my grief, I need to talk about Dad. He is still my father. No one else can take his place. While it no longer seems strange for me to speak of him in past tense, I am aware of people's awkwardness or confusion when I talk about him. But I need to talk about Dad and his role and continuing place in my life.

Openly communicating the experiences and emotions of death, or anything else, has never been easy for me. But the openness which it fosters I try to make the cornerstone for every relationship I have. This lesson of openness and communication is the gift my father left me in his death.

Like the healing, the lessons to be found in loss can take a long time. Sometimes they are mercifully slow. Death comes on its own terms. Since about all that most people can hope to do is to weather the experience, I have given little thought to what I might do differently if I were to relive this experience. The best we can do is to try to weave into our lives the lessons death thrusts upon us. The event of my father's death knocked down many of the barriers I had erected in my relationships. It allowed me to come closer to some people. It allowed me to see how rewarding openness can be.

I have come to understand that I can never be separated from the memory of the person I love. The predictable and traditional times of sharing, such as holidays, meal times, and weekends at our summer lake home no longer bring those powerful feelings of sorrow or loss. These events now give me a sense of peace and comfort.

Just as a living person touches us most deeply in unexpected ways, ways which often go unnoticed by others, my life is touched and my emotions ignited by unexpected events. Hearing someone tell Dad's jokes, passing someone wearing the scent of his cologne, or hearing one of his favorite pieces of music brings a lump to my throat and tears to my eyes. But I know now that not even death can destroy the power of the relationship with the ones we love.

EIGHTEEN

Julianne's Story

From the beginning I knew my grief belonged to me and that I was the only one who could work through it.

I was watching the evening news when the program was interrupted for a special report. The announcer said, "A DC-10 has crashed in Sioux City, Iowa. . . ."

Could George have been on that flight? I wondered as I watched the film of the crash. I erased the question and quickly turned off the television. Later, with the thought haunting me, I turned on the TV—only to watch the fiery crash all over again.

Pressed by an uneasy feeling, I called George's office. The voice on the other end told me something was terribly wrong. My husband and Gary, his boss, had not arrived at their destination, and they hadn't called to explain their delay.

I tried to console myself as I remembered the many times George had reassured me with "Don't worry; no news is good news." For the moment, all I could do was wait—just wait!

George's mother, Aunt Alta, and Uncle Paul were making their usual summer visit to our lakeside home. That evening Mom had already gone to bed, but Paul and Alta were sitting with me.

Fearing the worst, our son, Michael, and his wife, Wendy, arrived with our priest, Father Bob. With increasing hopelessness, after repeatedly watching the plane cartwheel down the runway and break into fiery pieces and listening to survivors report the gruesome details, we turned off the TV.

We waited for some news about George, but none came. Finally, after deciding to try to get some rest, Mike, Wendy, and Father Bob left, and Paul, Alta, and I retired. Again the dreadful thoughts crowded my mind. *Is he dead? Is he lying in a hospital—critically injured? Could he possibly be alive?*

I called my mother and sister, a few close friends, and our church prayer chain asking for prayer. Through the night I continued to call George's office and a number the airline provided, seeking some news, any news, about my husband. Shock began to set in, and though sleep did not come, somehow I got through that night.

The next morning there still was no confirmation that George had been on that particular flight, although by then we were fairly certain he was. I distinctly remember praying, "Lord, I am willing to accept whatever condition George is in."

My mother called and described a vision she'd had while praying. George, dressed in his usual cowboy hat and boots, and Jesus, with his hand on George's shoulder, were walking away from the site of the crash. I knew then, although it was not confirmed, that George had been on the plane and had not survived the crash. I also knew he was safe. He was with Jesus.

Soon after my mother's call, Michael arrived with Wendy, looking pale and drawn. He had talked with the airline. "Mom, it doesn't look very good!" he said. Our hope fading, we went to my bedroom and dropped to our knees. I cried out, "Jesus, Jesus, Jesus," over and over until the panic left and peace came. Soon after we received word. Though it was not confirmed, George was presumed dead.

The news media began calling, asking me for an interview. They called friends, neighbors, relatives, and it seemed, anyone who had the slightest connection with our family. I believed we should not make a statement until we had definite news. At midday the airline called to inform us that it was confirmed. George was dead.

The next day, particularly the afternoon, was very tiring and difficult, not only for me but for all my family. We found privacy in the sanctuary of my bedroom, and it was there we met to comfort each other and pray. It was there that we made the most difficult decisions regarding the final arrangements for George, my husband and my children's father. Together, sometimes through tears, we discussed the alternatives we had.

We took into consideration our feelings and needs, the feelings and needs of George's family, and what we felt George would want We also had to face our limited knowledge of his condition. A new closeness developed between us that afternoon, and based on mutual understanding, acceptance, and love for each other, we decided George's body would be cremated and buried in Lansing, our home for thirty-four years. The strength we all had to get through that period was incredible.

At a service on Monday, the song "Because He Lives, I Can Face Tomorrow" caused emotion to well up in me. But rather than sadness, I felt a wonderful joy. I will never forget how I was comforted as I found myself comforting others.

Our family drove to Saginaw to attend Gary's funeral, my husband's employer and traveling companion that fateful day. After our return to Lansing, I was handed George's personal effects. Holding that package in my hand, I was acutely aware of the finality of his death.

To avoid interference from the news media, we held a private interment prior to the Thursday memorial service. It was uncomfortably warm and there seemed to be no sign of relief. God saw our need. While we sat beneath the shade of a tent, a gentle breeze cooled us, and as we sang "It Is Well With My Soul," I felt the peace of knowing that my beloved husband was with our Lord.

The church overflowed. The air was hot and humid. A sudden cloudburst cleared and cooled the air. Again God had met our need, and again I experienced a song rising within me and found strength and comfort as I greeted and comforted others. I saw God working in so many wonderful ways, helping me, my family, and my loved ones. How proud George would be to see his family consoling and giving loving support to others.

I began to keep a journal. As I wrote, I sorted through many thoughts that were going through my mind and put them into perspective.

July 27—*If this pain is for nothing, I would swiftly end it. Yet my body struggles against it, not cooperating. Every muscle resists. My chest aches with a heaviness and a tightness I've never felt before, as though the world rests on me. I'm exhausted, but I can't sleep. There is an emptiness inside me as though part of me is missing, a part of who I am.*

My skin feels on edge, as though all my nerve endings are on the surface. I struggle on anxiously, not knowing what lies ahead.

I feel like I am crossing a rushing river at midstream. My footsteps are unsure. This path is new to me, and now and then I hesitate, not knowing if the next step I take will be my last. Yet there is something, someone, calling me to keep on. There is a hope. There is a rest.

Where can I find this rest? How will I enter into it? Giving up, letting go of the pain, is this the answer? If so, then I pray, "God help me, that I might find rest."

July 29—*I was exhausted today. My girls and grandchildren came to help sort through things in the apartment. I did little but watch. The pain wasn't so great today. Garrett brought more tears with his comforting words, "God is with you, Grammy." Then he asked his mother, "Does Grammy feel better now?"*

July 30—*More grief today in the form of anger. The pain is back in my chest tonight. My anger today was directed more toward George for leaving me than at anyone or anything else.*
  I want him back!

I knew my life would continue. Did I want to live in the past or move on to the future? I knew the choice was mine.

At first I didn't want to see George's clothes or anything that reminded me of him, but little by little I began going through his things, deciding what to do with them. Later I went through cards, letters, memorabilia, and photographs. My children and I each wrote a letter expressing our loss. All these I put in an album dedicated to George's memory. Difficult as it was, it brought more healing.

August 5—*Returning home was very difficult. My heart does not seem to release the grief so quickly now. I still can't believe this is real.*

August 7—*This was my worst day. I went to church, and wasn't hungry all day. I feel so separated, as if a part of me is being ripped out. The tears come and come.*

The handwritten notes and messages brought the most comfort. One very special friend sent me a note or letter every day for three months, encouraging me with special prayers, poems, and scriptures.

One particular scripture, Jeremiah 29:11–13, I held near to my heart: " 'For I know the plans I have for you,' declares the Lord. 'Plans to prosper you and not harm you. Plans to give you a future and a hope.' " This became my prayer.

Though at first I found it difficult to concentrate, slowly I began to read books and periodicals pertaining to grief, including *Afterloss.*

August 28—*Lord, my heart hurts. I feel very anxious. I can't believe George is not coming home. Oh, God, how can this be? I can hardly stand this pain. Oh, just to talk to George. To hear his voice. Every part of me screams No, No, No. "Blessed are those who mourn, for they will be comforted." "Surely he hath borne our griefs, and carried our sorrows."*

September 5—*Thirty-six years ago today, George and I were married. I feel sick in the pit of my stomach. My precious family remembered this day with a beautiful picture frame, cards, and calls. Michael brought me flowers and took me to dinner. How thoughtful! Bless them, Lord. Bless them.*

I feel such anger. I want to strike out and break something, anything. Today I stopped at a horse ranch thinking it would feel good to go riding. I haven't in years. They were closed.

My life feels so out of control.

People began to get on with their own lives, and the phone rang less often. I remember returning home and checking my answering machine, my heart sinking when there were no messages. I asked a close friend if she would commit to calling me once a day for a month. She was more than happy to do that. I found that people wanted to help but didn't know what to do. Another dear, longtime friend answered my calls for encouragement and prayers day or night, regardless of the hour.

September 13—*George isn't coming home. Oh, God, I want to scream. How it hurts! I don't know how I am going to make it. I know that without You I can't. God, I want George back!*

I had no unfinished business with George, but there was unfinished business. There were several unresolved issues that I found very difficult.

First, did he suffer? I had no way of knowing what he went through those minutes before the crash or if he suffered. All I had to go on was what the autopsy report said and what other people who had survived the crash reported. I found myself forgiving those I felt were responsible and asking God to forgive them.

Second, I didn't have an opportunity to comfort him or to say goodbye. Through prayer, God took me to the crash site. He allowed me to hold George and comfort him. Jesus, watching, stood beside me. After a time He ever so gently reached down and lifted me to my feet, saying, "It's time to go now." Together we walked away.

September 26—*It was better today. I went to prayer group, and I released more grief through prayer and felt God's comfort. It's curious. It came in the form of strength, as though He had placed a rod in my back to keep me strong.*

I was able to contact and talk with several of the people who had been in the crash and survived. I hoped that maybe they had seen George or talked with him. I felt a bond with these people. I prayed for them and their families.

I prayed, sometimes talking quietly with God, sometimes crying out to Him. I wrote to Him in prayer about my thoughts, my feelings, and my needs. I prayed the first thing in the morning and the last thing at night. I prayed on my knees, in the shower with tears streaming down my face, in the car, while walking, shoveling snow, stacking wood, sometimes shouting at Him with anger. When I could not pray, others did.

I counted the days, the weeks, and the months that passed. I knew there was a recovery process and that time was part of it. So I counted and figured I was that much closer to feeling better. But I didn't just wait for time to pass. From the beginning I knew my grief belonged to me and that I was the only one who could work through it. When others were once again busy with their own lives, I was still hurting. I knew that though I still felt the loss, my life also would go on. It was up to me to decide how I wanted to live it. God was doing His part; I must do mine.

October 26—*When I think of George, I feel the void, the absence, the loss. I miss the comfortable, safe, secure feelings I always had when he was here. Lord, it just can't be!*

I became aware of my need for male companionship but it seemed early to be thinking about another man in my life. I received a call from a friend of a friend. He left a message asking me to return his call. Several days later he called again, and I accepted an invitation to dinner. That was the beginning of a painful lesson. I was not ready for a new relationship. I was hurting and very lonely. His wife had died and he was hurting too. I began to experience emotions and feelings I hadn't felt for a long time.

October 28—*Went to church by myself. Lord, it's so difficult and I feel so lonely. George was always there beside me. I cried going to church, at church, and coming home.*

Later today I received and accepted an invitation to dinner from Franklin. That perked me up. He was a real gentleman. We shared our common experience of grief and our hopes for the future.

October 30—*Another date. There are physical and emotional feelings stirring in me.*

November 2—*Woke up missing George. Cried again. I so want to be held. God, show me Your perfect will. I feel so vulnerable. Help me to control my emotions. Shut the doors tight if this new relationship is not of You.*

For about six weeks the struggle was ongoing. I realized, finally, that my feelings were coming from a need to be loved and held again, and because I felt understanding and compassion for my new friend. I lost more weight and was exhausted. I continued to write in my journal, and I prayed almost constantly. I knew God had shut the door when I discovered Franklin was involved in another relationship.

December 18—*It's over. How foolish I feel and vulnerable I am. Everything he said I wanted to hear. God, please forgive me for getting so caught up in my own selfish desires that I failed to listen to Your voice and follow You.*

This Christmas will be so different without George. It doesn't feel like Christmas. I've not baked cookies or put up a tree, but I know it's okay. Selecting gifts and cards brought home the crushing realization of my loss.

December 22—*I need to be willing to serve God without a mate. But I still long for the companionship of a mate, and right now, that's what I miss the most.*

January 13—*My children are grown and my husband, at sixty, is dead.*

January 31—*I don't need someone else to be a whole person. Even with all my feelings and emotions, the flu I had and the headaches, I still feel great about myself, better than I have in a long time. I've decided it's okay to be single.*

Prior to the crash my life revolved around George, my children, my grandchildren, the church, and plans to build a new home. It was an orderly, safe life, and I found in it my main purpose of being and my greatest security. Now I can give thanks in all things, knowing God is involved in my life. Even in what seem to be the most insignificant details, He is faithful.

God continues to open doors for me to share His love and the hope He offers, and I have discovered He can and does use me with all my weaknesses. He does have a plan and purpose for my life. I thank Him for that.

NINETEEN

Marlene's Story

I'm going to die. Tell Marlene I love her.

I have a feeling I'm going to leave you alone."
Dave said those words to me one morning early in the spring of 1986. They frightened me, but I put them out of my mind. In May our daughter and son-in-law told us we were going to be grandparents, and later Dave said, "I'm not going to be a grandpa." Even though we didn't understand it then, I believe God was preparing us for what was going to happen.

Our last night together, we went for a walk on the beach, holding hands as we always did. We sat on a park bench and watched the sunset. We spoke of our love for each other.

The next day, July 24, started out as a normal day, a beautiful, sunny day. I kissed Dave goodbye that morning as usual. I told him I'd see him that night, and we left for work.

About 10:30 I received a call from my son. He told me that Dave's mom and dad had been in a car accident and they needed him to go to them. I called his employer, asking for the dispatch office since Dave worked in the field. My call was immediately transferred to the assistant manager who said, "Dave has been electrocuted, but he's still alive."

I remember saying, "But that's not why I called. I wanted you to let him know his parents have been in a car accident and they need him," as if my telling the assistant manager that I hadn't called to hear about Dave's accident would make what he was telling me not so. I remember pacing the floor by my desk and thinking *I can't stand losing him*. What began as a beautiful day had turned into a nightmare.

Both Dave's parents were in the hospital, his mom in critical condition. Dave, also in critical condition, was flown to a hospital in

Traverse City, Michigan, and later transferred to the University of Michigan Burn Center.

We were allowed to see him at the Traverse City hospital for only a few moments. Before we went into the emergency room to see him, the doctor talked to us. "He probably won't live," he said. "And if he does, he'll be paralyzed. The electricity went in through his shoulder and out his legs, crossing just under his shoulder blades. It severed his spinal cord. He'll lose both legs."

The drive to the Burn Center seemed to take forever. Our son Mike, our daughter Sandy, and our son-in-law Doug were with me.

The next time we could see Dave, he was in intensive care, and he was alert. The doctor talked to Dave and me. He told us that in order to save Dave's life, both legs would have to be amputated. The doctor told Dave he would have to decide whether to have the operation, and then he left us alone.

Because Dave was on a ventilator and couldn't talk, he wrote on a piece of paper some words I will never forget: "Do you still want me?"

"Yes, I still want you," I said. "I love you. I just want to take you home and hold you."

He thought about the decision he had to make. Then he wrote, "I can't choose to die." His decision was made. They would amputate his legs as soon as possible.

The pain we felt during the next ten days was almost too much to bear. I watched him lie there—a body once so strong and beautiful, now so badly broken. But even in the pain, there was an all encompassing love—from God, our friends, and our family. The love helped me get through the long months that lay ahead.

Our children were all at the hospital when the surgeon amputated Dave's legs. But it wasn't enough to save him. The electricity had been too devastating.

During the following days Dave and I were both ministered to several times by the elders of our church. During one of these times, I heard clearly in my mind the words, "He is going to die." God was preparing me for the decision that soon I would have to make.

The doctors said they would have to do more surgery. They needed to remove part of Dave's pelvis. We couldn't let them. He had been through too much. He'd had several surgeries and each time they found his condition was much worse than they had thought. In the beginning the doctor had told Dave he would have the use of his arms, but all his back muscles had to be removed, leaving him virtually helpless.

Our children, Dave's brothers, and I had to decide if we would agree to more surgery. We talked about what Dave would want. Long before his accident, he had made it very clear that he wouldn't want to live if he couldn't take care of himself. None of us had any doubt about Dave's wishes. And we were very sure of the decision we should make: no more surgery. We had to let him go. Up until then we had been praying for physical healing, but we began praying for a different kind of healing. "God, please take him home. He has suffered enough. Take him to be with you. Set him free."

After we gave our decision to the doctors, they said they thought we had made the right one.

I was able to be alone with Dave and tell him the things that were in my heart. I talked to him about the events of our life together that meant so much to both of us. I reminded him of the trip we made to Hawaii to celebrate our twenty-fifth wedding anniversary and that we had walked hand in hand on the beach in Waikiki. I talked about the years we'd spent together raising our four children and the love we'd shared.

Tears rolled from his eyes. He was saying goodbye to me, even though he couldn't speak. He had told me many times how much he loved me, and I knew that was true. Right after his accident, he thought first of me as he told his buddy who rescued him, "I'm going to die. Tell Marlene I love her."

We all said our goodbyes. He loved to hear our kids sing, and they sang one last time for him. During his last day on earth, our children played the guitar and sang to him, even though he was unconscious. They sang "Silent Night" because "we know you'll be with God this Christmas, Pop, and we won't be able to sing it for you then."

On August 2, 1986, after fighting gallantly to live for nine long days, Dave died. I was not with him. No one was. But he was not really alone. I know Jesus was there with him holding his hand.

Going home without Dave was devastating. Walking around our yard, looking at the trees and flowers he had planted and so lovingly cared for, I thought I couldn't stand the pain. I felt as if my life had ended when his ended. He was part of me and that part was suddenly ripped away, leaving a horrible emptiness. There was a huge hole in the pit of my stomach that I thought would never go away. I felt as if I was walking in a dream. This wasn't real. It couldn't be happening to us—we were so much in love. He was so young, only forty-four, and I wanted to grow old with him. I'd planned on it. Dave was my friend. My lover. My life. How was I going to go on without him? How could I live without him?

Eventually our children had to go back to their own lives—Terri back to Texas, Steve back to Iowa, and Michael back to college. Thank God, Sandy and her husband lived close by. I was grateful for that.

I was so afraid of being alone after they left. I wasn't afraid that someone would hurt me, but I was afraid of the loneliness and how I was going to make it alone. Who would do all the things Dave used to do? The northern Michigan winters can be very long. Who would plow the snow from the driveway?

Looking back now, I realize the first winter was the hardest time. My children were wonderful. For awhile they called me every day. Two wonderful friends stopped by or called every day for an entire year. I am convinced that without them and my children I would not have survived. This wonderful support made healing easier for me. I worked full-time before Dave's accident, and I went back to work a couple of weeks after he died. It was extremely hard for me to do, but it kept me busy and helped me heal.

I had to work through all the normal emotions of grief. I was angry. And I was angry with God. Why did He take my husband from me? We were so much in love. I asked God for answers. I felt I deserved them, but no answers came. I tried to rid myself of my anger and frustration by walking, and I walked a lot—even during blizzards. Finally spring came and I remember that on one of my walks on a beautiful spring day I thought *I've made it through my first winter without him, but how can the flowers be blooming and the birds singing? Dave is dead.*

Even though music has always been a big part of my life, after Dave's death I just couldn't listen to it. It hurt too much. Finally one day I made myself listen and let the tears flow. That was another door to walk through, a step closer to healing. After that it was easier and music is again a big part of my life.

A year passed before I could take his clothes from his closet. Even then I kept his shoes and his toothbrush. I just couldn't get rid of them. I would open his closet door and bury my face in his clothes just to smell him again. His clothes were proof that he had lived, that he had been a part of my life.

One evening when I was missing Dave and hurting so badly, I put his picture in front of me on the coffee table, and I talked to him. While I was talking, I could feel a stirring over my body. I knew Dave was there listening to me. I didn't want that feeling to end.

Shortly after Dave's death I prayed, "God, please, just let me know if he's all right. I need to know that." That night I had a dream: My son and I went to pick up Dave at work. He walked toward us, wearing his familiar hat and parka. He was smiling. I knew then that he was all right.

At times I felt God's presence, but there were also times when I thought God had deserted me. It seemed He wasn't there, wasn't listening to my prayers. One night when I felt particularly alone, I prayed, "God, why have You left me? I don't feel Your presence any more." Later that night, when I was tossing and turning in my bed, unable to sleep, the phone rang. It was a woman from our church. She said she knew it was late, but she had the strongest urge to call me to see if I was all right. God had been listening. He was with me. He still cared.

A year or so after Dave's death I was in St. John's, Virgin Islands, with a friend. We were part of a tour group. There was a plumeria tree nearby. These trees grow everywhere in Hawaii and have the most fragrant flowers I have ever smelled. When Dave and I were in Hawaii he picked the blossoms and gave them to me to wear in my hair. I hadn't seen a plumeria since we were in Hawaii and finding myself near one naturally brought back many memories. Then someone handed me a blossom. As I took it, the tears began to flow. I knew that somehow Dave had given me that flower. I knew he still loved me and cared what happened to me.

After I regained my composure, I looked for the person who had handed me the flower, and to my amazement, I didn't know who had done it. All my attention had been on the plumeria. I still have the blossom. It is dried now, but it still has its pink color. I know it was from Dave, and it reminds me of Dave's continuing love for me.

Shortly after Dave died, I went to a grief counselor. I would recommend counseling with a grief expert to anyone who has lost a loved one. And with the encouragement of a friend who had also lost a spouse, I joined a bereavement group. Slowly and with more tears than I can describe, I've put my life back together. I learned that you have to take one day at a time—sometimes one hour at a time. Anything more is overwhelming. I also learned you have to walk through the rain to get to the sunshine.

Now, almost five years later, I'm happy again. The pain is gone except for occasionally—like now, as I write this story. I have beautiful memories of our life together, and the sun is shining in my life again.

My children are a very important part of my life. I have two beautiful granddaughters, who love me very much. And I love them with all my heart. I travel a lot. Life is good again. It's very different from the life I had with Dave—but it's good.

I have changed from the person I was. I've become more independent. Of course, I had no choice if I was to survive. I believe I'm also more patient. I don't get as angry about things that really don't matter. Dave's death has made me realize that I will not live forever either, and I want to make the most of each day I have. It's hard, but I'm trying.

I still miss Dave and I will always love him. I thank God for the time we had together, and for the beautiful gift Dave was in my life. He taught me much about love in our twenty-six years together.

I made some mistakes along the way to the sunshine. I took some wrong turns, and I opened doors I should have left closed. One mistake I think I made was that in my overwhelming grief, I forgot that my children were also grieving. I feel I didn't offer them the support they needed. Hopefully they found it in each other.

Dave's mom and dad both survived their automobile accident with no major health problems. Although it was a very traumatic and devastating time for them also, they have dealt with Dave's death admirably.

I hope my story will help someone who has lost a loved one. I want them to know hope. Life will be good again, even though that may seem impossible. But it is possible. It takes a lot of work, and there are many doors to walk through. In the end, though, it is worth it.

TWENTY

Mary P.'s Story

Finally, it was coming clear.
God hadn't punished me—God loves me.

It was Christmas time and I was filled with pure joy. All four of my children were visiting for the holidays. Julie, an Air Force Academy graduate, was home on leave. She was enjoying her career as a captain in Intelligence. Tom had graduated from the University of California at Irvine and had achieved great success as a comedy writer and performer. Molly, age twenty-two, was working as a paralegal, writing a novel, and celebrating her fourth year of sobriety. And Michael was getting straight A's at U.C. Santa Barbara.

During the seventeen years I struggled to raise these children alone, I carried a basketful of resentment against my alcoholic ex-husband. They were ages three to eleven when I divorced him. I had no marketable skills and very little money, but I was determined to provide them with everything that children from a two-parent home should expect.

I am proud to say that professionally I succeeded far beyond my expectation. My children and my business were my life, and I succeeded in blending the rearing of outstanding children with working constantly. I never had any trouble with any of them except Molly, who got involved in drugs and alcohol in high school. When I put her into a treatment program for her dependency, I was exposed to the Al Anon twelve-step program. I even spent several years in therapy to help myself deal with my issues of fear and resentment, workaholism, and co-dependency.

That Christmas season, I was so grateful. I felt at last that it was my turn to live my life. Since the children were out of the home, I leased my home and moved in with Charlie, my best friend and business partner. I felt some discomfort about the living-together arrangement because of my religious and cultural background. But I was so happy and so in love that I was sure we would soon marry.

The Monday before Christmas, I went for a routine checkup. (Ever practical I went before the year's end so I could count the medical expense against that year's taxes.) I'd had a good-sized lump in my breast for several years, and my previous doctor had told me it was nothing to worry about. So when this new doctor told me I needed to have it biopsied, I practiced my positive thinking. I knew it was benign. In fact, the day after Christmas Charlie and I drove to Seattle for a ten-day cruise of the San Juan Islands. He had taught me how to fish for salmon, dig for clams, and be "first mate" on his wonderful wooden fifty-four foot trawler, the Tiger Bay. I was so happy I felt indestructible.

I had the biopsy surgery on January 10. When I awakened, the doctor told us the tumor was cancer and so advanced that I would have to have a modified radical mastectomy. I kept saying, "I don't want this. It can't be true." I was so horrified and frightened, I reverted to the behavior that had worked so often in the past. I became business-like. I appeared to be strong, and I did not let anyone know how scared I was. I did not tell my children or any members of my family. I researched all the medical data I could and agreed to have the operation in one week.

The nurse who did my pre-op admission the night before the surgery insisted that I tell my children. She pointed out that they had the right to know. So, feeling shame because I did not want them to feel any pain, I called my daughters. I was very grateful that they both came in time for the surgery. Their presence and love helped me so much, and I am sure it helped Charlie too. I did not tell my sons, or my parents, or any other relatives, or friends until a few days later. I lay awake worrying about everyone and how they would take the news. I couldn't deal with their fear. I had always been like the Rock of Gibraltar for all of them, and I felt I was letting them down.

I was a good patient. Charlie brought me home, and then I began chemotherapy. I handled the chemo fairly well, but I became more and more depressed. On the surface I was cheerful, religious, optimistic. Everyone was astonished at how well I was dealing with "it."

My doctors recommended that I talk with others who were going through the same problem, and I did. But I didn't reveal my true feelings to them either. The only person who was aware of my real terror and anger was Charlie. He tried to help by bringing home funny movies and waiting on me. I devoured books on self-healing and became convinced that I had caused my cancer and that I could cure it. When I took responsibility for causing the cancer, on the inside I knew absolutely that God had punished me for living in sin, for feeling pride in my body, especially in my breasts.

I tried to meditate myself to health. I prayed. I ate foods recommended for healing and wellness. And of course I did everything the doctors told me to do. But mostly I suffered silently with the guilt that I either had to marry Charlie or leave him.

Looking back now I can understand how the pressure built within me, until finally I had a terrible nightmare. I dreamed I was watching my operation. I could feel the knife cutting me. I could see blood spurting all over the bed. I was hysterical and awakened Charlie. I spilled all my feelings about why I thought God had taken my breast. I told him that he had to marry me immediately or I was moving out. His immediate reaction was to tell me to concentrate on getting well and that we would talk later. But once I had finally admitted these dark thoughts, I could not let them go.

It was very strained around the house. Before he had tried so hard to be a comfort to me. Now he retreated. The more he withdrew, the more upset I became. I really felt that I was losing my mind. I suspect the trauma of my surgery had brought up feelings Charlie had long kept buried, feelings having to do with his own experiences in Vietnam. Eventually he told me he had been contacted by an old college girlfriend, and he was interested in being with her. He said he wanted me to move out of his house.

Since I had never really dealt with my feelings about the loss of my breast, the shock of what I thought he was doing to me became my major focus.

I cried for days. I did not know where to go. My house was leased for three more years. I lay awake at night trying to figure how this could have happened. What did I do wrong? Of course, I did not want anyone to know.

After a few weeks, some of my old strength returned and I began to look for a place to live. I decided it had to be a refuge, a place of beauty and serenity, a healing cocoon.

I found a lovely little townhouse in the foothills, surrounded by beautiful flowers and streams. I could see the mountains from my bed. It felt right, so I made arrangements to stay with friends until I could move in.

Meanwhile I continued to have chemotherapy and I could not work. Charlie and I had been business partners in an architectural, construction, and real estate business. I did not have the energy or confidence to start over again. I really wallowed in self-pity. What was left for me to lose? I'd lost my breast, my health, my home, my man, my job, my femininity, my confidence, my financial security, and my future. I'd really hit bottom.

I began counseling with a therapist to help me adjust to the tremendous changes in my life. Since I wasn't working, I obsessed over the possibility that I would lose all my investment properties and everything I had worked so hard to accumulate for my retirement years. As a matter of fact, I did have to sell several properties, but I realized I might not even have an old age.

Finally I began to live in the *now*. With the therapist's guidance, I started to think about my childhood, my people-pleasing, my rigid religious beliefs. The therapy helped, but I was still suffocating in my grief. And my body ached from the loss of physical intimacy at the time I needed it most. I wanted to go to sleep and not wake up. I was angry at God. I had always been a good girl and worked so hard to raise my kids and please everyone. I felt I had lost everything.

I spent most of the early summer alone in my little house, recuperating, walking, reading, and writing—and doing a lot of crying.

One day I rented the movie *Field of Dreams*. In this story the main character builds a baseball field in his cornfield so that the ghosts of great baseball players of the past can come from heaven and play there. When everyone thinks he is crazy, he says, "Heaven is where dreams come true."

That night before the movie ended I wrote these words:

I have to figure out how to follow my dreams now so I can achieve a glimpse of what heaven will be like. I am concerned about my willingness to die at this relatively young age, and now this quote only serves to confuse the matter. If dreams only come true in heaven, why live a longer, difficult life. I am tired. There needs to be a reason to keep up the struggle. Maybe it is because I don't have any dreams yet.

Yes, that is it.

I have never taken the time to dream. I don't have any dreams, so what could I do in heaven? I need to spend time gently learning about myself, taking care of myself, loving myself, and I expect then I will allow myself to dream.

I need to pursue my own dreams, and not live my life through anyone else. Not through Charlie, Julie, Tom, Molly, or Mike.

Finally, it was coming clear. God hadn't punished me—God loves me. God is not some distant authoritarian father. God is in me. All I had to do was let go and let God.

I began to feel some hope. My stamina was returning. I was gratified that I had so many loving friends who helped me move, drove me to doctor appointments, brought me food and gifts. I began to be really kind and gentle with myself. I traveled. I filled my house with flowers, and ballerinas, and angels. I started courses in pottery and Japanese at the local college.

And—I don't know exactly when it began—I was laughing more.

But I had still another hurdle to endure, and that was on August 10. My daughter was deployed to the Persian Gulf. Again I was angry at God, and for a time I forgot all that I had learned on my path to recovery. I was glued to the television and was really frightened when the actual fighting began in January. But I had learned about my powerlessness. So each day I mentally placed her in God's hands. That helped so much.

Now I am living a spiritual and peaceful life that I never thought was possible. I have had reconstructive surgery. In early April Julie came home from the war and has been nominated for a Bronze Star. She and Tom both had magnificent weddings this summer and everyone said I looked great. My two new in-laws are everything I could have hoped for in spouses for my children, and I love them like my own. My two youngest are still a joy to watch as they become beautiful, responsible adults.

Charlie and I tried to put our relationship back together and even went to therapy together for awhile. He revealed that the temporary relief of the old college girlfriend was like a helicopter coming to take him out of the battle in Vietnam. He had grabbed for it, but had let it go. He wanted to try to make things work for us, but it was too late.

Recently, I opened a small real estate and land-use consulting office near my home. I am even contemplating dating again. I have so many things I must see and do that I find work an interruption. Yet it is wonderfully challenging in a very different way.

Writing this story caused a few more tears, but I'm proud of what I have accomplished. I know I had to learn a valuable lesson and sometimes I want to shout it out so that everyone around me will know.

But whether or not others know, I know. And that gives me the confidence and joy to embrace each day as if it were my last.

TWENTY-ONE

Marcia's Story

*I didn't blame God because I believed He
didn't take her; He received her.*

It was Sunday, January 24, 1982, 7:30 A.M.

A sheriff's officer was at our door with a message for us to call the Kansas City Police Department. While Mervyn, my husband, made the call the officer stood silently in our kitchen. I stood nearby, watching and wondering what this urgent message could possibly be about. *Is it about Kay? Has she been hurt? Is she ill or in the hospital? Why doesn't she call us herself?*

Mervyn slowly shook his head from side to side. The expression on his face meant something was seriously wrong. I was very alarmed. *We must get to Kansas City. Something must be terribly wrong with Kay.*

Mervyn turned to me, and slowly and tenderly he said, "Marcia, our little girl is gone."

"No. No! It's not true," I screamed. "She isn't gone. She's hurt, but she can't be *gone.*"

I felt my heart stop, and I couldn't breathe. I gasped for air. And through my tears, I screamed. Mervyn held me and said, "It's true . . . it's true. Killed instantly . . . massive head injuries . . . thrown from the car in which she was riding."

As the words tumbled from Mervyn's mouth, I could not believe them. "It isn't true," I cried. "It can't be true . . . I will not accept it." Kay, my soul mate, her dad's pride and joy, her brother Kent's closest friend—her beautiful life was over in an instant.

We were a young family, growing up together, and we were extremely close. We played, worked, laughed, fought, and loved together as no other family we knew. How could the three of us go on without our Kay? Why Kay? Why us?

Our beautiful twenty-four-year-old daughter was as beautiful on the inside as she was on the outside. She had a captivating smile that won everyone's heart and a tremendous desire to do and give her best—all of her life. She was organized and responsible beyond her years. She had a thirst for living and was driven in her quest, almost as if she knew her life would be short. She was the one who kept the rest of us lined out and told us when we were wrong. Kay had it all together.

We had mixed emotions when she moved to Kansas City in 1978 after graduating from the University of Kansas. We were excited for her because her future was full of hope and promise, but selfishly we wanted her to stay close to us in Wichita.

The day before the accident, Kay and I had our usual Saturday morning telephone conversation. She said, "Mom, although I'm all grown up, I still see you more often, and I am closer to my family than anyone I know." We talked about her hopes and dreams for the future. Her last words to me were, as always, "I love you, Mom."

As I search for words to describe the devastating days immediately following Kay's death, I can tell you it was only by the grace of God that I survived. I wanted her. I needed her. I missed her beyond all belief. Through the tears, I cried "Why?" but the answers did not come.

I didn't blame God because I believed that He didn't take her. He received her. What got me through the day was God's promise that because I believe in Him, one day I will see and be with my beloved Kay again.

But the days without her were meaningless. I longed for her weekend visits. I had always loved just being with her. It was *years* before I accepted that she was not coming home, not ever—not for the weekend—not for birthdays—not for Christmas. I would never see her smile or hear her laugh again. I would never see her in a wedding gown. She would never have our grandchildren.

She had been robbed and cheated of a beautiful life. And we had been robbed and cheated, too. It wasn't fair!

Missing her was the hardest part for me, and I couldn't and didn't know how to cope. All I knew was that I wanted her back, and I wanted everything to be like it was before. I saw the helplessness in my husband's eyes as he realized he couldn't "fix it" this time. I felt the sadness in Kent's heart, not only as he grieved for his sister, but over my shattered life as well.

I was numb and completely out of sync with the world. I would stand in the shower with the water running over me, as if to wash the pain away, screaming and pleading with God to let us have her back. I sat staring endlessly into space, wondering how others could go on living when life had stopped for us. I was nervous. I had nightmares. Noise bothered me. Idle conversation irritated me. I had absolutely no patience with those who made hurtful remarks, whether innocently or ignorantly. I was tired, and I wanted to get off the merry-go-round I was on. My husband was afraid for me to be alone.

What was I going to do? How could I live without her? I didn't *want* to live without Kay. I was obsessed with thoughts of her, and the details of the accident haunted me. Family and friends did the best they could to comfort, and the expressions of love and sympathy were overwhelming. But I simply couldn't get it together.

My devoted husband and our loyal, loving son became my only links to sanity and to the realization that life must go on. As the days and months turned into years, I had brave days and not-so-brave days. I did all the things well-meaning people told me I should do. I returned to work in our family business. I kept busy. I did things for others. I remembered the good times and tried to put the bad times behind me. Those who I relied on to be much smarter than I told me those steps would make things better—that time would heal—that I would get over it. But I didn't.

I began to think I was going crazy. The emptiness inside me grew deeper each day as I realized that none of these things was working to bring me the peace my broken heart needed for mending. The fact is nothing made it better. Time didn't heal; I was not getting over it.

I knew my family and friends were hurting, too, and wanted to help me. But the amazing part is that none of us knew how to help each other. It was almost as if we thought *If we don't talk about it or think about it, it will go away*. But I needed to talk about it. I felt *compelled* to talk about it—to read about it—to make sense of it—to find a way to give my days and nights meaning again.

I chose my sources carefully and self-protectively. I received tons of self-help material, but most of it did not speak to my heart and I put it aside. A special friend and young widow sent me a copy of the *Afterloss* newsletter, but it lay on my desk for a year before I opened and read it. To my surprise, and for the first time, this literature was different. Someone had written the truth, and the words gave me hope for the first time.

Afterloss said: "Grief is a process, not an event. Time doesn't heal. It's what we do with the time that counts."

Afterloss gave me practical, daily thoughts and applications that dealt with my pain and anguish. It said to be patient with myself and others, that everyone is different and our relationships are different. We don't all love and hurt and heal the same. Don't count on others to give meaning to your life. And whatever you do, *talk about the person who died*. I discovered that my feelings were normal, and this knowledge was my first step toward beginning to live again, instead of just going through the motions.

I believe we are put on earth for God's glory and to make a difference in this life. I have been blessed by loved ones whose unconditional love and undying friendship kept me going through the worst of times. I have been blessed because I have found others who understand my pain and have been given the knowledge to teach me to come to terms with it.

I wouldn't be writing my story if it weren't for Kay's death, and I pray that those who read it will be blessed and encouraged—and will come to believe that life can have meaning again and that peace will come into their hearts.

It isn't easy.

For some of us the process is very slow. The pain never completely goes away. I still miss Kay terribly. The missing is still the hardest part. There is so much I want to tell her and share with her. I want to tell her about Kent's upcoming wedding. I want to tell her how strong in spirit her dad is becoming. I want to smell her hair. I want to go shopping with her and eat a chocolate sundae with her, and laugh about why we shouldn't be doing it. I want to tell her I love her and feel her arms around me one more time.

But we must trade the facts of our lives for faith. I know now I don't have to know *why*. I only have to know that God is in control and, as I continue in my recovery, to have faith that He will guide me. Philippians 4:13 says, "I can do all things through Christ who strengthens me." I have faith that when I see Christ face to face all my questions will be answered. And I thank Him for never leaving my side, for blessing me through the lives of others, for His gracious love that never dies.

I wanted to do something special for Kay in her memory and in honor of her life, death, and eternal life. To honor Kay and in appreciation for the words God has given me to write, if you will begin your own healing process and begin to come to terms with your own heartache, if you will have a greater love for one another, an enriched sense of caring and sensitivity, a thirst for knowledge and truth, a deeper understanding of the blessings and grace given to us, then I will have accomplished my goal, and Kay will remain always in my heart and in yours.

TWENTY-TWO

Shirley's Story

The shock was so great,
my entire body was in pain.

It was a day full of thoughts of our firstborn, who we had so anxiously awaited twenty-five years before. May 1, 1991—it was one week until Robert Jr.'s birthday.

The day began with an appointment at the American Embassy in Tokyo. A fellow American, an English teacher, was to wed a Japanese. I was there to help them through the legal work. Robert Sr., Agricultural Attache, was at his desk, as is usual when he's in the country.

After my appointment I went to a book museum with two friends. We stopped at shops along the way back to the bus stop after lunch. At a kimono shop I found several obis and bought one for Robert Jr., whose stereo speakers needed new covers. This beautifully woven piece would do the job nicely, I thought.

After my day of walking and exploring, we ate a simple supper, and we didn't hurry to clean up afterward. It was while we were relaxing that we received the call—the call that said we would never speak to our son again, never again see the light in his eyes or the smile on his face, never again hear his quick laughter that was so dear. We would see only his still, lifeless body in a casket, so young, so handsome, but not our son. He was gone—murdered.

That was my aching unbelief. The shock was so great, my entire body was in pain. We needed to know what happened, what events led to a fatal stabbing.

Robert Jr. lived and worked in California. The bank where he worked had successfully gone through an audit, definitely cause for a celebration. Two supervisors arranged a party and included in it an early birthday celebration for Robert.

When the party was over, he left with one of the women, and

together they were confronted by her former boyfriend. She had rejected this man, and he was filled with jealousy and rage. An argument followed, and the boyfriend, a convicted armed robber, began shoving both of them. The woman ran to safety and locked herself in her car, leaving Robert down on the ground where he was stabbed.

How could she involve our son in her life in any way, we asked. They were friends, she said.

Yes, my mind goes over the scene, and I feel a rage. How does a mother endure? It's been four months and the pain continues. It isn't possible to be what I was before my son's death. The pain is so great; my entire nervous system is strung so tightly. In the beginning I couldn't unwind. Sleep was spotty.

I teach English in Tokyo for a Japanese friendship club, a popular form of business that caters to people looking for a social life outside of work. An intercultural outreach, it offers recreation and classes in many subject areas.

The support I received from two groups of students was of tremendous help. During the month following Robert's death while I was in California, they sent me telegrams and letters. I knew that after my return to the classroom they would tolerate my lack of enthusiasm for teaching as I groped through my grief.

The month of June was tortuous. I could barely make it through my classes. The anguish and pain were ever-present, and there were moments I felt like screaming. My students would have understood if I had. Their faces told me that.

It was a little easier in July. A pool party for the International Friendship Center had been scheduled before we got the call about Robert. Since I am the Embassy contact person, it wasn't something I could turn over to someone else. It went well. Just under 200 people attended.

During these two months, the assailant stood trial in California. A friend attended the hearings and reported to us by phone after each one.

No premeditation could be shown; therefore, murder in the first degree could not be proven. The verdict was voluntary manslaughter. He was sentenced to eleven years.

Yes, I wanted to see justice served. He deserved more.

Through Tokyo Baptist Church, I learned of professional help available to us. A family service counselor employed by the Foreign Mission Board of the Southern Baptist Convention could help us through those dark days. And our interim pastor, a retired Army chaplain, made himself available at any time I needed to call for help.

Robert wasn't our only child. His younger brother spent a difficult time alone in California, grieving for Robert. We kept in touch by phone. We returned to California in August and celebrated his twenty-third birthday at a pool party given by the church where we all were members before Bob and I left for foreign assignments. Our son's aunts, uncles, and cousins drove some distance to join us. That made it a real celebration.

The last weekend in August a cousin was married. The wedding was happy and joyous, and the couple so perfectly happy. I was so proud of them. The mood was warm and homelike.

We had to go to Robert's condo. His treasures were still there, and we had to decide what to do with them. That visit brought back the pain and anguish of our loss. I left Robert's picture on the wall.

I went to the courthouse where the hearing had been held to purchase a transcript of the trial. I had to reach a decision concerning what I should do about the sentence. Eleven years seemed a small price for the murderer to pay for the life of our son.

I contacted a lawyer friend, who invited me to meet with him, a colleague, and a public defender. They helped me to understand the law and the criminal justice system. They called the prosecutor and public defender of the case, who reaffirmed there was no evidence of premeditation.

They also made me realize that the assailant would be punished totally by the circumstances in which he would live for the length of his imprisonment. He will be forever reminded of the act that placed him in the state penitentiary among criminals who are willfully provocative of defensive behavior. He will be among hardened criminals.

At this writing, we haven't decided to take legal action to further punish our son's assailant. Our pain is great. Daily we try to remind ourselves that he's with our Lord and we'll see him again. I find myself wanting to see him now. It hurts when sometimes, forgetting for a moment, I think *I'll ask him when I see him* or *I'll ask him when he calls*.

Both women involved with Robert's death, the one who was with him and the one who hosted the party the night he died, are in psychiatric treatment. This is the unresolved area of the tragedy. I am not ready to speak to the one who involved our son in her life.

The person who made that necessary call to us was Robert's mentor and friend. He continues to be my friend and support. He grieves with me. I try not to grieve openly.

It seems impossible to get past the shock of losing a child. Many say, "Hold on to the memories of the life you had together. In time you will be restored to being a whole person."

But restoration comes ever so slowly. There are days when life is unbearable. Unmeasured, eventually the pain subsides. And God's children are in our midst, waiting to reach out.

A wonderful memorial service was held for our son on May 7, his twenty-fifth birthday. The church was filled to overflowing. The waiting room held more.

To know him was to love him, forever.

TWENTY-THREE

Sharon's Story

Others' eyes do not quite meet the eyes
of the mourner of an AIDS death.

In an earlier chapter of this book, I shared some poems I wrote after my husband's death. My brother's death, five years later, was different. His was a new kind of dying.

When my husband died, the funeral parlor was packed with family, friends, and co-workers who rallied to my support. When my brother died, the funeral parlor held only faithful family members, a few of his old friends, some family friends, and one lone co-worker, offering support.

When my husband died, people were loving, caring, supportive, their eyes full of tears at my loss. When my brother died, people were uncomfortable, detached, and absent, their eyes not quite meeting mine. Few seemed to believe his death was worth my grief.

When my husband died, he died very suddenly. I raged against his death, fighting its reality. When my brother died, he had suffered the torments of hell. I had seen him emaciated, his cheeks sunken, his almost-blind eyes straining to see, his almost-deaf ears striving desperately to hear. I welcomed his death, happy his suffering was over.

When my husband died, he died of a respectable heart attack. When my brother died, he died of AIDS.

The differences between dying respectably and dying from AIDS are numerous and definitely discernible. The difference in the number of people at the services is only one, and in honesty, could be explained. My brother, Walker Lynn Tuttle, had lived in Houston many years and had few friends left in Kentucky. Many of my friends knew I believed that Lynn was better off and they probably assumed I did not need the support I had so obviously needed when my husband died. They expressed their condolences. My company sent a generous donation to The Names Foundation, which was my brother's request. Also, not everyone knew of his death.

And Lynn and our family and his friends had had five years to prepare ourselves for his death. But I knew that five years was not long enough for Lynn to get used to this idea. It had taken him almost thirty years to learn to live with the fact of his homosexuality, and accept it, admit it, and be happy.

After his death, I determined to be as honest about the cause as Lynn had been. When people who read his obituary approached me to say they were sorry, they often asked the cause of his death. I looked them in the eyes and said, "He had AIDS." Many took this matter-of-factly, without blinking, but their eyes did not quite meet mine. One blurted out, "How in the world did he get *that?*" When I answered, the eyes slid away. Others' eyes do not quite meet the eyes of the mourner of an AIDS death, especially when they know how he contracted AIDS.

When my brother's illness was first diagnosed, and after the first shock and terror had abated, he seemed to rebound. He was a fighter with a strong desire to live a life of quality for as long as possible.

He continued working until almost the end. He attended plays, concerts, ball games, and horse races. He fought his disease with a holistic approach, by eating nutritionally, taking vitamins, exercising, maintaining a positive attitude. He took AZT. He came home to Kentucky often. And he never lost his wonderful wit and irreverent, quirky sense of humor.

But the disease continued its ruthless, inevitable course. Intermittently his efforts to fight and live life to the fullest were temporarily defeated by the weakening efforts of his immune system. He developed rashes, infections, and sinus problems, and lost weight. With the help of the dedicated Doctor Crowfoot, he managed to pull through time after time to fight and live again.

But as the time marched relentlessly on, the periods between hospitalizations shortened. Lynn grew weaker. His friends continued to die. And his personality changed. He became anxious, fearful, paranoid. He frustrated and angered easily. Considering that it was increasingly difficult for him to communicate because of his hearing loss and problems with his eyes, it was understandable. I believe that the brain tumor, mostly responsible for his death in the end, was at work during this time.

During one visit home he became enraged at me and our youngest sister over a disagreement about the decor of a play we had just seen. At another sister's home, he became obsessed with the idea that he was being treated badly because he was left alone while she and her husband worked. So, because of a disagreement, a misunderstanding, and his AIDS-induced perception of these events, my brother and his sisters were estranged for the last year of his life.

In notes found after his death, we learned some of his feelings: "When you become sick and lose your health, your job, income, status, and power, you become insecure, threatened, confused, depressed, and vulnerable." "I vacillate between rage, depression, and disbelief."

During a Cursillo (a Catholic religious retreat) that my sister, Camilla, and I attended, both of us experienced great joy, love, and forgiveness. We kept feeling strong, repeated inner messages that we should go to Lynn. We knew he was back in the hospital and doing very poorly. The next weekend we flew to Houston.

Our hearts broke when we saw him but gladdened at his absolute joy in having us there with him. We spent three days, communicating as best we could by getting close and talking directly into the hearing aid in his right ear. We talked for hours, sharing our feelings about the estrangement, sharing our concerns for him, sharing our love. We ran errands for him, straightened his room, plumped his pillows, held his hands. And we hugged him. We forgave each other the past and loved unconditionally in the present. We had a joyful reconciliation.

We stayed three nights, taking turns sleeping on a small cot in his room, listening to the piteous night sounds of his agony and pain. Chronic diarrhea caused him to get up several times during the night, stumbling and groping in his blindness, sometimes pulling the I.V.s from his arms. Sometimes he became confused and disoriented, imagining people were in his room. Once he fell out of bed. Camilla, a registered nurse, was of tremendous value at this time.

Dying can be gruesome in a lonely, mechanical, dehumanized, and impersonal modern hospital. But we were grateful for an AIDS floor in the Houston hospital.

Lynn was not a docile, passive patient. He did not take death lying down. Intelligent and well-versed in his illness and prescribed care, he expected that care to be given. He felt the loss of control, the isolation, the hopelessness, and what sometimes seemed to be the lack of caring. He asked questions. He voiced his opinions strongly.

This did not always endear him to the hospital staff. But there were caregivers on the AIDS floor, where death is ugly and inevitable, who cared. For them we were thankful.

Lynn desperately feared dying. He especially feared dying alone.

My sister and I felt the immediacy of his death. She talked about God with him, asked him to accept the Lord and to ask for His help right then and at the end. Lynn was never a particularly religious person, but we could tell that he was groping spiritually. So we hoped and we prayed. Later, in his notes, we read with some comfort: "a slow process of growth, of development, of dealing with reality, of accepting responsibility and often of gaining understanding acceptance of a higher power."

On the morning we left him in Houston, we left feeling guilty—as though we were deserting him to the mercy of strangers. But we had to go back to our jobs and families. We also felt joy and peace at our reconciliation, mixed with the almost certain knowledge that his suffering was almost over and the sadness that we might never see him again.

I remembered the lines of Dylan Thomas: "Do not go gentle into that good night. Rage, rage against the dying of the light." I knew that's what Lynn was doing. And I understood.

He died four days later, but he wasn't alone. Two of his brothers and two caring friends were with him.

During his years of AIDS, I had already experienced the shock, numbness, and suffering stages of grief. Out of necessity, I had come to an acceptance of sorts and, I believe, to some growth during our hospital stay. If I could ever believe that Lynn had come to accept his death, my recovery would surely come.

At the memorial service Lynn's family was there for him: his mother, his three sisters and their families, and three of his brothers and their families. One brother from Texas, my daughter from California, other out-of-state relatives, and our step-father, who was in a nursing home in the advanced stages of emphysema, were unable to attend. Loyal aunts and cousins and friends were there. Our seventy-two-year-old mother had always been especially close to Lynn. He had made an effort, out of his deep love for her, to remain close. She cried when she heard of his death. But at his service, she was silent, subdued, and disengaged, resigned to the latest sorrow in a life full of tragedy.

Also present at the funeral was the tension, in the air, a tangible feeling. Even some of the family members had difficulty meeting one another's eyes. Some of us stuffed and repressed and denied our feelings, keeping outwardly calm. Some of us remained proud and stubborn. Some of us avoided others of us. Some of us were emotional and cried. Some of us hoped. Some of us prayed. Some of us did several of the above.

AIDS patients are often referred to as victims. Lynn was another kind of victim also. Lynn and I and all our brothers and sisters are victims of our childhood, wounded by growing up in a war zone with alcoholic parents. Before they are adults, children of alcoholics learn how to repress, deny, detach, hope, pray—and how to survive. So it is with us. We are survivors, but there we were at the memorial service of our brother who did not survive. It was not a pretty picture.

The survivors and mourners of the AIDS dead suffer just as much as survivors of those who die from other diseases, like cancer. Often AIDS survivors suffer more. Yet we are often treated differently, with less concern and compassion, which causes us more grief.

Sometimes the message I felt I was getting after my brother's death seemed to be, "Why are you mourning? His death is no big loss; he deserved it, didn't he?" I have heard AIDS patients spoken of with contempt. Some people seem to think AIDS is a curse or a punishment from God because of the sufferer's lifestyle. I have heard other AIDS mourners say they felt rejected, avoided, even feared, as if *they* were contagious.

And how will we deal with our grief if someone doesn't help us along that labyrinthine road to recovery? The majority will have to work their way through the stages of grief while still facing their ambiguous feelings of having had a son or wife or child or whoever with AIDS. These feelings may encompass their own shame, guilt, futility, bitterness, and anger, or their own rejection of the dead loved one.

I give full credit and appreciation to the non-family mourners at my brother's service. They coped with a situation that could have been traumatic and messy. But they were there, probably because they could cope. Those incapable of coping did not come. Talking to understanding family and friends, ones who coped and came, gave great comfort to our family. I tried to talk to as many as possible and express my appreciation of their support.

We talked about how Lynn, during the early stages of AIDS, had bought a burial plot and arranged his funeral. Once he even talked of suicide. In the end, he changed his mind about both. He decided on cremation and requested that his ashes be placed beneath a bush near the finish line at Churchill Downs race track in Louisville. After his death, one of his brothers, who knew his wishes, traveled to Houston to take care of the after-death details, and took his ashes back to Kentucky.

As we stood beside his resting place, we listened to the beautiful sounds of:

> Amazing Grace! How sweet the sound
> That saved a wretch like me;
> I once was lost, but now I'm found,
> Was blind, but now I see.

Hearing these words of hope and promise filled my heart with comfort and gladness.

But I do not want you to be ignorant, brethren, concerning those who have fallen asleep, lest you sorrow as others who have no hope. For if we believe that Jesus died and rose again, even so God will bring with Him those who sleep in Jesus.
                                                         1 Thess. 4:13–14

Father Danny Goff offered us an exceptional and appropriate homily of brotherly love and forgiveness. After mentioning a few anecdotes about Lynn, he spoke about the need for forgiveness. He may have spoken on this because he knew our family was divided, not because of our brother's homosexuality, but because of misunderstandings, pride, anger, accusations, and recriminations resulting from other causes—stemming, I believe, from our background. Father Danny may have known that Lynn felt sorrow, as well as some responsibility and guilt for his family being apart. Lynn told my sister and me about his feelings during our last visit with him.

Father said that from what he could understand, Lynn wanted his family to come together and to forgive each other. He reminded us that life is short. He said we all needed to forgive each other and love each other. And he told us that is what Lynn wanted and that is what God wants.

On the day of my brother's memorial service, a devout lady, a member of my sister Camilla's prayer group, gave Camilla the following written account of a vision the woman said she had received on March 29, 1991, Good Friday, the day Lynn died.

I saw a man lying on a bed; he was eaten up on the inside with disease.

Next, I saw him crouched at the foot of the Cross and the blood of Jesus was gently falling on him drop by drop. His body became very clear; the spirit of the Lord cleansed him to such perfection that his body became transparent.

In the next scene the gates of Heaven were opened. Lynn, clothed in a white robe was lying prostrate before the throne. There was a calm peace in his spirit, a deep, deep sense of relief. The tremendous joy of being in the presence of God had not taken place as yet.

I asked God about the opened gates that I had seen months ago when I sensed Lynn was so close to death. I felt the Lord was saying, "He was close to death, but I gave him one more chance to reconcile with himself and with his family."

I strongly felt that he had a complete sense of total forgiveness toward every single family member. Over the past months, God gave him the grace necessary to totally forgive and unconditionally love his mother and all of his brothers and sisters.

One of his last prayers: "Someday, somehow, Lord, let my family know how sorry I am that I hurt them. I humbly ask their forgiveness. I forgive them and totally and unconditionally love them. O God, this is one of my last requests to You. I give this to You, Lord, and commend my spirit to You in peace."

TWENTY-FOUR

Jane's Story

I did not know of his illness until a few days before his death.
He had AIDS. He had chosen not to tell me.

I've lost four loved ones during my lifetime—my husband, my father, my mother, and my only child. I think that is more than anyone should have to endure. I've never wanted to study death or how it affects those who are left behind, but it seems I have become something of an expert. I haven't wanted to compare my grief experiences, but just the same I'm aware that each time there was a difference. In fact, there were few similarities.

After my husband died I was angry and frustrated. I was so miserable, no one could enjoy my company. He was only forty-eight. Scott, our son, was studying in Europe when his father died.

After about a year, there was a sudden, dramatic change in me, and I began to live again. I began to laugh and have fun. For about fifteen years I enjoyed life. During that time I grew very close to my son. We'd always enjoyed a very special mother-son relationship. We'd done many things together and found great pleasure in each other's company. Our relationship became stronger and more meaningful to both of us. I have many happy memories of that time. And during that time I remarried.

My family has always been close and loving. My son had grandparents, aunts, uncles, and cousins that loved him and me. From the time he was born, we thought he was special. We spent five of his preteen years in Big Bear where he became an avid skier. He attended high school in Long Beach and did his college work at Long Beach State, Chapman College, and the university in Vienna, Austria. He got his arts and science degree from UCLA and a masters from The Art Center in Los Angeles. Scott was a talented graphics artist and eventually established a fine reputation as a freelance artist working mostly in book design for many of the publishing houses in New

York City. In spite of the geographic distance, we remained close until we became estranged over an inheritance situation. That was a very difficult time for me.

We'd known since Scott's high school days that he had homosexual tendencies and his father and I were able to persuade him to have counseling. We hoped that therapy would help him change his lifestyle, but it became clear that he wouldn't. After his father died, I continued to try to convince Scott to seek help, but I wasn't successful. The situation was very difficult for me to handle alone. Eventually all I could do was try to understand and not condemn.

After I remarried, my father died. My reaction to his death was different from my reaction to my first husband's death. I had loved my father with my whole heart and his death left an empty hole. I grieved, but I was not angry, and I did not have the feelings of guilt I'd had after my husband's death.

Then my mother died. She had been so ill that at her death I felt relief. In the months following her death, I missed her, but I thought I was able to give her up because her suffering was ended. Now, though, I miss her very much, more than before.

My son's death was the most tragic and traumatic of all, and I felt the whole range of grief. I did not know of his illness until a few days before his death. He had AIDS. He had chosen not to tell me.

But just a few days before he died, one of his friends called me. I immediately flew to New York to be with him. He was gravely ill and unable to talk to me except for one brief conversation. Those last days with him were very important to both of us. We had a warm and loving reconciliation and expressed our love for each other. I will be eternally grateful that we had that time together.

My son died December 9, 1988. He was fifty-two years old.

Words cannot describe the regret and grief I felt. At first there was a strange numbness. Then came the incredible denial. There were so many emotions crowding in on each other, it was hard to know which ones were stronger. It was confusing and made it hard for me to accept reality. Scott was all I'd had for so many years that to go on without him seemed unthinkable and unacceptable.

I found some comfort in his friends. He had many friends and several of them became my good friends. They helped me through the first devastating year. I am better able to handle my grief now. More and more often I can replace the sad thoughts with happy ones. I do have many happy memories.

Keeping busy and finding new interests has helped me. I've discovered that my friends want to help if only I'll let them. For some reason I've tried to handle my problems alone, but that doesn't work. I need to talk, especially about the anger and the guilt.

I have received two special gifts from the tragedy of my son's death. My husband and I have grown closer. He is even more supportive than before and I can talk with him about my feelings whenever I feel the need. And I have come to realize that I have not really lost Scott. I know now that he'll always be with me.

It hasn't been easy to handle these emotions, but I'm doing better. I still have "down" days when I don't want to talk to anyone, but those days are getting to be fewer and farther apart.

I think I've come a long way.

TWENTY-FIVE

Florence's Story

My first night alone with my daughter was pure hell.
We wandered through the house like two lost souls.

It was Easter weekend. Mike had been invited to fly to Mulege, Mexico, with his friend, Billy, and Billy's parents in their light plane for a weekend of skin diving. I stood in the doorway that Friday morning, watching him trudge up the country road, a small suitcase in his hand. He turned and waved to me one more time. That was the last time I saw him.

Mike and Billy were inseparable. They were almost always together. They attended the same schools, jumped their horses in the same shows, helped the local ranchers cut hay, mucked out stalls together, and spent long hours just enjoying each other's company.

Mike was my Golden Boy. A handsome six-footer, fifteen years of age, he had dark brown hair and eyes and strong arms and legs from schooling horses and swimming. He was blessed with a sweet disposition, a wry sense of humor, and a great affection for animals and small children. Beside his horses, a large police dog, a golden spider monkey, and a medium-sized boa constrictor, he had a row of wire cages across the back veranda that housed a collection of mice, ground squirrels, and snakes he had rescued from the hay fields.

Like the proverbial Pied Piper, he had a following of neighborhood children. He spent hours explaining to them the lifestyles of his animals and their care and feeding. Usually when a child went home, a small new pet went along. More than one squeamish mother was surprised.

Those were the drug culture years, but Mike loved the good things of life: swimming and diving, tennis, and most of all anything to do with horses. He played polo with his school team on claimers from the quarter-horse track that he spent hours training.

I flew to Los Angeles that night to spend the weekend with my husband at Big Sur on the California coast. He was on assignment to the Hughes plant in Fullerton, and we were looking forward to spending a few days together after a month-long separation. At the end of a pleasant weekend, I called home late Sunday afternoon to check on our seventeen-year-old daughter, who had stayed at home to school her new jumper. Her friend Caroline answered the phone. She said a plane had crashed in Nogales, Sonora, and they were afraid Mike was on it.

In a state of shock my husband and I tried to contact someone who could tell us about Mike, but we were unable to get any further information. We didn't know if our beloved son was dead or alive. Immediately we began driving home, hoping with each mile that it was all a dreadful mistake.

But it was true! Mike was dead. While taking off the plane had crashed on the runway in Nogales and burst into flames—killing every one on board, three adults and five young people. This was not the aircraft he had flown south on. Others with their own private planes had joined Billy's family in Nogales. In a twist of fate, Mike had agreed to fly home with someone else.

In public we functioned automatically. We appealed to our congressman for help in obtaining the release of our child's burned body by the Mexican government. We drove to the Nogales Airport and watched F.A.A. officials supervise the removal of hundreds of pieces of burned metal from the air strip. I combed the remaining shards searching for some reminder of my child. Our family dentist, a friend and neighbor whose children had grown up with Mike identified Mike's body. He told me later that it was the hardest thing he'd had to do in all his years of practice.

We had a small private burial service, followed by a memorial service at our local church that was attended by hundreds of Mike's friends and classmates. We played recordings of his favorite music, "Aires from the Well-Tempered Clavier." Our friends tried to comfort us with kind and compassionate words.

The public mourning ended, and we were free of the constraints of controlled, civilized behavior. Mike's father and I spent long hours weeping, wrapped in each other's arms. Eventually he had to leave to finish his assignment in Fullerton. The workplace allows only so much time for grieving.

My first night alone with my daughter was pure hell. We wandered through the house like two lost souls. She blamed herself for all the petty quarrels she'd had with her brother, and the sibling rivalry they'd had in the show ring. She hurt because she would never be able to tell her brother she didn't mean it.

I hurt because my child was lost to me forever. I tried to ease the emptiness in my heart by going to the barn where Mike's favorite horse was stabled. I'm certain The Colonel understood every grieving word I said as I wept into his mane.

I dreaded nightfall. The lonely house and a quiet, subdued seventeen-year-old daughter locked in her own grief were more than I thought I could bear. I took long walks along the banks of the river. When I was well away from the house and no one could hear, I screamed like a banshee, over and over until my voice was hoarse and I was empty of emotion. Drained, I could then go home and fall into an exhausted sleep.

I went back to my job. My supervisors and co-workers tiptoed around me, not knowing that getting back to the regular routine was all that was keeping me sane! During the day I coped with my job as an employment officer with the State and the litigation that followed the crash. Callously, the insurance companies representing the builders and remodelers of the crashed aircraft attempted to contact me at my office the day following the crash. My compassionate boss refused to give them my home address and warned them not to call the office again.

Other than talking to my minister, I sought no counseling. I knew I wanted to go on living. I explored the hurt early on to determine if I could bear it. I knew it was not an impossible task.

I didn't realize how deeply my daughter was hurting. She managed to maintain her emotional equilibrium until her father decided to seek consolation in the arms of a sympathetic co-worker. The man who always wanted me to lean on him, and had complained "You are too strong," did a deft sidestep and let me fall flat. My beautiful daughter dropped out of school and spent a year with a group of flower children in Laguna Beach. Fortunately, they were compassionate and helped heal her bruises and make her whole again.

My grieving continued, not only for the loss of my son, but also for the loss of my husband and lover. Oh, I could function all right. By that time I was employed by the State of California and I went off to work each day, seemingly a normal person. I carried out my duties and obligations, but at night I wept large bitter tears of despair.

Finally, on the night Bobby Kennedy was assassinated, I lay in my bed watching the horror of that scene in Los Angeles. I shed copious tears. After a time I realized I didn't know why I was crying or for whom. Was it Bobby? His family? Mike? Or my lost lover?

That was the moment I let go of all my sorrow.

I'll always love Mike, and there will always be a place in my heart damp with tears for him. But I was finally set free from my poor, misguided husband. Months later he came to his senses after a disastrous marriage and quick divorce from his sympathetic friend. He sought a reconciliation, which to his surprise I rejected. We are friends even though I remarried ten years later. After all, together we had two children we both love. And he is proud that I successfully completed law school and passed the bar.

After all this time I still think of Mike every day with love and tenderness. His photographs hang on the walls and sit on tables. The wax flowers he pulled out of a trash can on his way home from school when he was a fourth grader are in a vase in my bedroom. The empty bottle of Jungle Gardenia perfume he gave me that last Christmas still has a faint scent.

He lives in the reminiscences we exchange when my daughter and I are together. For me there's great comfort in keeping Mike's memory fresh. Now, when I travel to far off places and see wonderful things, I think of the delight he would feel if he were there.

Mike was a wonderful child. We are fortunate to have had him those fifteen wonderful years.

TWENTY-SIX

Elizabeth's Story

I felt that my feelings of suffering and loss were invalid.
I was not able to mourn—only to feel shame.

I was eighteen and unemployed. I was living temporarily in my dad's motel room, sleeping on the floor. And I was pregnant, a child about to give birth to a child.

I felt very alone and frightened. The boy I'd been seeing, the daddy-to-be, left town when I told him I was pregnant. I thought I had only one option—abortion. And I thought I had to bear the burden by myself. Just the loneliness was overwhelming, but the guilt and shame were unbearable.

There wasn't time for realistic, careful thinking. By the time I was sure of the pregnancy, I felt I had to act quickly. If I reached the twelfth-week point, the abortion clinic wouldn't do the procedure. Numbly I went there, paid the money in advance, and when they called my name, "Elizabeth?" I followed the others in my group into the back.

It didn't take long. It hurt like hell. I walked out, still numb, feeling like I'd been violated. But it was over.

That night I developed an infection. For the next seven days I ignored the fever, the dizziness, the bleeding. Finally a friend took me to the emergency room. The doctors said I had waited much too long to seek medical treatment. The infection had severely damaged my reproductive organs. I might never be able to have children. I thought that was my obvious punishment.

Guilt became the focus of all my energies. The underlying grief and loss I swept away to a dark corner of my soul. My loss was not the result of a freak accident, an illness, or an inexplicable act of God. I had made the decision myself; therefore, my suffering and loss were invalid. I wanted to mourn, but I felt only shame.

Tragedy is a part of life that each of us learns to cope with in various ways. Some of those ways are viewed as normal and healthy. But after my abortion, I felt that the "normal" ways of coping were not possible for me. I couldn't mourn. I couldn't turn to my family for support and certainly I couldn't turn to my religion, or so I thought. I believed these ways of finding support and comfort weren't possible because my suffering was the direct result of my own choice. I was empty and alone.

When I agreed to write this story, I had no intention of describing my despair and despondency. In fact, I have spent many, many hours trying not to write this story. I wanted somehow to protect the memories that I've buried deep within me. But it has become painfully clear to me that emotional scars don't disappear just because they weren't acknowledged. I have learned that grief is not something that will just evaporate if it is ignored. It sits there waiting to overwhelm you again without warning.

Recently my best friend called to tell me that a mutual friend was having a baby. Much to my surprise, I felt an uncontrollable rush of emptiness crashing down on me. I began to sob. I was aware of a devastating void inside that I hadn't consciously realized still existed. Apparently when emotions are ignored, they inevitably continue to be manifested in a variety of different, sometimes destructive ways. When my sadness recalled that long repressed guilt, my grief began again, as though it was fresh and new and raw.

The circumstances of my life improved greatly during the next several years. I found a good job in a business I enjoy, have my own apartment, and am in love. My boyfriend is from Germany and was living nearby for three months. Much to my surprise—and his—the night before he was to return home I realized I was pregnant. My first thought was that a curse had been lifted and I was finally free of the guilt that had saddled me the past five years. Miraculously I was pregnant again, and this time I could share the wonderful event with someone I loved.

Soon, however, I had to face the fact that my boyfriend did not think a baby was a good idea. In the light of day and realism I could clearly understand his position, but this issue was something that to me transcended all rational thought and circumstance. I found it incomprehensible that he would expect me to give up possibly my last chance to give life to the soul that had been living quietly in my heart those last years. Of course, he couldn't understand, and I didn't know how to verbalize it so that he might understand. I had hidden all my thoughts and feelings deep inside, and I'd managed to keep them buried until I was forced to face the issue again.

The first pregnancy was suddenly as current an issue in my mind as though it had happened yesterday. Armed with nothing more than an inexplicable feeling that fate and destiny were on my side, I went to my mother and close friends with the announcement that I was having a baby. "Yes," I said, "I quit my job." "No. I don't know how I'll manage." "I don't know if my boyfriend will want to take responsibility." But I was determined to have my baby. Everyone showed remarkable support. In fact, they were far more supportive than I would have expected had I been able to think about what to expect.

A few days later I was on a plane to Germany. I intended to stay a week and then return home to create a life for myself that included motherhood. My boyfriend continued to object to our having a baby in view of our current circumstances and geographic distance.

While I was in Germany, I lost my baby. I woke up in a strange hospital, trying to understand the sights and sounds around me. I saw a nurse scurrying around the room and a woman lying in the bed to my left. I heard people speaking a language I didn't understand. I couldn't talk to them or ask them questions. My mind was in a fog and I didn't immediately remember what had happened. Within minutes the dreadful reality became clear and as I remembered exactly what had happened, those long buried feelings of shame, rage, and loss magnified and consumed me.

Losing a child before it is born is a uniquely awful experience. Most people don't acknowledge that a spiritual connection takes place between mother and child during pregnancy. They especially don't acknowledge this bond in those pregnancies that don't achieve full term. But there is a bond. I was touched by a bonding with the soul that lived for a time inside my body. When the physical embodiment of that soul was gone, and it was no longer a tangible life, I was lost and empty. I felt that even though my body continued to walk and talk, my heart was only a shell.

The emptiness felt like a gaping wound that could never be healed. Not only did I feel I was still being punished, but I also felt ridiculed for having believed that happiness was possible for me. Since I hadn't allowed myself to acknowledge these raging emotions during the first pregnancy, all my emotions were even more irrational now. Once again I was a messed up eighteen-year-old kid who couldn't do anything good or right.

But I was also fortunate. No one would allow me to slip too far. My boyfriend shared my grief and supported me when periodically I slipped back into my self-punishing role. I had friends who listened when I cried and didn't remind me this was my own fault or imply that I had to bear my burden alone. My mother and family didn't pass judgment, but constantly offered love and support. I came to realize that they shared my loss with me.

Obviously my loss is still very fresh, and I am not entirely certain I am finished hiding from my emotions. I still prefer to dull my senses most of the time rather than to risk sparking the tornado of feelings that I have found to be so powerful when they take over. But I think I've managed to strike a compromise with the demons inside that surface periodically. I am at peace with the soul that I haven't given life to, and I'm at peace with myself.

My experience and pain have forced me to find the Wisdom whose existence I hadn't acknowledged or experienced. Through Him I have found more strength than I believed possible. Certainly this issue is not entirely resolved, and I may always cry tears left over from the past. However, my suffering was not nearly as forsaking an experience when I finally learned how to share my burdens with the people who love me.

TWENTY-SEVEN

Lorene's Story

Where was my husband, my friend, my partner, the one I had shared my life with? He wasn't the man who was saying those hurtful things to me. That man was a stranger.

A song I hear frequently on the radio has the words "How am I supposed to live without you, after I've been loving you so long?" Today I can listen to the lyrics and smile, but it wasn't always so. In fact, for a time I couldn't turn on any music station without being torn apart by grief and pain.

My world crashed when my husband of twenty-six years told me he was divorcing me. I remember sitting there in total shock. A horrible, icy cold feeling enveloped me as he rambled on and on about "things" not being right. His five best friends were women I didn't even know! He seemed to want to be sure I understood that. "Lots of people get divorced," he said with what appeared to be a smile. "What's the big deal?" And he shrugged.

I sat there unable to speak, thinking I would surely die right where I was before the night ended. Where was my husband, my friend, my partner, the one I had shared so much of my life with? He wasn't the one who was saying those hurtful things to me. That man was a stranger.

We had gone through many difficulties getting together, but when we finally did, our hearts and souls were one. We were so close. Our children grew up sharing our joy and our struggles. We were partners in a dynamite business we started from nothing. And it had become a very profitable and creative endeavor for both of us. Everyone thought we were truly the ideal couple.

When I finally found my voice, I tried to talk to him. Surely he couldn't be serious. How could he just walk away after twenty-six years? But he didn't want to talk. Apparently he had said everything that was on his mind. He went calmly to bed as I lay in a heap, sobbing uncontrollably.

I must have cried for days. I don't remember those days too clearly. I was breaking into thousands of pieces and I actually hoped I would die.

My husband would not agree to counseling. He had made up his mind, and nothing and no one was going to change his plans. The only explanation he gave me was, "Our paths in life are going in different directions now." That was it?

Not long afterward I learned he had been living another life, a life apart from the one he shared with me. I knew he had been going through a period of discontent, but I had no idea it was that serious. I had tried to talk with him. I'd wondered why he was gone so much. Apparently he believed these other women understood him better than I did. He claimed innocence when I questioned him about spending so much time with one particular woman I thought was my friend. His reply was that she was his very dear friend, and I had no right to question or try to control who he spent time with. Not long after, he moved out of our house, and moved in with her!

During all this time, about one and a half months, I tried desperately to hold on. I couldn't think of life without him. I cried every night and most of the days. I couldn't eat or sleep, and I truly didn't care if I lived or died. My whole world was torn apart! I had not lived by myself since I was in my twenties, and suddenly there I was, in my fifties, alone. I felt completely helpless, totally frightened, extremely lonely, and so very, very sad.

I began to talk to God, and I began to realize that I really did not want to die. I wanted to live. But how? Total despair cannot be tolerated alone.

The day I sat down with my sister and two very dear friends and told them what I was going through was my first step toward recovery. The tears came again, but for the first time someone cried with me. They hugged me and kissed me. They told me they loved and cared about me. Gradually that terrible, icy cold feeling inside me began to go away, at least for a while. Words cannot possibly describe how their outpouring of love and concern helped me. Someone, three someones actually, really cared. I had thought no one cared.

I realized I had retreated into a world of my own, walling myself away from everyone. I did that partly because I was so hurt, and

We had loved watching and feeding the birds every day together. We had even named them. And now there was no one to enjoy the birds with! We'd had such wonderful companionship, not only because of the birds, but because of everything. That morning the realization of my loss was almost too much to comprehend!

My counselor said very quietly, "There's absolutely no reason why you can't sit down each morning and enjoy the birds by yourself." He was so right. And those quiet words showed me my next step.

I had to realize that my happiness doesn't depend on another person. It comes first from within me. Believe me, it wasn't easy, but each step I took in that direction helped me to become a stronger, more confident person.

The next aspect of my recovery the counselor helped me with was learning to deal with my grief positively. For weeks I had been driving blindly on the roads crying so hard I could barely see! I truly was a menace in my car—not only to myself, but to the other innocent, unsuspecting drivers. I knew it was terribly dangerous to do that and I asked my counselor to help me with my destructive behavior. He suggested a plan of action that worked for me. The first thing I needed to do was turn off the car radio that kept playing all those love songs. Then, when the tears began, I would say to myself, "Not now. I will deal with my despair and grief when I am safely at home."

He reminded me that I needed to acknowledge my grief. If I tried to shove it under the rug, my wounds would never really heal. This advice helped me to be somewhat in control of my actions and still allow time to deal with my tears. It was the kind of advice that one of my mother's favorite sayings gives: "Inch by inch, life's a cinch; yard by yard, it's hard." I learned to do it an inch at a time.

When I told my mother about my husband, she grieved too. She had loved him very much, and could not believe what he had done. What made it harder for her to accept was that she had just spent a wonderful Christmas weekend at our house and remembered well the loving cards he had given us and the feelings he had expressed. She felt betrayed too.

Deceit is hard to deal with, and Mother became very angry. That seemed to help her through her grief, but for some reason I wasn't able to get angry. I still feel the sadness, but that is getting better. Mother, who is eighty-seven years old and has been widowed more than thirty years, helped me greatly to take life minute by minute, or hour by hour—however much I could handle at a given time.

On good days I make a point of learning something new. It makes

partly because I didn't want anyone to know my husband ha⟨
me.

Divorce is a uniquely devastating experience. Not only do you
someone you dearly love, but you must deal with the unbearabl⟨
that he or she has rejected you. You're not loved anymore! It
hurts to remember how horrible that felt.

I knew it was critical that I come out of my lonely hole and
the support of family and friends. My wonderful sister and bro⟨
in-law opened their home to me every weekend. Their compas⟨
and understanding played a large part in my recovery. Every ⟨
my dear mother sent me loving cards of encouragement and
cern. Those cards decorated my dining table for a year. I read t
every day and felt loved! And my friends, my steadfast friends ⟨
always there. They called me on the telephone; they invited m
their homes for nourishment—for food, love, and companions⟨
They truly restored my soul.

As I look back, I see that period had a two-stage process.
family was there, comforting and loving me during the first stag⟨
survival. And my friends encouraged me as I stepped from mere
vival to moving back into life again. You always know your fa⟨
will stand by you, but when my friends came forward, it brough⟨
back to the real world of everyday life. I don't think I would ⟨
survived without my friends. And for the first time I really knew
meaning of Ralph Waldo Emerson's well-known statement, ⟨
friend may well be a masterpiece of nature."

Many years ago two very dear friends gave me a very large ant⟨
crock. Those words are printed on it. Even though these friends ⟨
always dear to me and I counted the crock among my treasures
was often aware of the words, it was not until I was so needy and
friends so giving that I fully understood them.

My family and friends helped me survive. With some small s⟨
of courage and hope, I allowed one of my friends to lead me ⟨
good counselor. I was frightened to death when I went for my ⟨
appointment and the tears flowed as I re-opened my wounds. Bu⟨
helped me so much in so many ways.

I remember going to his office one day blubbering like a lost s⟨
He waited very patiently while I struggled to collect myself and th⟨
in his kind, caring way, asked me why I was crying. I confessed I
been crying since I sat down for breakfast and my husband was
there holding my hand and laughing and talking with me about
birds.

me feel good about myself. I have learned to take charge of my life and to do all the things my husband used to take care of, including the car and small plumbing and electrical repairs. In other words, I've learned *everything*. When I look back now and think what a helpless mess I was then, I have to smile and feel proud of myself.

On bad days I seek the company of friends and family whenever possible, not to cry on their shoulders anymore, but to feel their warmth and love. I do this on good days too!

Another very positive step I took toward recovery was to make very definite changes in my home. When my husband left the house, I walked about my empty home crying continuously. Every thing in it was a part of a memory we had shared. Each picture, lamp, table, dish we had purchased together during many years of travel and life experiences. Oh, how I loved our special little retirement home that we had labored over and built with such joy and love! But could I ever be happy in it by myself?

Well I could! And I am. But it took over a year to feel happy there.

The first thing I did was change my bedroom. Every night when I went upstairs and climbed into that huge king-size bed I became instantly depressed. Not only was I cold with all that empty space around me, but I felt like an ant. So I sold the entire set. I was so happy when that bed of memories was gone. It didn't bother me at all to think I might have to sleep on the floor, nor was I troubled that I had nothing to put my clothes in. What was important was that the furniture I had shared with my husband was gone and would not be seen again!

I replaced that mammoth king-size bed with a small, Victorian-style white, wrought iron and brass day bed. Then I found a beautiful ruffled bed skirt and a yummy comforter covered with cheerful flowers and topped them off with several soft, plump pillows.

My clothes are stored in a charming rosy pink jelly cabinet and in an ivory chest decorated with delicate flowers. And there is a wee carved blue chest for wee things. To complete the room, I added a couple of converted antique oil lamps, some pretty scatter rugs, and two dried flower arrangements for the wall. My new bedroom makes me smile! It is very feminine and cozy and it's all me! It truly looks quite wonderful and in no way resembles the bedroom I used to share with my husband.

I also got rid of some dark, very masculine, leather furniture in the living room. Out it went and was slowly replaced by very warm, cheery pieces. My new couch is smaller and is covered in a fabric called "Mom's Quilt." It is so comfortable and really invites you to come and sit a while. I have a small plump chair done up in green and ecru mattress ticking and a great little wing-back chair in a complementary plaid. I got rid of the modern table and replaced it with a small antique one and added a beautiful old chest. I have always loved old things; they add so much warmth to a home. Besides it is such fun to canvas the flea markets with a friend to see what bargains I can discover.

Bit by bit the house that my husband once shared has evolved into a decidedly different home. It's *mine,* and it makes me feel *good.* It is my nest. My safe place. And I am not frightened or sad to be here anymore.

I have talked about various steps that helped me to regain a healthy mental state, but there is another very important aspect that I have not mentioned but that I truly believe helped save my life.

Back when I began counseling, when I realized that I did want to live, I knew that my physical condition was precarious as well as my mental condition. Stress and despair can kill the body as well as the spirit.

I had lost a great deal of weight and looked rather pitiful. I knew I had to become strong and healthy if I was ever going to be able to take care of myself and do all the things I would need to do to take care of my home. I was very lucky to be able to enlist the services of a superb fitness instructor at the health club where I had a membership. With his guidance and care, over a period of ten weeks I really began to feel alive again. Of course, I told him what I was going through so he could understand why some days I went to him looking and acting like a basket case. I can remember there were many days when I went in for my workout feeling like the dregs of the earth. But inevitably, an hour and a half later, at the end of my exercises, I would feel like a new person.

I have kept up with this program ever since. One and a half hours three days a week makes me feel so much better than I ever thought possible. Besides, I need these muscles to haul that coal, lift those bales, tote that wood, and do all those other things that make my life work. And I am not exactly a spring chicken!

My experiences actually began January 2, 1990. Now as I write these words it is September 1991. It has taken me this long to get back to living. In the beginning, I didn't think I would be here today, nor did I care if I weren't.

But, I am here, and I'm glad I am.

I didn't want to write this story because I did not want to remember the pain. But, you know how it is. "Funny things happen on the way to the forum." My dear friend Barbara called once again urging me to tell my story. Finally I said I would write it tomorrow (that's today) "if it rained!" I made that promise knowing that it was going to be bright and sunny all day (because I had just heard the weather report).

Well, the Lord works in strange and mysterious ways. When I awakened to grey skies, I said to myself, "The sun will come out." I put on my work clothes, happy to be rid of a promised writing task, and set about preparing to do fall maintenance work. Guess what! It started to rain! I came in the house and looked at the clock. *Oh Lord, I guess I have to take pencil in hand and write my story.* That was six hours ago.

Well, I'm glad I did it. I do not by any means consider myself a professional writer, but I pray that my story will give others going through a similar experience that one ingredient that makes a real difference: *hope*. Writing my story has helped me to see how far I have come from such unbearable misery. Yes, I do, indeed, have scars. There will always be moments or days of sadness. But that is life and I can accept it. Now I thank the Lord every day for my health, my home, my family, and my friends.

God bless!

Book Three
Reaching for Recovery

TWENTY-EIGHT

One Day There'll Be an Empty Chair

Is it going to happen?
Yes, one day it's going to happen.

We were sitting on our porch early one Saturday morning, sharing a cup of coffee and the morning sun, when my husband looked over at me and gently said, "You know, darling, one of these days one of these chairs is going to be empty!"

I looked at him, quizzically. *What was he trying to tell me? Had he been hiding something?* I searched his face.

Our screened-in porch is sparsely furnished. Private and secluded, tucked into the side of the mountain, it overlooks the pool, the gardens, and the valley below. It's our special little place, and we've kept it fairly simple. It's where we go on weekends, where we can tarry over coffee and each other.

And there are two matching chairs—a *his chair* and a *my chair*—and that's about all. There are also a few small tables holding the gentle clutter of books and manuscripts waiting for weekend catchup time and, of course, five little dogs, sprawling in the rays of contentment and love, who tag along wherever we go.

We were tarrying on that gentle spring morning, enjoying the freedom from office pressures, basking in our private world. Then Jacques spoke of the chair that will be empty one day. For a fleeting moment I could almost see it. I could picture one chair empty and one chair full. Then my heart began to ache.

"Darling, why do we have to talk about this *today?*" I said, and standing up, I put down my mug, folded the paper, excused myself, and left our private place that had suddenly become unfriendly. The truth of his statement brought a sadness that hung in the air for the remainder of the day.

That evening my thoughts returned to the unfinished subject of the morning. And I began to think about just who might be sitting in the full chair. Would it be me, or would it be my darling? My first impulse was to hope that he would survive me. Then, remembering the horrendous pain of grief still fresh in my mind and mentally picturing him sitting there alone, I had mixed feelings. I wanted to protect him from the pain of grief and loneliness, but at the same time I wanted to protect him in a different way by being the first to go (as if we have that choice).

He had tried to broach this subject on several other occasions, tenderly coining a phrase he called "after us." But I wasn't ready. I always put off any such discussion with, "Oh, let's talk about that later, darling. Let's don't spoil this beautiful day," and I knew better.

Why is it that we are so reluctant to discuss death? We all know that we come into this world alone and that one day we will have to leave in the same way—alone! *We need to learn how to be alone.* We need to begin to find peaceful solitude in our aloneness *before* the other chair is empty. And then, when the time comes—as it will for each of us—it won't be quite so terrifying.

Growing up I often heard discussions about wills and things that go with them. The discussions centered mostly on making decisions about your wishes and putting them in writing. Mother had read one of those articles detailing all the reasons why you should have a will. She had been strongly convinced that she and Daddy needed wills, and she mentioned it on a regular basis. She was right, of course, but Daddy, for some unknown reason, seemed to think wills weren't all that important. He was a brilliant, college-educated man, a mechanical engineer, but he was totally uninformed about the impact of unresolved legal issues that can befall surviving spouses and families. He had the opinion that if everything was jointly owned there was no need for a will. "Why fatten some lawyer's pocket?" he often said. Of course, he was wrong.

When he asked Mother one year what she would like for her anniversary gift, she giggled and shot back, "A will!" It got to be the family joke: Daddy wants a Porsche; Mother wants a will. And the joke persisted: Grandad wants a hammock; Maymo wants a will.

He woke one morning, suffered a massive heart attack, and died later that evening. He was only fifty-seven. Fortunately, he had granted Mother her anniversary wish. I know the importance of wills and trusts and, yes, we each have both.

That Saturday morning on the porch, and all the other times

Jacques tried to discuss planning and preparing, of course I knew he was right. We need to take time to plan, to face the inevitable, and to face it as thinking, mature adults. We need to plan for the time that will come to us all, the time when we must say goodbye, the time when one will leave the other to carry on alone.

But this conversation about the chairs was something much more. His "one of these days . . ." remark introduced other, more latent fears. Right in the middle of a beautiful Saturday morning, it introduced the subject of death and final separation. It introduced thoughts of loneliness, sorrow, and despair. It introduced the subject that so few of us are willing to think about, much less discuss: The experience that waits for us all; the time when we must say goodbye.

Dear brothers, you are only visitors here.
1 Pet. 2:11 TLB

Of course, Jacques was absolutely right. One of these days there *will* be an empty chair. That is the way it's meant to be. Life is rich with comings and goings. Some are temporary and some much more permanent. This is why I have included the next two chapters.

My conscience will haunt me if I don't take some time to share some of the valuable lessons we've learned along the way. Some lessons are of a spiritual nature and some are just plain practical. We hope you will benefit from some of our mistakes.

At 7:30 P.M. the night before my mother died, we went out to select "the right funeral home." What a nightmare. I still can't believe it. I did not want to turn my mother's body over to a stranger or to someone I didn't feel comfortable with. Was I still protecting? You bet I was!

We learned in the hardest of all ways that funeral arrangements should have been in place much sooner. Much unnecessary emotional stress could have been avoided if we had only addressed this imminent need earlier! We were simply naive and uninformed (and exhausted). We'd been unable to find the time and energy to do anything but care for Mother's pressing human needs and to somehow try to gather and preserve sufficient strength to make it through each day.

Exactly three years and two nights later I found myself trying to help two young adult, unmarried sisters from New York City who had recently lost both parents during a three-month period. Their father died of brain cancer in July. Their mother had died three months earlier. Understandably the two sisters were in such a state of grief and emotional devastation, they didn't know which way to turn. Nor was their anguish made any easier by the countless legal matters left for them to resolve. They had no family or friends to help them. Neither of them was in any way prepared for the untimely deaths of their parents. And neither of them had been able to return to work.

They told me they were hiding in their apartment and crying most of the time. "We don't even know how to pray anymore," one confessed.

It was a heartbreaking situation.

We sent them all of our *Afterloss* material by overnight express, along with a draft of a chapter from this book. They know that we are here to help them in any way for as long as they need us. Many of the things they've told me are sore reminders of my own feelings of abandonment and pain immediately following the loss of my mother.

"I need to know where she is now," one sister said, speaking of her mother.

The other sister cried out in pain, "And all those empty caskets! How was I supposed to know how to choose a casket? I don't know anything about caskets."

I could relate. But hopefully you will learn from our experiences and won't ever have to stumble through that misery in quite that way.

Let's return for a moment to the conversation my husband tried to have with me on the porch and the subject of the chair that one day will be empty. How should intelligent, rational, mature people deal with the subject of death? First, we need to stop hiding from it, or pretending that it will never happen. We need to stop making comments like, "Can't we talk about this later, darling." Then we need to be realistic about life and also about death. Some simple planning can save you and your loved ones untold misery and pain at a time when sorrow abounds.

In response to my husband's comment that early spring morning, eventually I got around the whole dismal subject by asking him to make a tape. "Tell me everything I would need to know or watch out for if I have to go on without you. Give me the dos and the don'ts," I asked. And he has done that.

I have no idea what he said in the tape, and I may never know. I have no desire to listen to it now, but I am comforted by the knowledge that it is there should I need it. I know he has prepared several of our children for this future time as well. My husband is a realist. He is not one to be caught unprepared, neither is he one to leave important matters to chance or, as could be the case if he didn't prepare, to others. He doesn't leave decision-making in the hands of unqualified or uninformed people.

Once again he has taken charge. So should you and I. I have made a tape for him. Since my husband presented me with his tape, there have been no more discussions on beautiful Saturday mornings about the chair that will be empty some day. We have adequately dealt with the subject.

In the tape I made, I *felt* like singing the first line from the song, "You Better Watch Out!"—watch out for the "three-month-widower's pitfall." But I didn't. I just thought about it. I taped some of my music instead. He's aware of the three-month pitfall. Three months after a loss is the time when so many grieving widowers get "caught." A widower is at his most vulnerable stage three to four months after the death of his wife. He is depressed, sad and lonely, and probably tired of trying to manage alone—tired of living alone, sleeping alone, eating alone, cooking alone. And he is probably also tired of eating what he cooks. So along comes a friend who says, "I've got a lady you've just *got* to meet." That's okay to a point.

The problem is that the widower, driven by his loneliness, often moves too quickly and soon becomes involved in a new relationship that culminates with "I do" months before he has completed his grief recovery. The formation of a new relationship cuts short the process of grief recovery. And he commits himself to living the rest of his life with a premature decision made during the height of his loneliness and vulnerability. Unfortunately this is a fairly common occurrence, so widowers, *beware*. It goes without saying that widows also should proceed with caution when it comes to getting involved prematurely.

As I mentioned earlier, we have found most funeral directors and their associates to be among the most caring and compassionate people we've ever met. I strongly recommend that you select the funeral home you want to serve you and your family *before* your time of need!

There is no more difficult and painful time for a family than the period immediately following the death of a family member. *And during this most difficult of all times, you don't want a stranger assisting you or your family when, with a little foresight, you can have a friend instead.* Choose a funeral director and get acquainted. No doubt you will find that person is guided by compassion and sensitivity, a professional who will serve you and your family well before, during, and after the formalities.

Funerals are held to benefit the living, not the dead. Many people these days are planning ahead and making their own funeral arrangements so their loved ones won't be burdened with this added responsibility at the time of death. Doing that allows you to think about what would best comfort your loved ones.

Pre-planning your funeral arrangements can be a special gift from you to your surviving loved ones and, when you think about it, it is really no more unusual than buying a life insurance policy or making out your will. How benevolent to handle the funeral details this way. When you take the steps to make these necessary arrangements, you can put the matter out of your mind, feeling the peace that will come from knowing that you have planned and prepared wisely.

Call around and ask questions. Find out about prices and services. Before you make your final selection, you might want to know if the funeral director provides grief recovery assistance to your survivors. Of course, you can visit the director or ask a representative to come to you. I guarantee, funeral directors won't bite!

In spite of some of the stories you may have heard, the members of the funeral industry are not in business to get rich. Many have talents that could earn them much higher salaries in other fields of endeavor. Most have selected their profession because they are such caring, sensitive people. And they are dedicated to helping you.

Often funeral homes are willing to help with the many forms that have to be filled out after a death. I've known of directors who, after the primary service, help bereaved families by driving them to the court house and assisting with handling the multiple legal documents and issues that must be resolved.

I also feel it is appropriate for each of us to make a determination about the disposition of our bodies and to then make our wishes known, in writing, to a family member *and* to the funeral director. I have seen widows weep and lament about having no option other than to make a choice between burial or cremation for their husbands. And I'm sure that later they spend many tormented, sleepless nights wondering if they made the right decision. We need to assume the responsibility of making that choice ourselves ahead of time. We ought not leave that important decision to someone else.

And what about your wishes for an open or a closed casket? I urge you to make this decision too, and then translate it into written in-

structions so that when the time comes for you to leave this earth, your bereaved ones will not have to decide for you and then anguish over whether or not they decided correctly.

A little common sense now will save your loved ones from having to go shopping for a funeral home at 7:30 P.M. on the eve of your death or the day following and then try to make other determinations, while wondering what you would want them to do. And they won't have to listen later to old man guilt's taunting accusations about what should or should not have been done. (*You should have taken the watch and left the ring.*)

Recently the headmaster of a Christian school in the east died unexpectedly at his home. Of course the local authorities had to be contacted, and the following morning the coroner called a funeral director who came for the body.

Since neither the headmaster nor his widow had made prearrangements, she was uninvolved in the selection of the funeral director. She had to release the body of her beloved husband to an undertaker who was a total stranger. (In the event of no prior funeral home selection, in some communities the authorities choose the funeral home on a rotating basis.) Our daughter, who is associated with the school, was with the widow when this happened. It was a stressful time for the grief-stricken widow, partially because the funeral home chosen by the coroner would *not* have been her choice had she been involved in the selection.

The headmaster was well-known and highly respected in the community. He had scores of friends. The seating capacity provided by the funeral home was not sufficient to accommodate the number of people who attended the funeral and, as a result, many had to stand throughout the services. There was *nothing* right about this selection that unfortunately was made during a time of great duress by a total stranger.

You also should give your family some guidelines about the kind of casket you feel is appropriate. Some survivors, in their grief, lose all perspective and want to provide the very best. You should express your feelings about what you feel is appropriate.

There is a new kind of service available that you may want to consider also when making arrangements. It was conceived and developed by Merrill Womach, a well-known tenor. "The Tribute" program is being offered now by several companies.

The concept first occurred to Mr. Womach during the public mourning of President Kennedy when he realized that the commemoration of so-called "ordinary people" after death is just as important to their families as the commemoration of celebrities is to their loved ones and followers. After allowing the idea to incubate for a while, he sought a method of making tributes available to everyone and anyone. (Incidentally, his personal story of survival after the crash of his private plane is told in his book, *Tested by Fire*. I recommend it highly.)

These companies will prepare a video tape of your life or the life of your loved ones. You select up to fifteen photographs, and if you want, you may also select background music and a Bible passage. With the help of Federal Express, the turn-around time can be as short as two days, making it possible to have a video for viewing during the service.

I can't begin to describe the impact of these tribute presentations! They are so powerful; you really have to see one to understand. They focus on the life of the deceased rather than the death. They help us to remember all of the love between the laughter and the tears. I believe sample tapes are available for viewing at participating funeral homes and the names and addresses of the companies that provide this service as well.

And one final thought: If you don't have a will, I urge you to make one! Make that a number one priority. Otherwise, your personal effects might very well be distributed according to the laws of your state.

I've included some of these personal accounts to show you what can happen. Make your own prearrangements. Don't put it off too long. And when it's done, you can forget about it and get on with your life. Your survivors will appreciate this loving kindness more than you can imagine.

I have come to believe that the least painful and most effective, lasting grief recovery will come to those of us who begin to prepare ourselves in advance for the time ahead when we will each have to face the loss of loved ones.

Doing that is not being morbid. It is being honest and realistic.

TWENTY-NINE

Now That the Chair Is Empty

Now is your time of grief.
John 16:22 NIV

After my loss I was not aware that there were steps I could take to help myself. Most of the people I speak to now have the same misconception. This is one of the compelling reasons for writing this book.

I've often heard that the greatest fear of mankind is the fear of being abandoned. Haven't we all felt abandoned at some time or other? Isn't feeling abandoned a major part of grief? Isn't this the cruelest of all abandonments? There's no other way to rationalize it, we have been left behind, and we have been left alone. For the moment—for many moments—we have lost control of our lives, our futures, our joys, at least for a while. And as we pace from room to room, our wounds still raw, our chests heavy with aching hearts, that empty chair, that symbol of bereavement, sits there, mockingly, a daily reminder affirming our loss and our anguish. The empty chair is a silent symbol that our lives will never, ever be the same again.

Just one glance in its direction is enough to make our knees buckle, our tears flow, our minds ache. We face it in the morning when we go down to breakfast. We face it in the evening when we sit down to dinner. We face it in the library as we try to concentrate on the evening news. We face it in the living room, in the bedroom, on the patio.

And in our minds? Yes, the empty chair is always in our minds—this soundless, tormenting, dreaded empty chair. We can't move it or hide it or avoid it or pretend it isn't there. So how do we continue, day after day, to face it and still keep our sanity?

We begin by making that chair our own. We sit down right in the middle of it—right there in the room with our grief. We sit in the chair and look our grief right in the eye. Feel it! Face it! Challenge it! And stop being afraid of it. Let grief reign for awhile. Experience it. Let it pull us, tear us, tug and toss us. We give grief its day and soon we'll have ours. Then we can make some important decisions about ourselves and our future.

This is the way it is with grief. There's no way around it, or over it, or under it. The only way to survive grief is by walking *through* it— yes, through it. Step by step, moment by moment, day by day, like the spent winds of a sudden storm, finally grief's fury is no more; and then comes the calm. Then you will look back and say, *I have met and mastered my grief. I have made it to the other side.*

> *Yea, though I walk through the valley of the shadow of death, I will fear no evil: for thou art with me; thy rod and thy staff they comfort me.*
>
> Ps. 23:4 KJV

Do you believe this? I believed it, but I never really understood it until I needed to know what it meant. It was after my loss that I desperately needed to know, for as never before I needed comfort.

Since logic plays no role in the early days of grief, it didn't help when I tried to comfort myself with thoughts like *Well, be thankful you still have the rest of your family,* because my heart had stopped listening to my mind. It seems that when we are grieving we can think only of the one who is gone, not of those who remain. The single thought we have is that our loved one is suddenly gone and there is no way to find him or her ever again. We're still here but now he or she is *there.* But where is there? Where's the loved one gone? What is he or she doing in this new setting? We have many questions. Our world has been turned upside down. Nothing makes any sense anymore. Nothing works. Some days nothing even matters.

It's almost like the dream we've all dreamed, the one in which we suddenly realize we are lost. There are no familiar faces, no recognizable streets or places. We feel disoriented and out of touch with the things we learned to trust in life. We feel afraid and alone. We desperately need reassurances and answers. But many of us receive no reassurances; we hear no answers.

In her book, *To Live Again,* Catherine Marshall describes the same kind of experience and how desperate she was for reassurance and answers. "In a childlike way I began pleading with God for some glimpse of Peter, for some knowledge of his new setting, of what he was doing. The response came in a vivid dream. It was a dream with a self-authenticating quality. Now, years later, every detail is still clear. Of no other single dream in my life can I say that. I also learned from it some of the details of the life we are to lead after death that have rung true with the testing of time. In the dream I was allowed to visit Peter in his new setting. First I searched for him in a large rambling house with many rooms and airy porches. There were crowds of people about, but Peter was not among them.

"Then I sought him in the yard. Finally, at some distance, I saw him. 'I'd recognize that characteristic gesture—that certain toss of the head any time,' I thought, as I began running toward him. I found myself able to run with a freedom I had not known since childhood. My body was light; my feet were sure. As I drew nearer I saw that Peter was working in a rose garden. He saw me coming and stood, leaning on his spade, waiting for me. I rushed into his arms. Laughing, he pulled me close and rubbed his nose on mine."

God answered Catherine's prayer: Peter in a rose garden. How perfect. How comforting. Many of us, like Catherine Marshall, long to know where our loved ones are and what they are doing. We may feel somewhat frightened or abandoned because they've gone on and we have been left behind, left to persevere. We find ourselves standing at the gate to nowhere, feeling frightened and isolated. And we hate it. We hate all of it. We can't find the path back to the good old days where love and security were a way of life. We can't find a way back because, as I've mentioned before, *we aren't supposed to go back. We cannot go back and we must begin to accept that.*

This is the point we miss in those early days of grief. We're supposed to move on with our lives. But who feels ready to do that? Who can do it? "Not me," we say. "Not yet." And that's okay. We don't have to take on tomorrow immediately or the rest of our lives. We have to take on just today or just the next few minutes. The minute-by-minute we can handle for a while. We don't have to take on any more. Let's not even try.

Don't worry today about your strength for tomorrow either. God gives us strength for today, for the challenge of the next moment. We need to remember that. It is all we need to know. It's all we need to receive.

It's so easy to think: *How can I go through life now without him? How can I ever live without her?* (I asked myself these questions over and over. It doesn't help. It hinders. But I didn't know any better then.) Rather we must learn to adjust so that we can live the next minute without him or her. This you and I can do.

One thing I learned after my loss was that we have to treat ourselves and our recovery as an important project for a while. Most of us have difficulty deciding that taking care of ourselves isn't selfish, but it isn't. In a sense we must become our own caregivers. We have to feed us, and exercise us, and at times, even put us to bed. At least we have to do these things until we are strong and well again. Sometimes we even have to push us out the front door to get us involved in life again—often before the griever in us thinks we're ready. In a sense, we become both puppet and puppeteer.

This is how we begin. And we do it by putting one foot in front of the other, one step at a time. It sounds simple; it isn't. But we can learn to do it. And as we begin to overcome, as we face our fears and our grief, minute by minute, He is there to give us the strength we need. You may doubt and wonder about this truth at times. Most of us have. But He *is* there. When you reach the frontier of your need, He will fill you with His strength. Still He does not do for us what we can and must learn to do for ourselves.

> Jesus commanded the lame man,
> > *"Rise, take up thy bed, and walk."*
> > > John 5:8 KJV

> To the man with a withered hand He said,
> > *"Stretch forth thine hand."*
> > > Matt. 12:13 KJV

> To the blind man He whispered softly,
> > *"Go, wash in the pool of Siloam."*
> > > John 9:7 KJV

In the early days of my grief I spent many hours sitting alone in our music room with a head full of spiritual truths, but with not a clue as to what I could do physically to help myself. I have driven along the crest of a mountain encouraging myself with thoughts that began *maybe if I did this* . . . or *perhaps if I tried that.* . . . But all the while my heart was empty of my Lord.

I've felt the scales tilt out of balance in both directions. I know now that such imbalance is not the way to healing. The important thing in recovery is a blending of human footsteps with the direction of the Divine. We have spiritual needs, but as human beings living on earth, we also have human needs. We may have kids to feed or bills to pay or illness to cope with. And sometimes we have hearts that ache.

I believe we restrict or postpone our grief recovery if we attend to one aspect of it and ignore the other. Go with God; don't try to do it without Him. But we also need to make the human motions. We've got to put one foot in front of the other. The most effective and permanent grief recovery comes to those of us who strike a balance between our work and the Lord's work.

> *Yea, though I walk through the valley of the shadow of death, I will fear no evil: for thou art with me; thy rod and thy staff they comfort me.*
>
> Ps. 23:4 KJV

But how? When? Just what is the rod? And what does the staff have to do with my grief? I wondered too. I was especially curious about the spiritual significance of the rod and the staff. How could they be used to comfort the bereaved? I wondered about the human application. And so I began a study of this magnificent psalm. And the Lord, being who He is, guided me to my answers.

When Jesus was with us, and teaching in parables as He so often did, He would use a natural phenomenon to give us a spiritual truth. As we would grasp one, we would understand the other. Let's read this psalm from the shepherd's point of view. And then let's find the spiritual truth in it.

Among those of us living during this century, few have had an opportunity to observe or understand the intimate relationship between a shepherd and his flock. Missing this, possibly we have overlooked the true significance of the Twenty-third Psalm. And if we were raised in suburban settings, probably we also had no way of becoming familiar with the management of land or livestock. We have no way of knowing about the characteristics of a flock of sheep. Most likely we have never thought about how a good shepherd keeps his flock moving, or how he protects them, or why they need green pastures and still water.

David, the psalmist, was both a shepherd and the son of a shepherd. He knew everything about protecting his flock. As we learn more about David and his frame of reference, this psalm suddenly takes on new meaning. Its message of spiritual comfort inspires us as we find our way through grief recovery. It wasn't until I began an in-depth study of this psalm that I learned why the shepherd must anoint his flock with oil, why he takes them through the valley, and how he deals with a wandering, wayward member of his flock. And it wasn't until I began this study that I learned that the rod and staff have everything to do with comfort and healing. Now, for me, they have come to illustrate the perfect blend of the human with the Divine. From the spiritual standpoint, the rod is a symbol for God's Word, and the staff is a symbol for the Holy Spirit.

Looking at it from a human point of view through the eyes of a shepherd, the rod is a weapon for defense. The staff is a tool for guidance and reassurance. During grief recovery, it's very helpful to use both images, the human and the spiritual.

> *Rise, take up thy bed, and walk.*

For a little while, let's become children again. Let's experience the nature of the true Comforter. Let us look at the relationship between the shepherd and his lamb.

In his beautifully written and illustrated book, *A Shepherd Looks at Psalm 23,* Phillip Keller, an experienced shepherd, tells us that during the time this psalm was written, when a shepherd was afield with his flock, he could carry only the barest of essentials: his rod and his staff.

The shepherd considered his rod, his main weapon of defense, an extension of his arm. He relied on it to guard himself from danger. It was a symbol of his strength, authority, and power, and when necessary, he used it to discipline wandering, wayward sheep and to protect his flock from danger, repelling dogs, coyotes, and snakes. With the touch of the rod he protected the flock.

With the touch of His Rod, the symbol of His Word, God, the Master Shepherd, protects us. When we study His Word, He speaks to us, touches us, comforts us—protects us.

Only a shepherd carried a staff. It was usually a long slender stick with a crook on one end, shaped to meet the shepherd's own individual needs. Often the staff was used to lift up a baby lamb if it had become separated from its mother, and then used to place it gently back alongside the dam. The shepherd could move the lamb without touching it with his hands and avoid leaving his scent on the lamb. He wanted to eliminate any risk that the dam might reject her lamb. The shepherd also used his staff to guide and reassure his flock as they moved down a new path, perhaps a dangerous one, and to reach out to bring a shy or timid lamb near to him for close inspection. With the touch of the staff, he reassured his flock.

With the touch of His staff, which is the Holy Spirit, He reassures us. Our precious Father tenderly leads us down our new and difficult paths saying, "This is the way, walk ye in it." His Spirit continually guides our spirits. Through His Word our Comforter guides those of us who need to be comforted with the touch of His staff. And in our times of need, our Shepherd brings knowledge and wisdom—spiritual nourishment—to you and to me. Oh how we need this nourishment!

"I will not leave you comfortless," our Lord promises. To this we say, "Search me, O God, and know my heart." He knows the condition of our hearts. He also knows how to heal them.

Often we have heard healing grievers say, "Something was holding me up," or "Someone was there helping me." In the beginning God supplies our strength and courage. As we work through our grief, we become stronger. As we use our courage, it begins to strengthen and increase. We realize we no longer need to feel we are adrift. We have *not* been abandoned. He is there guiding and supporting us. We can feel safe again. And soon we will also feel strong again.

So take a new grip with your tired hands, stand firm on your shaky legs, and mark out a straight, smooth path for your feet so that those who follow you, though weak and lame, will not fall and hurt themselves but become strong.

Heb. 12:12–13 TLB

Put yourself in the care of His rod, the Word, and His staff, the Holy Spirit, and be at peace. Then rest in the presence and sweet assurance of His tenderness and care. We can think of it as a crossroad. It is the perfect time to begin to trust Him as never before and then to experience the excitement of following Him. But first we have to stop doing things our way and try His. Aren't we all under His sealed orders? How can we follow our Lord unless we pledge Him our total obedience? Become as a child again. Become His lamb. Follow your Shepherd, for God has said, "I will never, never fail you nor forsake you."

In the final analysis, your grief recovery depends on *you,* just as mine depended on *me.* God is there to guide you toward recovery and He will do many things for you, in you, through you, as you begin taking those first steps to help yourself. But remember, you must do your part. Just as Christ expected the lame man to pick up his bed and walk, you too must make your own human effort. We each have spirits, but we also have human hearts. We have souls, but we also have human minds. All of us need to be nurtured for future use. Under God's direction, under the care and protection of His rod and staff, let's begin.

Thy rod and thy staff they comfort me. He gently lifts us from our beds of pain.

Thou preparest a table before me in the presence of mine enemies. Even while our enemies—grief, pain, and devastation— are present, He attends to our needs.

Thou anointest my head with oil. He pours His Spirit into our spirits.

My cup runneth over. He continues to fill us with His spirit until our grief and sorrow have been washed away.

Surely goodness and mercy shall follow me all the days of my life; and I will dwell in the house of the Lord for ever.

The Living Bible paraphrases this psalm with very comforting promises:

Because the Lord is my Shepherd, I have everything I need! He lets me rest in the meadow grass and leads me beside the quiet streams. He restores my failing health. He helps me do what honors him the most. Isn't this our mission? Especially now?

Even when walking through the dark valley of death I will not be afraid, for you are close beside me, guarding, guiding all the way. Help us to always remember this, Lord.

Because the Lord is our Shepherd, we have everything we need. He promises rest and restoration, that He will guard us, feed us, guide us, that we will be the recipients of goodness and unfailing kindness, and that we will live in the house of the Lord forever.

Does this mean that God will move upon the sorrows of our minds, filling the voids with His love? Does this mean that soon we can begin to put our tears behind us, moving out into new life, un-afraid and whole, and that one day we will even smile again?

Yes, this *is* what it means, and so much more. What a promise! What comfort! Let Him anoint you. Ask Him to take over. Hold nothing back, because when we ask, we receive. This is the Lord's promise. This is the way of Love.

His anointing may be the grace to get through the next day, the courage to let your tears flow without apology, the strength to rise up from your bed of grief and walk free. Remember He said to one in need, *"Pick up your bed and walk."* His message is the same for us today.

If you are anguishing over an empty chair, let go and let His peace begin to enfold and surround you. Put your hand in His and let Him lead you from loneliness to solitude. Invite Him to join you in that solitude, for the One who is greater than any other promises that He will always be beside us, that we need only to reach out and He is there. In my desperation I reached out to Him as never before, and He has made my life a benediction. He is waiting for you. Just talk to Him. It's so easy. And so comforting. Go ahead. Talk. He is listening.

Lord Jesus, come now and sit beside me, right here in the empty chair.

THIRTY

And Jesus Went Forth

*Most assuredly, I say to you that you will weep and lament, . . .
and you will be sorrowful, but your sorrow will be turned into joy.*

John 16:20

"And Jesus went forth." I never paid much attention to what those four words really mean until after my loss, when I began to search for new meaning in every facet of my life.

After John the Baptist's death, Jesus longed to go away and hide Himself, to be alone with His grief. But the crowds were always following Him, making it virtually impossible for Him to retreat to the desert to mourn His lost cousin and good friend. Instead of hiding and allowing Himself to plunge headlong into grieving, He "went forth." He went out among the crowds, ministering to their needs and ignoring His own.

Those of us who have felt the sting of death have spent long winters of devastating grief, experiencing every facet of its pain. We, too, can come forth again, although changed, bringing new resolve and armed with new purpose.

You read in chapter 8 about the death of little Annie. Do you recall the wise words Denny spoke to Terry when she told him she thought she couldn't ever be happy again? Did he understand? Yes, he did. The baby was his child too, and he was hurting just as much. But he also understood something else. He knew that he and Terry needed to heal. Lovingly he said to her, "You have to want to get over your grief and you have to work at it." And she began to do her grief work. She began to write, recording the things she wanted to remember, like Annie's personality traits and various little anecdotes. Terry decided to reinvest in her life and its experiences. She took walks; she made an effort to thank the people who had been so kind to them. She began to face those emotional situations that were so stressful.

And she forced herself to get out into the world again, to stop isolating herself. She went forth.

Dear friend, don't closet yourself at home. Don't allow yourself to hide with your pain. Find a reason to get out of the house or an excuse to get up in the morning. And (this may sound strange, but it is very important) you must continue to feed your body. If you can't sit at the same table just yet, you can fix a tray. Or you can call a friend and say, "I need to be with someone. Let's go out for dinner." We're all aware of the benefit of discussing a problem with a friend; often just expressing our thoughts aloud brings a new solution. What we need is someone to just listen for awhile. We all need human closeness in our lives. Make the first move yourself if need be. Right now your friends may feel awkward approaching you.

And talk to your loved one.

Remember in chapter 19 the night Marlene missed Dave so much she thought she couldn't bear it. "I got his picture," she told us, "and sat it in front of me on the coffee table, and I started talking to him. And while I was talking I could feel a stirring over my entire body. Somehow I knew Dave was there listening to what I was saying."

And remember in chapter 13 when V. J. got up early one morning feeling that she was supposed to do something? She took her little dog, Ziggy, and headed for the Santa Rosa mountains and then, up there on that mountain top, she talked to Peter. She told him everything—what it had been like since he'd been gone and about her fears, anger, and sorrow.

And at the end she said, "And if I could change anything since you died I'd change . . . I'd . . . why, I wouldn't change anything. I'm glad for everything I went through, because now I don't have to go through it anymore." She went out and faced her pain head on. V. J. went forth.

I talked out loud too, and it helped. "Mother," I asked, "how did you make it after Daddy and Russ died?" Then I remembered her garden. She got up and forced herself out the back door and went into her garden, and there she worked. She dug and planted and raked, and then she dug some more.

She talked to God in that garden. And she talked to her lost husband and her lost son, whose plane exploded somewhere on a mountaintop in Vietnam. Often she would forget to stop and eat, but later in the day, when she walked back into her empty house, she was blessedly exhausted—physically and emotionally. She would bathe and put on something pretty, even though her man was no longer there to see her. And she would eat, always on her nice china, always on a place mat, always with a linen napkin. Then she would be tired enough to sleep—one of the things that is often difficult after a loss.

That is how she did it. She dug her way to freedom right there in God's sweet earth.

And now, *how about you?* How are you going to do it? At this moment you needn't know exactly. You just need to know that you will. I knew that the way through my grief would not be found digging in a garden. I had to find my own way—just as you must.

Don't be dismayed if your mind tries to tempt you into some bizarre behavior. Just don't follow it! There were even days when I would try to fool myself by pretending that Mother was still alive, that she wasn't around because she was back in Indiana visiting friends. I desperately tried anything to escape the unceasing bombardment of the piercing emotional pain.

I had to reach out and ask for the Lord's help. I even got down on my knees and gave Him the rest of my life. And He took it. Now He is patiently showing me how to use it. "But I have no talents," we say. God isn't looking for our talents; He's looking for our poverty. That is where He works best—in the fresh, fertile soil of a committed life.

"He took unto Him the twelve," and who did He choose for His twelve to instruct in His name, to represent Him, to carry His message forward? He chose a middle-aged, unpredictable, rough-cut fisherman who had lived a tough life; two successful brothers, fishermen known for their large catches and their astute business dealings; a leader of the underground, who was an impetuous, irritable, at times even violent, man; and his opposite, a cautious, deliberate, doubting man. He chose a rich tax collector, a racketeer, a man who was impressed by wealth and who had made money a god. He gathered together twelve regular guys and they had more influence on the future of our world than any other group of men in the history of mankind. He said, "You have not chosen Me, I have chosen you."

When you ask God to move into the void in your life, He'll do it. Then He'll show you His world and your place in it. Remember, He did not promise to deliver us out of trouble. He promised to deliver us *in* our trouble. He promised to guide and help us. This is the way of the Lord. And always acknowledging our free will, He goes where He's invited.

Perhaps now is the time for you to ask Him into your life. It is so simple: "Father, show me Your will for my life—my life after loss. Show me what I can do for You, Lord." Ask Him aloud or silently. However you ask, He will honor your prayer. Wherever you are, He will hear you and respond. He will hear your heart speak.

So many times I thought, *Lord, where are You now? How can You let me suffer like this? Won't You take my pain away?* Why didn't it occur to me that He was suffering too? Why didn't I remember that when we hurt, He hurts? Why didn't I remember that He knows all about suffering and pain?

Why didn't it occur to me that He was there beside me, helping me carry my burden? Hasn't He told us to cast our burdens on Him? Hasn't He promised to bind up our wounded spirits, to wipe away all tears from our eyes? These are not hollow words. These are promises of truth and hope. These are His commitments to you and to me.

Didn't He say that He will make all things new again? Then, could He make me new again? Can He make you new again? Surely He can do all these things and more. Why didn't it occur to me that perhaps something good could grow from my pain and suffering— that out of the ashes of fire and torment could emerge a new person, perhaps one who is stronger and wiser, ready to move in new directions, ready to live a more meaningful life?

I overlooked the obvious because, like so many of us, I could not think clearly in those early days of grief. But He was there beside me all along as I struggled down the long, lonely halls of grief, unaware that an end to the pain would finally come. But there could be no freedom until I had fully tasted the bitter gall of grief and drunk openly from its cup of sorrow.

In my desperation I reached out and I just asked Him to show me what I should do with the rest of my life. It was as simple as that. And He did make me new again. He helped me as I struggled to get myself back together so I could follow the path He laid out before me.

Until now you have not asked for anything in my name. Ask and you will receive, and your joy will be complete.
                                                        John 16:24 NIV

I was shocked and even a bit dismayed when I heard the silent command, "It's time to get to work."

Wait a minute, Lord. I'm not ready for this yet. I'm still grieving. I seriously wondered if I could go back again.

Can we go back? No, we don't go back, do we? We can't. We just think at times that we do, or we try to. And then we have to re-learn what we already knew: Living is a forward motion. We have been inexorably changed by our loss—changed in many ways we haven't yet discovered. Our whole life's focus has been altered or blown apart. We are not the same person we were before our loss, and we cannot go back to living in the old ways.

We may live in the same house or work in the same building or talk to the same people, but we are different now. Our loss has made us into something new. Some days we may feel terrified of the new person growing inside of us or irritated by the person we can no longer count on at times or control or at times even like. But the afterloss me and the afterloss you is who we are now, who we have become.

If you believe deep in your heart that your life and your happiness ended the day your loved one died, I want to bring you hope. And if you believe there isn't much left in your world now but loneliness and grief, I want to offer you a new perspective. If a thief suddenly appeared at your door, you would not willingly allow him to rob you of your present assets or those of your future, would you? In the same way, we must not allow another kind of thief, grief, to rob us of the future, ours without our loved one, when we can find a new sense of peace and contentment if we do our grief work now. We must not allow this thief to rob us of our chances to become whole again.

Unresolved grief robs us of future peace and contentment. It actually steals life in that a person may be living but isn't alive. That almost happened to me. Don't let it happen to you. When that thief of grief comes knocking at your door, don't give up all you are to this intruder. Don't give him your chance to live again, or your chance to love again, or your future. Don't give him your *you*.

Our Lord charged, "Get thee behind me, Satan!" We too must learn to say, "Move along, thief. I have something worth saving, something worth fighting for." That something is your *you*. It's my *me*. It's the force of our lives. We will need it for the days and years ahead. We don't need to know precisely how to use that force right now, we just need to remember that it's there, that it belongs to us, that it's valuable.

All during the period of my grief work, I talked to myself. I said:

You'll bring no honor to the legacy of her life by hiding.

Are you going to spend the rest of your life running safe little errands?

So what if you do break down and cry?

Your family needs you to be there for them again.

Focus on the world of the living, not on the world of the dead.

Start focusing on what you have, not on what you've lost.

You are wasting your life!

Pursue the things you care about but be selective.

You need to find out who you are now that she is gone.

Lord, please help me!

In my own way and in His time, I began to creep out of the shell I'd been hiding in and began to "go forth." It wasn't easy. And it certainly wasn't any fun. It was empty and lonely and even frightening at times. But remember that it was there, in that once empty office of mine, in that new environment that I had created for myself, that the idea for *Afterloss* came into being. It took root in the new soil that I had turned when I struggled to find my new self after my loss.

The lyrics from Neil Diamond's exquisite song, "You Don't Bring Me Flowers," come to mind again: "Used-to-be's don't count any more." It's important for us to identify and begin to sort out our own "used-to-be's." All of us have our beautiful memories to savor, to hold close to our hearts. Nothing, including time, can take them from us. Memories caress us with gentle comfort, and they are ours to remember and cherish forever.

If we have loved and have been loved in return, we have climbed the highest peak. "And the greatest of these is love." Our memories are like the wheat, bringing us strength and renewal. But we must learn to separate the wheat from the chaff. We must begin to separate the memories from the used-to-be's. This stays, but that goes. This is the wheat, but that is the chaff. This is a memory, but that is a part of my past, a used-to-be. We can no longer live with used-to-be's. Let them fade away.

As we begin to prune and separate and put aside our used-to-be's, we slowly back away from the past and begin to move forward, discovering new reasons for being alive and new vistas to explore until that time when we shall all meet again. Soon, maybe not today if your grief is still fresh but perhaps next week or next month, it will be time for you to begin to go forth too.

Do what you know you must do.

Don't hide. Make a commitment to yourself, or to your family, or to your lost loved one, and especially to God, to try. All that waits at the end of the rainbow for those of us who do not go forth is loneliness, anguish, and despair. And we already know about them.

So give Him your hand, your todays, your tomorrows. Give Him your grief, and He will give you His peace.

Jesus went forth, and now, so can you. Follow Him.

ed under its aged oak beams. And there were sundry other
utbuildings and even a beautiful pond bordered with bullrushes.

We moved our family into that old farm house, built stalls in the
d white barn, and raised our children in an atmosphere of health,
appiness, and hard work. Appropriately we named our home "Wal-
n." We left the "jet set" for the "horse set" and traded the Cadillac
r a truck. We went from silver forks to pitch-forks; we moved from
e conference table to a dinner table (an old oak one with funny
aw feet). We exchanged office hours for round-the-clock hours and
aded our alarm clock for a rooster. We stopped chasing airplanes
d began chasing horses; we moved our office from a designer
uilding into a converted garage, and traded lunches at The Club for
ndwiches prepared on our own homemade bread.

A son we named Christian was born in our farmhouse home while
s brothers and sisters waited on the other side of the bedroom door
greet him. After Christian's peaceful birth, the young doctor re-
rned the envelope my husband had given to him. "Oh, I *couldn't*
ke any pay," he explained. "It would spoil the joy of my first deliv-
y!"

Those were halcyon days—days filled with challenge and hard
ork. Those were days of freedom and happy hearts. We took con-
ol of our time, took charge of our own production, and reclaimed
ur lives. And we learned many lessons during those challenging
ears, two of which are *the importance of freedom and the value of
me.*

We've always placed a high value on our time but have paid only
ight attention to the exactness of the hour, that is until almost six
ears ago here in California. Since then, we've always known when
's 3:05 P.M. sharp. We had moved next door to a very nice couple.
oy and his wife lived in the last house on the lane, the house that
utts right up to the side of the mountain. And every afternoon at
recisely 3:00 P.M., Roy left his house to walk his dogs, Bo, Mike,
nd Precious. (Yep, Precious). Bo, the tall, black, standard poodle;
Mike, the short, white-haired something-or-other; and the little
ainty one who, as you may have guessed, answers to "Precious." I
ouldn't even attempt to describe her lineage. A motley crew indeed.

It would take Roy and his three dogs five minutes to reach our
ate. Our dogs would wait all day for this moment. The ceremony
tself actually began about 2:45 with a short prelude. First they'd
ace. Then three dogs would take the back of the house and two
ogs the front, each watching carefully from a different window.

THIRTY-ONE

The Road of the Rest
of Our Lives

Thou wilt make known to me the path of life.
Ps. 16:11 NASV

. . . And when she finally looked up she could see a long, v
stretching out into the horizon. And she knew that this m
road of the rest of her life. And she saw the road begin an
saw it end. And she came to understand the message sl
gather that night: that we must not in any way waste the
the road of the rest of our lives.

Almost a century and a half ago, Henry Thoreau, the
ist and writer, in his quest for freedom chose to l
chaos and pace of the world for the simplicity of the
Later he wrote about his reasons: "I went to the woods b
wished to live deliberately, to front only the essential facts of
see if I could not learn what it had to teach, and not, when I
die, discover that I had not lived."

Twenty-two years ago, we left too! And we were also searc
freedom. But we left a much more cynical world, a more
pace, a more warped and distorted system of values. And, lil
reau, we found freedom—exactly fifteen acres of freedom. H
instead of finding it in the woods, we found it in the countr
farm, a horse farm.

We found freedom bordered by white, wooden fences. We
fields of green peace where children could roam with golden
ers and quarter horses; we found a century-old farm house
and serene under the shade of a huge willow tree. There was
nificent three-story barn where, later, two daughters would b

They'd signal back and forth as dogs somehow do. About 2:50 they'd move into position, each one posted like a sentry beside a glass door. And there they'd sit like statues and wait. At 3:00 they'd stand up and begin getting restless and at last, *exactly* at 3:05 P.M., when their moment had finally arrived, they'd go into wild ecstasy, jumping, spinning, sometimes sitting on each others' heads, anything to get someone to open the door so they could tear out, stand by the gate, and bark their heads off.

This ridiculous ritual has been going on for almost six years. That is until three days ago. That day at 2:30 P.M., our dogs seemed to sense that something had changed. There was no pacing. There was no running to the doors or watching out the windows. All five dogs moped around the house. Somehow they seemed to know that Roy and their dog friends would not be walking by the gate that day. Somehow they seemed to sense a fact that we had yet to learn—Roy died the night before.

For our friend Roy, gone were the lazy afternoon walks. Gone were the mountains and the songs of the birds. Gone was the warmth of the midday sun and the camaraderie of the motley crew.

And once again, the importance of time moved sharply into focus, like a thunderclap.

Why is it that everything in life seems to have a bottom line, including time? And the bottom line in this case is the indisputable fact that, like Roy, we will all be leaving here one day. And until that day, we have something very precious: a span of time, a span of time between now and then that I call *the long white road of the rest of our lives* because this is the way God has taught me to think about it. I can see it in my mind, stretching out there ahead. Untraveled. Unmarked. Uncluttered. Fresh and clean and new. Filled with opportunities. Filled with promise. Filled with Him!

Have you ever wondered what's waiting for you on your road? I've been walking on mine for a little over three years now. At times, looking back, I can hardly believe some of the things that have occurred and yet I know they did. I was there! Three years ago I thought I would never again know happiness, know the way it feels to smile, know the joy of laughing aloud. At first I thought that grief was the cross I would have to bear for the rest of my life. But instead, *grief was the cross that led me to a closer relationship with Him* and the subsequent birth of the *Afterloss* ministry. I also thought I was permanently trapped in my grief prison. But instead, He offered me the key that led to my freedom when He sent me back to work. In the middle of my struggle with grief, I found a beautiful gift—the gift of knowing my Lord in a whole new way.

Many others who have shared their stories of recovery in this book have also found unexpected gifts. Florence, who lost her teenage son in a plane crash and later her husband by divorce, continued on with her education, entered law school and graduated, and is now in a thriving law practice. Terry and Denny now have three beautiful little boys. Toni has one, too. Sharon went back to school, graduated from college, and is now in her English Master's program. Julianne remarried (after she told us it was okay to be single). And Diane is working as an editor of a Christian school newsletter along with us in the *Afterloss* Recovery Program. Shirley is teaching in Tokyo and plans to be in this country in May. David and Scott are both working as senior staff for members of Congress in our nation's capital. Georgann has gone forth to help upgrade airline safety. And V. J. has resumed her singing career, in addition to conducting interviews for her daily radio program. She recently announced her engagement.

All of these have found gifts in their loss. Just as I did, they have discovered something new either in themselves or in their lives after they lost their loved ones, after they made the decision to rededicate themselves to their futures. These people have triumphed over tragedy.

It may seem strange to call them triumphant, but be assured that those of us who have suffered the trauma of losing a loved one and little by little, moment by moment, step by step have come up from the depths of despair once again know how it feels to be part of the human race. And that's the triumph!

My mind slips back over the past four years and embraces the many heroic, grieving people I've met. And as I study the faces in the pictures of some of their loved ones—a baby girl, a baby son, an older son, a grown daughter, a husband, a father, a brother, a mother—my heart goes out to each of these brave survivors who have, in spite of their pain, learned how to go on with their lives. They've learned how to trust again, how to love again, how to *live* again, how to go forth.

Rereading these twenty-two stories in Book Two is an indescribable experience. These accounts of such tremendous loss and pain made me wonder if so much pain should be contained in one book. *Lord, how much pain can a person bear?* But He kept sending more and more people across my path.

I recall each touching story told often through painful tears. I remember, too, the prayers that were silently offered as each loss was described. I think about the harsh sentence of grief that was inflicted on each survivor. I am comforted and grateful to be able to tell you that not one of these prisoners allowed their sentence to become a lifetime condition. They valiantly fought their way to freedom. And so can you.

Each one of the survivors told me that writing about their loss was an experience filled with deep emotional pain, and that they cried off and on during the whole time they were writing. Lorene and Elizabeth almost gave up on telling their stories, both saying, "I just *can't* relive all of that pain again." But somehow the Lord convinced them that they could (or should). Sharon locked herself in her bedroom all one weekend and wrote. A note came yesterday from Shirley in Toyko saying, "I cried buckets—but strength came from writing it. I know you understand."

Do you wonder why? Because each survivor wants to share what they discovered during their journey—it is their serenade to freedom—and they all are saying just about the same thing: *there is a life to be lived after a loss and that life can be good again.*

Freedom waits while we discover that we can't go back to living the way we did before our loss. Freedom waits as we watch and learn from those who have blazed the trail before us. Freedom waits as we learn to channel our pain and sadness into new directions.

There is an open road waiting out there for each of us. It's our uncluttered, clean tomorrows. It's the road of the rest of our lives, the road we no longer have to walk alone unless we choose to. It's the road where blame and guilt and fear no longer walk beside us. It's the road of freedom.

This is the road we walk with God, where we dwell in His promises, walk in His light. We can put our burdens down now, trade our sadness for a new peace—the peace that only God can give, and walk out into the night, unafraid.

> Oh, let the song of God enfold you.
> Let Him have the things that hold you.
> Let Him fill your heart and satisfy your soul.
> Give Him all your years of sadness,
> And all your years of pain,
> And you'll enter into life in Jesus' name.
> —J. Wimber

Epilogue

The *Afterloss*® Credo

I need to talk about my loss.

I may often feel the need to tell you what happened—or to ask you *why* it happened. I am struggling with many *whys*. I may need to ask this question again and again until either I find the answer or I am able to accept the fact that there is no answer.

**I may frequently need for you to listen while
I explain what this loss means to me.**

Each time I discuss my loss, I am helping myself to face the reality of the death of my loved one. I may cry when I talk about my loss . . . I hope you don't mind and I hope you won't feel too uncomfortable. Tears are an important part of my recovery, tears also help to relieve my stress. You may want to cry along with me. It's very comforting when you do.

**Try not to judge me now—or think that I'm behaving strangely.
Remember that I'm grieving. I may even be in shock.**

I am struggling to cope with many frightening thoughts and unwanted feelings, and to live in a world that now no longer includes my loved one. I may feel overwhelmed. I may feel afraid, I may even feel guilty. I may also feel rage or deep despair. And I may confuse easily. I may realize I am becoming more and more forgetful, and at times I may even believe that I am losing my mind. But above all, I hurt. Grief is a pain that is unlike any pain I have ever felt in my life.

**I need to know that you care about me. I need
to feel your touch, your hugs.**

But don't worry over what to say to me about my loss. I won't remember anyhow. I need you just to be *with* me. (And I need to be with you.) And please don't leave me alone for long periods of time feeling that your presence would be an intrusion. More than ever

NOTES

NOTES

Epilogue

The *Afterloss*® Credo

I need to talk about my loss.

I may often feel the need to tell you what happened—or to ask you *why* it happened. I am struggling with many *whys*. I may need to ask this question again and again until either I find the answer or I am able to accept the fact that there is no answer.

I may frequently need for you to listen while I explain what this loss means to me.

Each time I discuss my loss, I am helping myself to face the reality of the death of my loved one. I may cry when I talk about my loss . . . I hope you don't mind and I hope you won't feel too uncomfortable. Tears are an important part of my recovery, tears also help to relieve my stress. You may want to cry along with me. It's very comforting when you do.

Try not to judge me now—or think that I'm behaving strangely. Remember that I'm grieving. I may even be in shock.

I am struggling to cope with many frightening thoughts and un-wanted feelings, and to live in a world that now no longer includes my loved one. I may feel overwhelmed. I may feel afraid, I may even feel guilty. I may also feel rage or deep despair. And I may confuse easily. I may realize I am becoming more and more forgetful, and at times I may even believe that I am losing my mind. But above all, I hurt. Grief is a pain that is unlike any pain I have ever felt in my life.

I need to know that you care about me. I need to feel your touch, your hugs.

But don't worry over what to say to me about my loss. I won't remember anyhow. I need you just to be *with* me. (And I need to be with you.) And please don't leave me alone for long periods of time feeling that your presence would be an intrusion. More than ever member, too, the prayers that were silently offered as each loss was described. I think about the harsh sentence of grief that was inflicted on each survivor. I am comforted and grateful to be able to tell you that not one of these prisoners allowed their sentence to become a lifetime condition. They valiantly fought their way to freedom. And so can you.

Each one of the survivors told me that writing about their loss was an experience filled with deep emotional pain, and that they cried off and on during the whole time they were writing. Lorene and Elizabeth almost gave up on telling their stories, both saying, "I just *can't* relive all of that pain again." But somehow the Lord convinced them that they could (or should). Sharon locked herself in her bedroom all one weekend and wrote. A note came yesterday from Shirley in Toyko saying, "I cried buckets—but strength came from writing it. I know you understand."

Do you wonder why? Because each survivor wants to share what they discovered during their journey—it is their serenade to freedom—and they all are saying just about the same thing: *there is a life to be lived after a loss and that life can be good again.*

Freedom waits while we discover that we can't go back to living the way we did before our loss. Freedom waits as we watch and learn from those who have blazed the trail before us. Freedom waits as we learn to channel our pain and sadness into new directions.

There is an open road waiting out there for each of us. It's our uncluttered, clean tomorrows. It's the road of the rest of our lives, the road we no longer have to walk alone unless we choose to. It's the road where blame and guilt and fear no longer walk beside us. It's the road of freedom.

This is the road we walk with God, where we dwell in His promises, walk in His light. We can put our burdens down now, trade our sadness for a new peace—the peace that only God can give, and walk out into the night, unafraid.

> Oh, let the song of God enfold you.
> Let Him have the things that hold you.
> Let Him fill your heart and satisfy your soul.
> Give Him all your years of sadness,
> And all your years of pain,
> And you'll enter into life in Jesus' name.
> —J. Wimber

middle of my struggle with grief, I found a beautiful gift—the gift of knowing my Lord in a whole new way.

Many others who have shared their stories of recovery in this book have also found unexpected gifts. Florence, who lost her teenage son in a plane crash and later her husband by divorce, continued on with her education, entered law school and graduated, and is now in a thriving law practice. Terry and Denny now have three beautiful little boys. Toni has one, too. Sharon went back to school, graduated from college, and is now in her English Master's program. Julianne remarried (after she told us it was okay to be single). And Diane is working as an editor of a Christian school newsletter along with us in the *Afterloss* Recovery Program. Shirley is teaching in Tokyo and plans to be in this country in May. David and Scott are both working as senior staff for members of Congress in our nation's capital. Georgann has gone forth to help upgrade airline safety. And V. J. has resumed her singing career, in addition to conducting interviews for her daily radio program. She recently announced her engagement.

All of these have found gifts in their loss. Just as I did, they have discovered something new either in themselves or in their lives after they lost their loved ones, after they made the decision to rededicate themselves to their futures. These people have triumphed over tragedy.

It may seem strange to call them triumphant, but be assured that those of us who have suffered the trauma of losing a loved one and little by little, moment by moment, step by step have come up from the depths of despair once again know how it feels to be part of the human race. And that's the triumph!

My mind slips back over the past four years and embraces the many heroic, grieving people I've met. And as I study the faces in the pictures of some of their loved ones—a baby girl, a baby son, an older son, a grown daughter, a husband, a father, a brother, a mother—my heart goes out to each of these brave survivors who have, in spite of their pain, learned how to go on with their lives. They've learned how to trust again, how to love again, how to *live* again, how to go forth.

Rereading these twenty-two stories in Book Two is an indescribable experience. These accounts of such tremendous loss and pain made me wonder if so much pain should be contained in one book. *Lord, how much pain can a person bear?* But He kept sending more and more people across my path.

I recall each touching story told often through painful tears. I re-

They'd signal back and forth as dogs somehow do. About 2:50 they'd move into position, each one posted like a sentry beside a glass door. And there they'd sit like statues and wait. At 3:00 they'd stand up and begin getting restless and at last, *exactly* at 3:05 P.M., when their moment had finally arrived, they'd go into wild ecstasy, jumping, spinning, sometimes sitting on each others' heads, anything to get someone to open the door so they could tear out, stand by the gate, and bark their heads off.

This ridiculous ritual has been going on for almost six years. That is until three days ago. That day at 2:30 P.M., our dogs seemed to sense that something had changed. There was no pacing. There was no running to the doors or watching out the windows. All five dogs moped around the house. Somehow they seemed to know that Roy and their dog friends would not be walking by the gate that day. Somehow they seemed to sense a fact that we had yet to learn—Roy died the night before.

For our friend Roy, gone were the lazy afternoon walks. Gone were the mountains and the songs of the birds. Gone was the warmth of the midday sun and the camaraderie of the motley crew.

And once again, the importance of time moved sharply into focus, like a thunderclap.

Why is it that everything in life seems to have a bottom line, including time? And the bottom line in this case is the indisputable fact that, like Roy, we will all be leaving here one day. And until that day, we have something very precious: a span of time, a span of time between now and then that I call *the long white road of the rest of our lives* because this is the way God has taught me to think about it. I can see it in my mind, stretching out there ahead. Untraveled. Unmarked. Uncluttered. Fresh and clean and new. Filled with opportunities. Filled with promise. Filled with Him!

Have you ever wondered what's waiting for you on your road? I've been walking on mine for a little over three years now. At times, looking back, I can hardly believe some of the things that have occurred and yet I know they did. I was there! Three years ago I thought I would never again know happiness, know the way it feels to smile, know the joy of laughing aloud. At first I thought that grief was the cross I would have to bear for the rest of my life. But instead, *grief was the cross that led me to a closer relationship with Him* and the subsequent birth of the *Afterloss* ministry. I also thought I was permanently trapped in my grief prison. But instead, He offered me the key that led to my freedom when He sent me back to work. In the

The Road of the Rest of Our Lives

Thou wilt make known to me the path of life.
Ps. 16:11 NASV

. . . And when she finally looked up she could see a long, white road stretching out into the horizon. And she knew that this must be the road of the rest of her life. And she saw the road begin and she also saw it end. And she came to understand the message she was to gather that night: that we must not in any way waste the steps on the road of the rest of our lives.

Almost a century and a half ago, Henry Thoreau, the naturalist and writer, in his quest for freedom chose to leave the chaos and pace of the world for the simplicity of the woods. Later he wrote about his reasons: "I went to the woods because I wished to live deliberately, to front only the essential facts of life, and see if I could not learn what it had to teach, and not, when I came to die, discover that I had not lived."

Twenty-two years ago, we left too! And we were also searching for freedom. But we left a much more cynical world, a more fevered pace, a more warped and distorted system of values. And, like Thoreau, we found freedom—exactly fifteen acres of freedom. However, instead of finding it in the woods, we found it in the country, on a farm, a horse farm.

We found freedom bordered by white, wooden fences. We found fields of green peace where children could roam with golden retrievers and quarter horses; we found a century-old farm house, solid and serene under the shade of a huge willow tree. There was a magnificent three-story barn where, later, two daughters would be married under its aged oak beams. And there were sundry other outbuildings and even a beautiful pond bordered with bullrushes.

We moved our family into that old farm house, built stalls in the old white barn, and raised our children in an atmosphere of health, happiness, and hard work. Appropriately we named our home "Walden." We left the "jet set" for the "horse set" and traded the Cadillac for a truck. We went from silver forks to pitch-forks; we moved from the conference table to a dinner table (an old oak one with funny claw feet). We exchanged office hours for round-the-clock hours and traded our alarm clock for a rooster. We stopped chasing airplanes and began chasing horses; we moved our office from a designer building into a converted garage, and traded lunches at The Club for sandwiches prepared on our own homemade bread.

A son we named Christian was born in our farmhouse home while his brothers and sisters waited on the other side of the bedroom door to greet him. After Christian's peaceful birth, the young doctor returned the envelope my husband had given to him. "Oh, I *couldn't* take any pay," he explained. "It would spoil the joy of my first delivery!"

Those were halcyon days—days filled with challenge and hard work. Those were days of freedom and happy hearts. We took control of our time, took charge of our own production, and reclaimed our lives. And we learned many lessons during those challenging years, two of which are *the importance of freedom and the value of time.*

We've always placed a high value on our time but have paid only slight attention to the exactness of the hour, that is until almost six years ago here in California. Since then, we've always known when it's 3:05 P.M. sharp. We had moved next door to a very nice couple. Roy and his wife lived in the last house on the lane, the house that butts right up to the side of the mountain. And every afternoon at precisely 3:00 P.M., Roy left his house to walk his dogs, Bo, Mike, and Precious. (Yep, Precious). Bo, the tall, black, standard poodle; Mike, the short, white-haired something-or-other; and the little dainty one who, as you may have guessed, answers to "Precious." I wouldn't even attempt to describe her lineage. A motley crew indeed.

It would take Roy and his three dogs five minutes to reach our gate. Our dogs would wait all day for this moment. The ceremony itself actually began about 2:45 with a short prelude. First they'd pace. Then three dogs would take the back of the house and two dogs the front, each watching carefully from a different window.

NOTES

NOTES

before, I need to be with people who care about me. And if you can't be with me, your phone calls, your letters, or even short notes sharing your thoughts and feelings about the loss of my loved one will help me far more than you may ever know. It's very comforting to me to know that you share my grief.

Sometimes when you ask what you can do to help me, I honestly don't know.

There are many days when I don't know what my needs are anymore. I don't have the answer to a lot of questions right now. Often I can't answer you because my mind behaves as though it has shut down. It's very helpful when you can take on this initiative for me. And even though you may have asked me to, please don't always wait for me to call upon you when I do need some help. It is so hard for me to think or to plan right now.

I need for you to believe in me and in my ability to get through this grief in my own time and in my own way.

And please don't tell me that it's time for me to get on with my life. I am probably already saying this to myself. Each of us is different. Each loss is unique. I may move through my grief more quickly than another or I may move more slowly. I just need for you to be patient with me now—for you to try to understand.

Please don't tell me that you know just how I feel. No one will ever really understand just how I feel.

And in your desire to comfort me, don't offer comments like, "You're attractive, you can marry again," or "Now, now, don't cry—you must be strong," or "You can always have more children," or, unbelievably, "You're lucky it was only your mother."

Please don't tell me, either, that this death was really God's will—or that He needs the presence of my loved one more than I do.

This causes me to doubt God during a time when I need Him the most. And please, don't suggest that I take a pill or offer me an alcoholic drink to "help" me get through this trying time. Rather, encourage me to eat properly, to rest and to exercise and, as much as I am able to, to maintain a healthy lifestyle.

**Don't be concerned if you think I am getting better and
then suddenly I seem to slip backward again.**

Grief makes me behave this way at times. I am learning that the waves of grief will come and go in my life, but they won't always come with such force or such frequency—and one day, hopefully, they won't come at all.

**And finally, please give me the time I need
to grieve and to recover.**

I want to get on with my life, as has often been suggested, but I know that first I must walk through the dark shadows of my grief. I need to meet it head-on and to master it—not to pretend that it isn't happening, not to hide my pain deep within me where it will fester and erupt later. I will never recover from my loss if I do not complete the work of my grief. And, although it is almost impossible for me to believe this now, I know that one day my grief will end.

Most of all, thank you for just being my friend.

Thank you for your patience, thank you for being here for me, for caring, for helping, for understanding. Thank you for praying for me. And remember in the days, weeks, or years ahead—after your loss—when you need me as I have needed you, I will understand. And then I will come and be with you.

About the Author

Barbara LesStrang is president of Harbor House Publishers, Inc., of Boyne City, Michigan, and its affiliate, Harbor House (West) Publishers, Inc., located in Rancho Mirage, California. In 1989 she founded the *Afterloss®* Recovery Program and serves as the publisher of *Afterloss,* the program's monthly newsletter.

A native of Grand Rapids, Michigan, she attended the University of Michigan, and has been vice president and director of marketing for The Great Lakes Press and director of marketing for The Campus Inn Hotels. She is a biographee of record in Marquis' *Who's Who in American Women.*

She and her husband, Jacques, Chairman and CEO of the publishing companies, have raised seven children, Christian, David, Linda, Paul, Steven, Diane, and Michelle, and live in Rancho Mirage, California.

Afterloss, the monthly newsletter, brings helpful, comforting, and encouraging information about how to recover from grief and bereavement. Subscriptions are available at a cost of $24 for six months or $45 per year. Gift subscriptions are also available and a card will be sent advising the recipient of the gift.

For additional information or to order subscriptions, write to:

Barbara LesStrang
The *Afterloss* Recovery Program
Harbor House (West) Publishers, Inc.
Box 2545
Rancho Mirage, CA 92270

NOTES

NOTES

NOTES